# Development Methods
# and Approaches
## Critical Reflections

# Oxfam GB

Oxfam GB, founded in 1942, is a development, humanitarian, and campaigning agency dedicated to finding lasting solutions to poverty and suffering around the world. Oxfam believes that every human being is entitled to a life of dignity and opportunity, and it works with others worldwide to make this become a reality.

From its base in Oxford in the United Kingdom, Oxfam GB publishes and distributes a wide range of books and other resource materials for development and relief workers, researchers and campaigners, schools and colleges, and the general public, as part of its programme of advocacy, education, and communications.

Oxfam GB is a member of Oxfam International, a confederation of 12 agencies of diverse cultures and languages, which share a commitment to working for an end to injustice and poverty – both in long-term development work and at times of crisis.

For further information about Oxfam's publishing, and online ordering, visit www.oxfam.org.uk/publications

For more information about Oxfam's development and humanitarian relief work around the world, visit www.oxfam.org.uk

# Development Methods and Approaches
## Critical Reflections

Selected essays from *Development in Practice*

Introduced by
Jo Rowlands

A Development in Practice Reader

Series Editor
Deborah Eade

**Oxfam**

First published by Oxfam GB in 2003

© Oxfam GB 2003

ISBN 0 85598 494 5

A catalogue record for this publication is available from the British Library.

Available from:

Bournemouth English Book Centre, PO Box 1496, Parkstone, Dorset, BH12 3YD, UK
tel: +44 (0)1202 712933; fax: +44 (0)1202 712930; email: oxfam@bebc.co.uk

USA: Stylus Publishing LLC, PO Box 605, Herndon, VA 20172-0605, USA
tel: +1 (0)703 661 1581; fax: +1 (0)703 661 1547; email: styluspub@aol.com

For details of local agents and representatives in other countries, consult our website:
http://www.oxfam.org.uk/publications

or contact Oxfam Publishing, 274 Banbury Road, Oxford OX2 7DZ, UK
tel: +44 (0)1865 311 311; fax: +44 (0)1865 312 600; email: publish@oxfam.org.uk

Our website contains a fully searchable database of all our titles, and facilities for secure
on-line ordering.

The Editor and Management Committee of *Development in Practice* acknowledge the
support given to the journal by affiliates of Oxfam International, and by its publisher,
Carfax, Taylor & Francis. The views expressed in this volume are those of the individual
contributors, and not necessarily those of the Editor or publisher.

Published by Oxfam GB, 274 Banbury Road, Oxford OX2 7DZ, UK.

Printed by Information Press, Eynsham.

Oxfam GB is a registered charity, no. 202 918, and is a member of Oxfam International.

# Contents

# Contributors

**Jens B. Aune** is a researcher at the Centre for International Environment and Development Studies (Noragric) at the Agricultural University of Norway.

**David Booth** is a Research Fellow at the Overseas Development Institute; he was previously Professor of Development Studies at the University of Wales Swansea.

**Paul Castelloe** is Co-Director of the Center for Participatory Change in the USA.

**David Ellerman** was, until his retirement, Economic Advisor to the Chief Economist at the World Bank, and has written widely on economic democracy.

**Patricia Howard** is Professor of Gender Studies in Agriculture and Rural Development at Wageningen University in the Netherlands; she formerly worked for the FAO.

**Allan Kaplan** is a consultant and writer on development, and founder of the Community Development Resource Association (CDRA) in South Africa, which seeks to build the capacity of organisations engaged in development and social transformation.

**Robert Leurs** is a Lecturer in Participatory Development at the University of Birmingham, UK.

**Malcolm MacLachlan** is Associate Professor of Psychology at Trinity College, University of Dublin, Ireland and is currently Chairperson of Trinity Development Co-operation.

**Matthew Maury** is the Southern Africa Regional Director for Habitat for Humanity International, and has worked with various development NGOs throughout Asia, Africa, and Latin America.

**Susan Maury** is an Organisational Development consultant who focuses on helping development NGOs become learning organisations.

**Marion N. Meyer** is serving with the Mennonite Central Committee as the emergency-response coordinator for Central America and Mexico, based in Honduras.

**Tlamelo O. Mompati** lectures at the University of Botswana in the Department of Social Work.

**Eliud Ngunjiri** is Executive Director of Resources Oriented Development Initiatives (RODI), an NGO in Kenya.

**Penny Plowman** is a development consultant to NGOs and international agencies in the field of gender and development.

**William Postma** was, at the time of writing, Bangladesh Country Director of the Christian Reformed World Relief Committee (CRWRC).

**Grant D. Power** is currently a consultant for NGOs involved in community-based, sustainable development in the USA and East Asia.

**Gerard Prinsen** was, at the time of writing, Training Coordinator for Extension Workers in the Ministry of Finance and Development Planning in Botswana.

**Maureen Raymond-McKay** was, at the time of writing, studying at Trinity College Dublin in Ireland.

**Jo Rowlands** is a Policy Adviser on Gender and Participation in Oxfam GB's UK Poverty Programme; formerly she worked for Voluntary Service Overseas. She has written extensively on gender and empowerment issues, with particular reference to Latin America.

**Naresh C. Singh** was, at the time of writing, Program Director for Employment and Sustainable Livelihoods and UN Activities at the International Institute for Sustainable Development in Canada.

**Hugo Slim** is Senior Lecturer in International Humanitarianism at Oxford Brookes University, UK, a Trustee of Oxfam GB, and an International Adviser to the British Red Cross.

**Genese Sodikoff** was, at the time of writing, studying at the University of Michigan in the USA.

**Barbara P. Thomas-Slayter** is Professor of International Development in Clark University's Department of International Development, Community and Environment. She is author or editor of several books on gender, ecology, and development, including *Gender, Environment and Development in Kenya*, and *Feminist Political Ecology, global issues and local experience*. She has recently served on the Board of Directors of Oxfam America.

**Thomas Watson** is Co-Director of the Center for Participatory Change in the USA.

**David Wield** is Professor of Innovation and Development at The Open University in the UK, and Co-Director of its International Development Centre.

# Preface

## Deborah Eade

---

> We shall have to acknowledge not only the scope of our professional methods
> but also their limits. It has been said that economics is a box of tools.
> But we shall have to resist the temptation of the law of the hammer,
> according to which a boy, given a hammer, finds everything worth
> pounding, not only nails but also Ming vases. We shall have to look,
> in the well-known metaphor, where the key was dropped rather than
> where the light happens to be. We shall have to learn not only how to spell
> 'banana' but also when to stop. The professionals, whom a friend of mine
> calls 'quantoids' and who are enamored of their techniques, sometimes
> forget that if something is not worth doing, it is not worth doing well.
> (Streeten 2002:110)

This Reader explores some of the tensions between the broad values-based *approaches* to development that contributors to *Development in Practice* tend to advocate – sustainable, people-centred, participatory, empowering, transformative, gender-equitable, inclusionary, and so on – and the contemporary *methods* and *tools* that are used to put these approaches into practice. As we shall see from the essays included in this volume, some of these tensions are creative, others less so.

While development agencies are never monolithic, and will often accommodate competing or even dissonant views, their policies and practices do nevertheless reflect their fundamental understanding of their mission of development, or the 'humanitarian imperative'. Whether or not they make this explicit, these agencies basically subscribe to a normative mission: that is, they have an idea of how the world should be, they know what they believe is 'wrong' with the *status quo*, and then decide how best to apply their resources to improve matters. The underlying principles that govern the approach taken by a given agency seldom change dramatically over the years, although they will gradually evolve over time; by contrast, the methods and tools by which these are translated into practice are more than likely to change, frequently and sometimes quite abruptly, in response to new ideas, fads, or funding pressures. These dynamics may produce relatively trivial discrepancies between what an organisation says and what it does, but may if unchecked lead to 'role strain' or more serious disjunctures between its beliefs about itself, its public persona, and the directions in which its ground-level practice is taking it.

There are three contrasting positions concerning the methods and tools used by the development industry at project level, as opposed to the way in which policies evolve and are articulated by specific agencies. The first is to treat them as though they were politically value-free alternatives which confer 'objectivity' or perhaps some kind of academic respectability on the practitioner and on his or her observations. It is therefore quite possible for an agency to hold that development policies are inherently value-laden, while at the same time implicitly adopting a technocratic view of the tools that it uses on the ground.

The second is to see specific methods and tools as embodying the 'hidden agendas' of the organisations that were originally associated with or now promote them, and hence as not remotely neutral. In this sometimes rather conspiratorial reading, a tool that originated in, say, the corporate sector, is inherently 'contaminated' by the for-profit hallmark it bears, and is therefore unfit for use by the non-profit sector. Among some Southern organisations, this may play out, for instance, as viewing gender analysis as an attempt to 'impose Western feminist' views. Among Northern NGOs in particular, unease with logical framework ('logframe') or with managerial methods deriving from New Public Management (NPM) often resonates with a declared preference for 'bottom–up' or 'participatory' methods, and with a concern for 'downward accountability' to those intended to benefit from the agency's assistance, rather than accountability to donors.

The third and probably most common position (to paraphrase from the introductory essay to this Reader) is that of a pragmatic but none-too-rigorous eclecticism – agencies take what they like from the *smorgasbord* of tools and methods on offer, and leave aside the bits that they find unpalatable. This allows them to pick and mix in response to local requirements or preferences, rather than following a single inflexible line. But it can also lead to rather mongrel forms, such as 'bottom–up and top–down strategic planning, ... participatory logframes, ... [or] participatory impact assessment sitting alongside milestones, indicators, and targets set by [outside agencies]' (Wallace 2000: 37). And once the links between methods and the values that inform them are ruptured, or if the methods themselves are poorly understood or wrongly applied as a result, the overall approach becomes incoherent and directionless.

Which brings us to the question of approaches. On this front, development agencies tend to be more descriptive than analytical – they are better at saying that they promote development that is 'sustainable' or 'rights-based' than at explaining what they believe development is, or to which (if any) theory they subscribe. To an extent, such agencies can justify this by arguing that their purpose is to get out and change the world, not to sit back and theorise about it. Some might add that the age of 'grand theories' came to a close in any case with the collapse of the Berlin Wall. But it is unwise to divorce action from theory, or to ignore the ideological baggage that specific methods bring with them. To do so is to risk 'depoliticising development' (White 1996). In her introductory essay to an earlier title in this series, *Development, NGOs, and Civil Society*, Jenny Pearce illustrated the profound dangers of ignoring the larger politics at play and basing action on implicit assumptions, rather than on critical analysis. Taking issue with those who believe that the challenge for the future is not an intellectual but a problem-solving one, she wrote:

> ... I would argue that there is a serious intellectual challenge, and that sorting it out is as important as getting the praxis and attitudes right. It might not be an empirical research problem as such, but it is about where NGOs ultimately decide to locate themselves in the global system. This raises not abstract, theoretical questions but core issues, such as: what and who is your work for? Among other outcomes, the failure to ask such questions has led to the false linguistic consensus of the 1990s and, to be somewhat harsh, to an intellectually lazy reliance on a handful of concepts and words as a substitute for thought. This has weakened and confused practice and, I would argue, contributed to the present crisis of legitimacy within the NGO sector. (Pearce 2000: 32)

She concluded that '[m]aking assumptions explicit is one way of identifying differences, clarifying choices, and ultimately fostering debate and cooperation among people who are committed in some way to building a better world' (Pearce 2000: 40).

One can certainly make a very plausible case, as Thomas Dichter has recently done (2003), that one fundamental reason why aid agencies find it so hard to make explicit their understanding of development is that their own institutional survival depends upon the *status quo*, and on conducting business more or less as usual. While development organisations have proliferated around the world, those that have *deliberately* put themselves out of work could probably be numbered on the fingers of one hand. If global inequalities are deepening even as the development industry expands, it is at least worth asking, as Arturo Escobar and other post-development thinkers have done, whether 'the problem' will ever be addressed by 'more of the same', or whether a more radical re-think about the function of international co-operation is required.

Be that as it may, development agencies are here to stay for the foreseeable future, and it obviously does therefore matter that they should be principled and professional, rather than expedient or amateur. Indeed, considerable progress has been made over the last two decades to raise standards in both the humanitarian and the development fields. There *is* a difference between gender-blind and gender-sensitive approaches to development, just as there is a difference between applying 'blueprint' approaches that do not take local views into account and seeking to put one's resources at the disposal of disadvantaged people in their own efforts to change their quality of life. The real point made by the contributors to this Reader, and reinforced in the introductory essay by **Jo Rowlands**, is that while techniques and methods alone do not add up to a coherent approach, beliefs about development are worth little without the skills to put them into practice, and the wisdom and humility required to learn from experience.

## References

Dichter, Thomas (2003) *Despite Good Intentions: Why Development Assistance to the Third World has Failed*, Amherst, MA: University of Massachusetts Press.

Pearce, Jenny (2000) 'Development, NGOs, and civil society: the debate and its future' in Deborah Eade (ed.) *Development, NGOs, and Civil Society*, Oxford: Oxfam.

Streeten, Paul (2002) 'The Universe and the University', *Development* 45(3) 107-12.

Wallace, Tina (2000) 'Development management and the aid chain: the case of NGOs' in Deborah Eade, Tom Hewitt, and Hazel Johnson (eds.) *Development and Management: Experiences in Value-based Conflict*, Oxford: Oxfam.

White, Sarah C. (1996) 'Depoliticising development: the uses and abuses of participation', *Development in Practice* 6(1) 6-15 .

# Beyond the comfort zone: some issues, questions, and challenges in thinking about development approaches and methods

## Jo Rowlands

*'If the only tool you have is a hammer, you tend to see every problem as a nail.'* Abraham Maslow

*'Common sense is the collection of prejudices acquired by age eighteen.'* Albert Einstein (attributed)

## Introduction

I have believed for many years that human beings are generally highly resourceful, intelligent, and creative. The more I have seen during my working life, which has given me opportunities to experience life in many parts of the globe and under many different circumstances, the more I have been reinforced in this belief. Unless their abilities have been badly interfered with, human beings are capable of evaluating and judging complex circumstances and acting on their conclusions – even where the range of actions available to them is limited by inequality and other circumstances. Any course of action is contextualised within culture and personal life trajectory – so people don't always act in the way that someone with a different story might expect. I recently had the opportunity to listen to a highly placed member of staff in the Ugandan Ministry of Finance talking about the choices made by poor people in Uganda in chopping down trees. She said that the Ministry used to believe that poor people did not act rationally (because they were destroying their own resource base), but that the more detailed picture which the staff were able to see as a result of their Participatory Poverty Assessment process showed that poor people act as rationally as it is practicable for them to do within problematic circumstances where it is impossible to look beyond the immediate needs of survival. She acknowledged that it was the policy makers' lack of understanding of the full reality and stark choices confronting poor people that was the problem. I am interested in finding approaches to development and methods with which to work that will enable us to free up that human resourcefulness, intelligence, and creativity in ways that bring the achievement of human rights and social justice closer to reality.

In this introductory essay, I will touch on many different aspects, perhaps thinking about approaches and methods not as 'science' but as 'art'. I want to challenge the notion that methodology is somehow neutral; to unpack some of the assumptions that lie behind development interventions; and to explore how power is embedded in everything that gets done. I am also concerned with the process by which priorities are identified and by whom, and concerned also with the elusive challenge of scaling up small progress. I shall take a particular look at participatory approaches, and touch on evaluation and learning. I want to throw many questions into the open: this is an essay that is full of questions. Many of the essays in this volume help to bring those questions back down to the ground again. I will not attempt to draw a complete picture, but I do want to add a degree of complexity which goes beyond what most accounts of particular approaches or methods allow for. I will delve as far into that complexity as space allows, but I shall not attempt to produce many tidy resolutions: readers will have to provide those for themselves, as far as they are able to.

## Not neutral, not in isolation

'Approaches' can refer to a wide spectrum of things. They might be empowering, participatory, gender-equitable, people-centred, inclusionary. Or they might be the reverse of each of those: disempowering, top–down, male-biased, formulaic, exclusionary. Or, of course, they might be (and often are) a combination of these, whether intentionally or not. Any approach has behind it a set of values, beliefs, and attitudes that give it its flavour, set its tone. This is a fundamental point to be clear about: approaches to development are not neutral. If an approach has a transformative agenda, it is in a particular direction, towards a change in power relations or resource allocation. If the approach largely tends to maintain the *status quo*, in so doing it is supporting the maintenance of a particular set of power relations and resource allocations.

Approaches provide a rough guiding framework within which specific methods and techniques can be used. Methods, then, are the step-by-step specifics of how an approach is put into practice at the 'coal face', at the 'kitchen sink', on the 'factory floor', or in the 'field'. Problems can arise when the method is not compatible with the values, beliefs, or attitudes on which the approach that is being used ultimately rests. In a top–down approach, the use of a method which encourages individuals to identify what they want to have happen, but in a context where their wishes will not be realised, can lead to frustration, disillusionment, and non-cooperation. Equally, in a participatory approach, a method which privileges some people's participation over that of others, such as one that requires the ability to read, although not everyone can do so, will not achieve the participation intended.

Problems may also arise when the approach used and the methods employed *are* compatible, but the individuals using these methods are insufficiently skilled or insufficiently self-aware for them to be truly effective. Participatory and inclusionary approaches are particularly vulnerable to this difficulty. The intent may be there, but here the methods cannot be separated from who is using them: where they 'sit' in the power relations of the context, how aware they are of that, what their skills are as facilitators or enablers of the participation of others, how willing they are to step out of their own 'comfort zone', and so on.

Within any given approach, how do we choose the methods that we use? And what factors influence how we apply them? These choices are not always clear or conscious. If we are really honest about it, many of us probably often choose methods because they are familiar and draw on skills that we feel confident about; or because we perceive that the funders require them.[1] We therefore cannot extract the user from the equation. Methods may be quick to use, or cheap to use. We might choose them because they have been tried and tested: they have a track record which gives them credibility. We might choose them because they are not too disruptive of the *status quo* – or conversely because they *are*. We sometimes choose particular methods because we can't think of anything else. The point is, how aware are we of what forms and informs our choices? And how transparent is this to anyone else? People trained in qualitative approaches within the social sciences learn that the quality of the research and its results can be deeply affected by the degree of awareness with which these kinds of issue are considered. Realistically, most 'practitioners' operate within constraints of time and resources that affect the choices we make; we also operate within political contexts that shape our choices.

As to the application of methods, there is the issue (mentioned earlier) of the level of skill with which they are used. There are other issues as well, including flexibility and the ability to adapt a given method according to responses and circumstances. And there are other potentially controversial elements: with how much commitment and/or passion is the method applied? Here we enter into the relationship between the individual(s) engaged in the activity and the nature of the subject material or the kind of change being addressed. I don't advocate the energy of passion as a necessary element for effective action: it depends hugely on the purpose and context of the activity. Undoubtedly there are some areas of undertaking where passion would be unhelpful or counter-productive, or could lead to errors of judgement and mistakes. There are other contexts, however, where commitment – as long-term dedication and passion, as energy and drive – contributes positively to the achievement of change, bringing capacity to confront obstacles and be resilient in the face of set-backs.

## Assumptions

Approaches to development, and the methods that flow from them, are profoundly shaped by assumptions that are made about people. Inclusionary and participatory approaches have a firm foundation in an assumption that human beings have capacities and value and potential, and that for many, these are limited by being in a position of powerlessness, vulnerability, or material poverty. Gender-equitable approaches are based on assumptions that men and women have equally valid needs, potential capacities, and contributions. They look for ways to redress the power imbalances that usually favour men over women. These assumptions can mean that conflicts of interest have to be recognised and addressed. Assumptions are also made about processes, such as how change happens or how learning takes place. Assumptions are made about what can and cannot be done. All of these shape the nature of the approach and the choice of methods.

Where do these assumptions come from? Some are based on experience or sound research and evidence from elsewhere. Others are based on beliefs and values – some of which can be based on stereotypes and misinformation. There have been plenty of examples of this over the years. A classic assumption is that of availability of time – usually the time of women, but also of all poor people. How many projects have tripped up over this assumption, only to find that the women's labour is not available at the point when it is needed: they are too busy doing their own work? Maybe some people used to make the assumption that poor people are poor because they sit around doing nothing all day; or, just as inaccurate, that they are doing things with their time that have less value than the project activity. I would like to believe that these particular assumptions are no longer made. Assumptions about what is and is not possible are sometimes based on a careful situational analysis (which can be vulnerable to the oversight of a key factor), and on knowledge and beliefs about how learning and change happen. This can lead to inaccurate assessments of what can be achieved. My favourite example of this comes from a women's group whom I visited in the course of doing research in the state of Puebla in Mexico. I met the women some three years after the completion of a pig-rearing project. The pig idea had been a disaster: everything that could have gone wrong apparently did go wrong. The project had been closed down and judged a failure. Yet when I met the women, they were full of energy, ideas, and enthusiasm, and they had embarked on a different project of their own, had raised their own funds, and had begun to generate income from it. In talking the whole experience over, it was apparent that they had learned all sorts of things from the 'failed project' which were now standing them in good stead. Despite the 'failure', these women had developed confidence, and above all a sense of themselves as able to act in order to meet their own needs. With the passage of time, it was clear that the earlier project had been a resounding success – just not in raising pigs!

One of the columns in the matrix of the Logical Framework is labelled 'assumptions'. The tool as a whole has attracted much criticism over the years, but this seems to me to be one of its strengths: to have a tool which systematically encourages you to become aware of the assumptions being made throughout a planning process seems like an excellent idea.[2] The existence of an assumptions column, however, cannot provide a substitute for the awareness and understanding of assumptions that are needed in order to fill it in. That requires an openness of mind which the tool itself cannot provide. It also requires a willingness to revise the assumptions when they prove inaccurate and, on the part of institutions, a willingness not only to allow revisions but to welcome them as evidence of learning and experience.

## Power

I cannot go much further in exploring the issues of development approaches and methods without stopping to explore the critical issue of power. All approaches to development have power embedded in them. The question is, what sorts of power do they encompass, who is powerful and who is not, and does that power help or hinder? It is well recognised that powerlessness is a central element of poverty; any focus on poverty, inequality, injustice, or exclusion involves power and power relations. But despite this acknowledgement, power is insidious and often remains invisible (or 'under the table', to borrow an image from VeneKlasen with Miller (2002)). Approaches that pay explicit attention to power relations, and acknowledge and address the power dynamics within which they operate, are more likely to contribute to change. But consideration of power also needs to be part of the solutions being sought and the methods through which this is done. We are not talking merely about 'power over' here. Approaches and methods are needed which reinforce and strengthen other forms of power that will contribute to lasting solutions through their enhancement – the power of people acting collectively to make change happen, and the power of people knowing and demanding their rights in ways that cannot be ignored.[3] Participatory and inclusionary approaches and methods can be a channel for positive changes in power relations – but even with those approaches, there is nothing automatic about it. I shall return to this later. What matters is that power needs to be recognised and addressed.

One way in which some approaches address power is to focus on particular arenas in which it shows itself. This has been seen in relation to gender, with many instances of gender and gender relations being put intentionally into the foreground and built into the methods so that the power issues cannot be ignored. There have also been many instances where gender issues have been present in the rhetoric, but in practice, when methods are applied, it has been possible for them to be deliberately or unwittingly ignored (Longwe 1997). It matters, therefore, to be deliberate in making the links between the theoretical approach and the implementation of that approach in 'real life' and not to be naive about the tendency of existing power relations to distort and divert the best-intentioned approach.

## Who sets the agenda and priorities?

Power comes to the fore again when we consider where agendas for change come from. Who identifies and ultimately decides what is needed in a given context, or which/whose needs should be given priority over which/whose others? Local, national, and international political agendas shift and change all the time, and are constantly interpreted and acted upon by a wide range of actors. So much of what actually happens is shaped and influenced by political timetables and considerations: When is the election? Who needs to be able to show that they have achieved what kind of results? Whose political future is at stake? Budget allocations at each level shift accordingly. Approaches to development need to be able to work within this shifting power context, and to develop strategies for functioning within it. Analysis and understanding are important, since they affect people's view of what is 'possible' and therefore 'worth attempting'. Sometimes, because of the values and beliefs underlying an approach, the response has to be 'it looks impossible, but we're going to try to do it anyway'. This can be very effective! Jubilee 2000 certainly faced considerable criticism for having unrealistic goals which were too complex for the general public to understand when it started its campaign to 'drop the debt' for the poorest indebted countries. Yet it succeeded in mobilising considerable popular opinion in support of an economic agenda of considerable technical complexity. Despite not achieving everything that it had intended, Jubilee 2000 made significant and continuing impact, educating many thousands of 'ordinary people' about significant global issues in the process.

The formal political arena is only a part of the picture. Approaches need also to work with, through, and around informal political forces. This includes intra-household relations and power dynamics within communities. In particular, the fact that conflict is often an underlying issue is something that in turn has an impact upon the effectiveness of development work. Many approaches try to work around this; but how many are robust enough to allow or encourage that conflict to emerge and to be dealt with? How many development practitioners are highly skilled in conflict management and mediation?

The people who set priorities for change on behalf of others very often have good intentions, but do not always have sufficient information or the skills to interpret it accurately. It is, however, possible to play a supporting or even catalytic role without basing one's support on a particular specific outcome. This prioritises process over output, so that an overarching approach (such as empowerment or inclusion) can shape the work without imposing particular agendas in a predetermined way. This is more of a challenge for organisations working within inflexible objectives-focused systems – but I hope it is a challenge that we can rise to, rather than an excuse for continuing on the same path as before.

# Who implements the agenda?

Much development work falters when the people entrusted with actually implementing change do not have 'ownership' of the task with which they are charged. So often, approaches and policies which have been carefully crafted do not lead to the changes intended, because key individuals did not have the commitment or the skills or the knowledge or the wish to see to it that change happens. They may have the wish but not the time, because (as is common in development contexts, whether NGO or government) they are working on a short fixed-term contract or are subject to relocation. They might be field staff who are already fully occupied but are expected somehow to find space for a new initiative. They might be activists who want change to happen but do not have the particular skills needed. Or they may be local government planners who have been given a set of policies from higher up that they are supposed to implement, but don't know enough about conditions on the ground to interpret the policy into realistic plans. Any approach would benefit from seeing that these individuals (or groups) are stakeholders in the undertaking, just as much as the supposed 'beneficiaries'. This is a perspective which could help to unblock some of the blockages that get in the way of many potentially positive development initiatives – as has been proposed recently in relation to gender mainstreaming (Howard 2002). If you take people out of a box called 'resisters', and consider them instead as stakeholders in the process of gender mainstreaming, it becomes possible to think deliberately about their needs as stakeholders and devise a strategy to address those needs.

This does not apply exclusively to gender mainstreaming. During my recent visit to Uganda, referred to earlier, to learn about the Participatory Poverty Assessment (PPA) processes there that have informed their Poverty Reduction Strategy Paper (PRSP), I and a group of Oxfam UK Poverty Programme partners had the opportunity to meet a district planner who had been one of a group trained in participatory methods and had facilitated the PPA activities in his district. The findings of the PPA had been fed into the process nationally, but it was also clear that his own district-level plans had been shaped significantly by the local findings, and that his own work as a district planner had been profoundly affected by the participatory research process. Clearly this individual had become an advocate for the approach to development represented by the PPA process. He could see how it helped him to do his own job more effectively.

There are challenges to be met when the implementation of particular projects, activities, or initiatives becomes a full-time occupation. Organisations get formed and individuals get paid to do the work that perhaps they have hitherto been doing on a voluntary basis. Or someone gets paid to do work that previously someone else had been doing on a voluntary basis. Through implementing the approach to change, social relations and sometimes cultural relations are changed. Individuals may then become dependent on the ongoing existence of the activity or organisation.[4] Certain kinds of work become 'professionalised' or 'technicalised'. Once the livelihoods of individuals are at stake, it is easy for work to become led by what will attract funding, rather than by what most needs to be done. It can happen that organisations lose their connection with the grassroots, and lose legitimacy as a result (Whitehead 1995). This may eventually undermine the effectiveness of the approach.

How do implementers obtain the necessary support for what they do? How can skills and capacities be developed when they are the less tangible, more ephemeral skills and capacities of facilitation, strategic thinking, organisational development, or counselling? Or when the nature of the change being sought requires personal changes on the part of the implementer? This is the case with gender, where all individuals are embedded in the existing power relations, whether they know it or not, and the extent of their awareness and their ability to confront the need for change in their own attitudes and behaviours can make all the difference to their ability to support others in a process of change. Individuals can attend training courses, but the real development of skill often comes through doing the thing, and then exploring what happened and deliberately learning from experience. Investment in staff is needed. In management contexts, the idea of having a mentor, or coach, is now quite widely accepted in some quarters. The idea of accompaniment[5] as a role that can usefully be played has become quite common in some development circles. This is when an organisation has a regular relationship over a period of time with someone who can provide informed critique, ideas, encouragement, and support for the building of capacity consistently, from a position of knowledge of and support for the organisation's work. Is this an approach in itself? Maybe. It certainly isn't just a method or technique for doing something. It is certainly a kind of relationship, and it challenges the more conventional relationships of power that characterise interactions between many funding bodies and the organisations they fund.

# 'Scaling up' and 'skilling up'

There was a considerable debate a few years ago about how to 'scale up' the effectiveness of development interventions. I remember feeling nervous about it at the time. On the one hand, one would not want to argue with the need for change to happen on a far greater scale, if the conditions of life for millions of poor people and communities around the world are to improve. But there was something in the concept of 'scaling up' that sounded too close to the undertaking of mass programmes, imposing them from above, or replicating something that had worked in one place across many places, whether it would be effective elsewhere or not.

It seems to me now that there are two kinds of 'scaling up'. One is the adoption by governments of pro-poor policies and practice, with the systems that are needed to go with it, where implementation can be at local level and adapted to local realities. This can work to the extent that resources and political will permit, and clearly there are serious limitations to both of those factors in many places. There is a lot to be said for taking this approach. Only the State, in most contexts, has the potential reach and resources to introduce large-scale change. There are, however, dangers of failure inherent in this approach. The political danger of failure is one. The danger of greed and corruption diverting resources is another. This is a risk whenever 'free' resources are moved from one place to another; it can be found in government, NGOs, international agencies, and private business, North or South – anywhere where money can be used to buy support or influence, impose policies, create or silence opposition. So if 'scaling up' involves any significant transfer of resources, especially where there are organisational inefficiencies and inadequate controls and accountability, corruption presents a risk to its effectiveness.

There is another practical risk in 'scaling up' which becomes immediately apparent when you try to adopt something on a large scale: suddenly you need the skills that were being used in the small-scale activity, but you need them quickly and widely. Very often, the skills in question will be ones that take time to develop; they will be available only in small quantities, or they will be expensive to buy in. Your whole 'scaling up' endeavour will then depend on whether you can get away with poor skills to implement with, or how quickly and effectively you can train new people – and often you find that what looked like a promising approach is deemed a failure, when it is not the approach that was the problem, but the lack of sufficient people with adequate skills, knowledge, and resources to implement it effectively. It now becomes clear why 'tools' and 'methods' that are simple and can be replicated with very little training are so sought after. And why efforts to take effective work 'to scale' so often founder.

The other approach to 'scaling up' has, to an extent, generated its own momentum, although there is plenty of scope for more. That is the 'scaling up' that can happen through the sharing of knowledge and information about what has been tried, with what success, and for that to be tried all over the place by people who are motivated to implement change. One example of this has been the rapid and spontaneous spread of ideas about the potential of microfinance schemes. This involved a very good idea, of providing small loans to women, which was implemented in some instances, with a very high profile internationally in the development 'community'. There are many impressive cases of effective adaptation of the idea to local circumstances in different places around the world. Sometimes the approach was replicated in rather uncritical ways which over-simplified and lost the nuances of local interpretation – and because it is difficult to admit failure with an approach that has been so clearly successful in other instances, it took a while for a more critical attitude to the good idea to emerge. I suspect that the microfinance idea is most effective when sufficient attention is given not just to the adaptation process, but also to the needs for learning and 'skilling-up' that, if attended to, help to ensure effective use of any method being introduced. This kind of 'scaling up' works because people are motivated to achieve change and will look actively for ideas and inspiration that will help them to figure out what might work in their own circumstances. It is most effective when a good idea or approach or method is not simply replicated, but is tested and adapted to suit the specific circumstances.

Another example of an approach being scaled up by example and by the momentum of a good idea is that of Participatory Budgeting. From its beginnings in Porto Alegre in Brazil, this approach to the active involvement of citizens in financial decision-making and priority-setting has spread with varying success to more than 70 towns and cities in Brazil and is now spreading farther afield. It is currently being piloted, in quite different ways, in Manchester and Salford in the north-east of England.[6] Different places use the tools of the budget matrix and community meetings in their own way, with varying annual cycles of consultation and a range of ways of engaging with more conventional democratic processes and structures. In the UK, although it is too early as I write to assess how well the approach will 'fit' with the cultural context(s) and existing system of representative democracy, there is great interest already from many local authorities. If the approach is seen to work and to be adaptable to the UK context, the idea will need very little active promotion to be taken up and tried by others. As with the example of microfinance cited above, this kind of 'scaling up' risks failing though misapplication and misunderstanding, and through the idea spreading faster than the detailed understanding of the characteristic features of the idea and its application that makes it work. Perhaps every apparently good idea needs a label attached to it saying 'Warning: effective only if applied with skill and used in a way that adapts it to local circumstances'.

## Does the wheel need to be re-invented?

An exact reproduction of something that worked in one place in a different place can work if the circumstances are similar enough, or the issue being addressed is sufficiently technical in nature. I certainly would not argue for starting from scratch on every occasion as if this were the first time. But where human beings and human societies and cultures are the context, there is much room for unrecognised or 'invisible' differences which mean that things are not as similar as they might appear at first. Access to the ideas, knowledge, thinking, and experience of others is a crucial resource to spare us unnecessary re-inventing; case studies are most useful if they try to distil the essential elements that would be needed for replication beyond their particular culture and context. If we are to be successful, we need also a capacity, and willingness, to think afresh for each set of circumstances. Then we can work out which elements of other people's experience to keep, or at least try to replicate or adapt, and which elements we should not use.

On occasion, it will be a positive process to re-invent something that others have tried. This is particularly true if it is the *process of working it out* that gives us the skills to apply whatever it is in practice. Mistakes have an important role to play here. If we can use them, mistakes can be the richest source of learning about what works and why.

In the context where I work in the UK, there is currently a strong government emphasis on the idea of *'best practice'*, with great importance placed on identifying and disseminating 'best practice' in many fields. This is somewhat helpful in supporting the dissemination of possibly productive ideas for others to use, adapt, and build on, but the concept of 'best practice' implies that there is one approach or method that is 'best' in some universal way – a blueprint which can and should be followed. This is seriously problematic; it may undermine the flexibility that is needed to achieve specific things with particular people in particular places. At the opposite extreme, however, would be an attitude that believes each situation to be so unique that there is little to be learned from others. This would lead to much unnecessary effort to work everything out from the beginning, which in most circumstances will not be the most effective use of limited resources. 'Good practice' is a more useful concept, which allows the experience of others to provide a set of possibilities against which the needs of the particular context and circumstances can be tested. 'Good practice' still supposes a particular set of values and priorities – how else do you know it's good? – which may or may not fit other circumstances, but it allows for the possibility that there may be more than one way of doing something.

## Participatory and inclusive approaches

One example of the second approach to 'scaling up' described above has been the way in which participatory approaches have spread over the past 20 years. From being a rather radical and idiosyncratic, different way of working, participation has slowly taken the path towards the mainstream, to the extent that now the use of participatory approaches and methods is expected and encouraged in many situations. Interesting ideas and a different kind of methodology were attractive in appearing to hold out the hope of more innovative action and a closer match between the locally experienced needs and resources and the 'solutions' attempted. One of the characteristics of participatory approaches that appealed to people working in communities and at the 'grassroots' was their potential to address some of the power dynamics that had been sabotaging attempts to bring change through more conventional approaches. 'Participation' held out the possibility of actively engaging excluded and powerless groups and individuals, such as women, tribals, young people, older people, people with disabilities, other minority groups, into the centre of development processes. Methods could be chosen to facilitate active participation, and to include the voices and priorities of people otherwise ignored. These approaches were and continue to be full of potential. There are many, many instances now of such approaches and methods leading to programmes and priorities that are very different from what they would otherwise have been. It is no wonder that the ideas spread far and wide across the globe.

However, it is clear also that participation is not a panacea. As with any other approach, there need to be positive results. Participatory methods are vulnerable to being applied mechanistically and without the levels of awareness, self-awareness, and skill required on the part of facilitators. Or they can be applied without sufficient local knowledge for the power dynamics to be visible, leaving local people vulnerable to inaccurate assumptions (Mompati 2000). In such cases, they can be used to put a 'gloss' of participatory democracy over processes that continue to reproduce existing power relations. So the simple fact of using participatory methods is not sufficient to ensure that participatory *approaches* will be applied successfully. Neither, of course, is the mere use of the language of participation sufficient; for many agencies, 'participation of beneficiaries' means joining in their pre-determined projects, or being consulted, which may happen just so that the participation 'box' can be ticked, rather than being enabled to engage in social processes from a position of greater strength (White 1996). Participatory methods can also be used as one-off exercises, putting a participatory gloss on information extraction, which does nothing to address power relations and can bring problems to the surface which are then left unresolved (Jackson 1997).

Participatory methods may themselves become structures: for example, the participatory-budget matrix referred to above was developed to facilitate a complex process of citizen participation in a normally non-participatory process. This is a rare example of a formalised type of participatory decision making, which is significant because of the general lack of variety in decision-making structures in international development thinking, much of which assumes mono-cultural 'villages' or 'communities' as the basic unit.[7] An institutionalised process can be very beneficial in overcoming the resistance of individual prejudice. Once the process is institutionalised, however, there is a danger of rigidity, which could begin to work against the participatory ethos. There have also been many instances where supposedly participatory methods have been used to gather a range of information and opinions or ideas which are then used to legitimise a more conventional programme. In these cases, the methods have become separated from the approaches from which they originated, which often means that the aspects of critical analysis and reflection have been diluted or removed. This creates a dissonance that is felt keenly by the people whose opinions and inputs have been sought, and can contribute to a lack of cooperation the next time the methods are tried with them. For participatory approaches to be sustainable, people need to see the results, or at least see that results will be forthcoming, as these approaches require an investment of time and effort that could easily be directed elsewhere if no positive change emerges.

For participatory approaches to be successfully 'scaled up', there needs to be some way of creating or accessing a sufficient pool of adequately trained and/or experienced people to apply the methods effectively. If this is not achieved, success will be limited, and the attempt to include people who are not usually reached will become self-defeating. If it is not done well, people will say that the approach does not work.

One challenge for the 'community' of participatory approaches is that of 'quality control' and standards. Many individuals and organisations have invested time, creativity, and resources in training and communicating about what makes effective participation. However, there are still many forces pushing for the 'quick fix' and trying to use participatory approaches and methods without investing in the learning and experience required to make them effective. This is partly an issue of time-scale and funding patterns. If you are reaching for deep change in social and power relations, a three-year funded project is not going to be enough. Yet very few funders are willing to contemplate the funding horizons of 15–20 years that might be needed for sustainable and significant changes to which participatory approaches have the potential to contribute. For the smaller organisation that is dependent on project funding, the inability to take the longer view and plan accordingly is debilitating. I know from my own experience as a development worker in a small NGO that there is very little time left for getting on with the work, once the necessary fundraising and consequent reporting obligations have been complied with. This is not a new criticism, and some funders are trying to think differently. There must be ways of applying the ideas and attitudes of participatory approaches to the relationships between implementing organisations and the funders that satisfy the needs for accountability and probity associated with a funding relationship, but do not stifle the creativity and energy needed for effective work on the ground. Power and control is an issue in the funding relationship, just as much as between the development worker and a community.

Another challenge for participatory approaches is perhaps naivety. The power issues are real ones; participatory approaches will not make it possible to slide round them, but will make it more likely that they will become visible and need to be addressed. The results of participation can be hard to predict, which is unsettling (if not outright threatening) to any politicians or others who have a personal investment in the *status quo*. It is certainly the case that some people with power stand to lose out if more equitable arrangements are to be implemented. For changes to be effected, these issues have to be confronted and addressed. Let us be clear about this: participatory approaches, if they are to be inclusionary and transformatory, are no easy option – although they are profoundly inspiring and satisfying when they work well.

## Rigorous pragmatism?

For many people and organisations working in development, there is a constant tension between wanting to do the best job possible and needing to get things done, to get results, to meet objectives and targets. Participatory methods can help to get some things done more quickly, such as identifying the facets of a complex issue in a meeting or workshop context – although I have not encountered any attempt to systematise the things to which that applies. The general perception, however inaccurate, is that they slow things down, and are therefore a luxury. How many of us have compromised in the face of time-related pressures or financial constraints – whether or not that compromise was justified? Perhaps we know how something should be done, but how we can actually do it within the constraints we face is a different matter. The idea of doing something to a 'good enough' standard was very helpful to me, although it can be useful only within a framework of agreed minimum standards and a level of clarity of purpose and values. It also needs an accurate assessment of what can be achieved through different methods, given the available time and other resources. Otherwise, how do you judge what 'good enough' is? Without that framework, and the underpinning purpose and values, how do you distinguish between being tokenistic, for example, and doing a quick job that is actually sufficient for the immediate need? There are many occasions where the choice is between being thorough and idealistic, and being pragmatic and getting something done. How do you distinguish between when the former is needed and when the latter is sufficient? Pragmatism so often wins out in organisations that are objectives-driven. I would feel more comfortable with this if there were some way of ensuring that pragmatism is 'rigorous pragmatism', based on good analysis and transparency, rather than expediency – although this would not avoid the important questions about who takes the decisions, who is accountable to whom for the consequences, and so on what basis and in whose interests is even rigorous pragmatism being invoked.

## How do we know? Monitoring, evaluation, and impact assessment

To know whether any approach or method is effective, some kind of evaluation is needed. But evaluation itself needs approaches and methods in order to be undertaken. Where these can be consistent with each other, so much the better. Evaluation has been driven, to a large extent, by the need to demonstrate whether a particular approach or method is valid and effective, to justify replication as well as to justify expenditure and provide accountability. 'Top–down' approaches have tended to be evaluated through approaches that attempt to demonstrate 'proof' that the intervention led to the outcomes. Fortunately, this rather rigid approach has been challenged, and there is a growing understanding and an emerging consensus that 'proof', especially in social development, is an inappropriate aim for evaluation. Instead, evaluation can test the logic of the situation, and whether it was likely that the intervention or activity contributed to any changes, and whether this was a positive contribution (Roche 1999). With participatory and inclusionary approaches, evaluation that can explore 'multiple subjectivities', rather than aiming for 'objectivity', is far more conducive to learning, which is increasingly becoming the prime purpose of evaluation. If change is positive, then the 'ownership' of being able to attribute causality becomes less critical, and it is more useful to use evaluation processes to contribute to the 'deep reflection'[8] that will help the positive aspects of processes of change to be internalised and embedded in everyday practice, and help to enhance the possibilities of effective replication and adaptation.

Evaluation has relied heavily on the existence of aims or goals and objectives being stated clearly at the beginning of the programme or project. Many an evaluation report has been written lamenting the absence of clarity of aims and objectives, and some evaluators have concluded that no judgement can be reached in these circumstances. With participatory approaches, a somewhat different attitude to objectives is required, since at least some of the concrete outputs and outcomes will be determined by the people who participate as the undertaking progresses. Objectives may shift and evolve as the programme moves forward. Objectives may need to be more process-oriented, which will require indicators concerned with the *nature* of a change rather than the specific change. So, for example, with the Mexican 'pig-rearing project' referred to earlier, the objective, instead of being the establishment of a viable pig-rearing business run by the women's group, might be the successful and independent generation of income by the women in the group, together or individually. Whether this was though rearing animals or through running a local bus service (as another women's group in Mexico had successfully done) would be immaterial.

Monitoring has been in many respects the poor relation of the 'M&E' pairing. If, however, monitoring can incorporate evaluative elements throughout an ongoing process, learning can be immediate and can allow adaptation and refinement to become a more fluid feature of a programme of activity. The ultimate test of any approach or any set of methods lies, however, in what difference they have made. Impact assessment needs to look not only at what changes have occurred, who is better off and who is worse off, but at the relationship between the approach and methods used and the changes that have been achieved. Perhaps the change has happened despite the methodology, rather than because of it!

## Conclusion

No methods, even when they are good ones, can work to obviate the need for good, contextual, analytical, purposive thinking. The best methods do not automatically enable us to address power imbalances or move us towards change and social justice. Methods need to be applied in the context of a clear approach, based on values and purpose, if they are not to become rigid and reinforcing of existing relations. But even when clearly placed within a thought-through approach, methods and tools may fail or be counter-productive if they are used without skill, or are implemented by people with different purposes and intent.

There are challenges here for practitioners, activists, and researchers. A balance is needed between self-analysis and self-awareness (which can become 'navel-gazing') and purposeful action. It can often be better to get something wrong and learn what would work better, than to spend too long agonising over getting exactly the right approach and methods. Will the approach we are taking and the methods we are using make a difference to what happens? Are they likely to contribute to transformative, positive change? For this, both the approach and the methods need to be complemented by strategies and tactics in their use: we need to continue to apply fresh thinking as we learn from our own experience and that of others. The learning process, for individuals and organisations, needs to become far more strongly embedded in the approaches and methods used.

There are more questions than answers in this essay, more issues raised than conclusions reached. Some knowledge and experience, and maybe answers, can be found in the pages that follow.

*'Everything should be made as simple as possible, but not one bit simpler.'*
Albert Einstein (attributed)

## Notes

1 Tina Wallace (2000) discusses the commercial and even military origins of some approaches and methods adopted by NGOs and questions their applicability to transformational agendas.

2 The Logical Framework, or LogFrame, has been particularly associated with an approach to development that has been much criticised as top-down and technocratic. I will not rehearse the arguments here. The Framework has been used in combination with a participatory model, but it seems to me that its greatest weakness is the reliance on linear logic, and how difficult it is to make it work in a way that shows change as a multi-causal, multi-actor phenomenon.

3 I have explored the various forms that power can take in Rowlands (1997) and Townsend et al. (1999). See also Kabeer (1994).

4 Or organisations like them. I count myself among this group.

5 The Spanish, *acompañamiento*, works

better than its rather awkward English equivalent; it communicates the notion of an individual or organisation respectfully 'walking alongside' another, providing the knowledge, skill, or challenge needed to empower the organisation or individual being supported to make a change, think bigger, develop a strategy or whatever it is that is needed, but as part of an essentially peer relationship. *Compañero crítico* ('critical companion') is also used in this way.

6 And very likely in other places of which I am unaware.

7 My thanks to Julie Jarman for this point.

8 Bloch and Borges (2002:464).

## References

Bloch, Didier and Nora Borges (2002) 'Organisational learning in NGOs: an example of an intervention based on the work of Chris Argyris', *Development in Practice* 12(3&4): 461-72.

Kabeer, Naila (1994) *Reversed Realities: Gender Hierarchies in Development Thought*, London: Verso.

Longwe, Sara (1997) 'Evaporation of gender policies in the patriarchal cooking pot', *Development in Practice* 7(2):148-56, reprinted in Deborah Eade (ed.) (1997) *Development and Patronage*, Oxford: Oxfam GB.

Howard, Patricia (2002) 'Beyond the "grim resisters": towards more effective gender mainstreaming through stakeholder participation', *Development in Practice* 12(2):164-76.

Jackson, Cecile (1997) 'Sustainable development at the sharp end: field-worker agency in a participatory project', *Development in Practice* 7(3):237-47, reprinted in Deborah Eade (ed.) (1997).

Mompati, Tlamelo and Prinsen, Gerard (2000) 'Ethnicity and participatory development methods in Botswana: some participants are to be seen and not heard', *Development in Practice* 10(5):625-37, reprinted in Deborah Eade (ed.) (2002) *Development and Culture*, Oxford: Oxfam GB.

Roche, Chris (1999) *Impact Assessment for Development Agencies: Learning to Value Change*, Oxford: Oxfam GB.

Rowlands, Jo (1997) *Questioning Empowerment: Working with Women in Honduras*, Oxford: Oxfam GB.

Townsend, Janet et al. (1999) *Women and Power: Fighting Patriarchies and Poverty*, London: Zed Books.

VeneKlasen, Lisa with Valerie Miller (2002) *A New Weave of People, Power, and Politics: An Action Guide for Advocacy and Citizen Participation*, Oklahoma City: World Neighbors.

Wallace, Tina (2000) 'Development management and the aid chain: the case of NGOs' in Deborah Eade, Tom Hewitt, and Hazel Johnson (eds.) *Development and Management: Experiences in Values-based Conflict*, Oxford: Oxfam GB.

White, Sarah (1996) 'Depoliticisation of development: the uses and abuses of participation', *Development in Practice* 6(1):6-15, reprinted in Deborah Eade (ed.) (2000) *Development, NGOs, and Civil Society*, Oxford: Oxfam GB.

Whitehead, Christine (1995) 'Emergency Social Funds: the experiences of Bolivia and Peru', *Development in Practice* 5(1):53-7.

# Dissolving the difference between humanitarianism and development: the mixing of a rights-based solution

## Hugo Slim

Some months ago, I spent a morning in the public gallery in Courtroom One of the UN's International Criminal Tribunal for Rwanda in Arusha. Sitting behind the gallery's glass windows, I watched three UN judges holding court in front of an enormous UN flag, listened to the prosecution questioning an anonymous Rwandan woman, Witness J, who was hidden from view and protected by armed guards. I met the eye of the former Bourgmestre of Mabanza Commune, who was being tried on eight counts of genocide, murder, extermination, crimes against humanity, and grave breaches of Common Article 3 and Additional Protocol II of the Geneva Conventions.

A few days later, having driven a few hundred miles north, I sat observing a meeting of elders from a pastoralist community in Kenya. Gathered under a tree, they sat together on land which had once been held in common by their people and been grazed accordingly by their cattle. Bordering a river, this land was an important route to a valuable water source for their herds. Meeting in this spot where they, their fathers, and grandfathers had grazed their herds in years gone by, they were now trespassers. Some years ago, as part of the increasing privatis-ation and sub-division of so much pastoralist land in Kenya, this land had been demarcated without consulting the great majority of pastoralist elders and was now the property of the wife of the former Minister of Land – the same Minister who had overseen this policy of land 'reform'. As the meeting went on, passions rose about the continuous threats to pastoralist grazing lands from such misplaced land policies and their attendant abuses of political power. As speakers warmed to their theme, a number of elders reminded the meeting that they were a warrior people and that, while they would continue to pursue legal and peaceful means to secure their land rights, they would eventually resort to violence if their efforts were persistently frustrated.

First published in *Development in Practice* 10 (3&4) in 2000.

NGOs have been, and continue to be, intensely involved in both Rwanda and Kenya, working in the aftermath of genocide and in the struggle for land rights respectively. Responding to the Rwandan genocide with relief assistance to civilians and with advocacy to support the indictment and trial of *génocidaires*, NGO actions are labelled 'humanitarian'. Working with pastoralists on matters of land rights and livelihood, their activities are characterised as 'developmental'. This distinction is an old one. It is also an essentially unhelpful one, which implies that these two activities represent different professions with distinct values. For too long, using these terms has played into the hands of that dreadful tendency to dualism which dogs the Western mind and has led to the pernicious idea that humanitarianism and development are radically different moral pursuits. The ethic of the humanitarian has been presented unthinkingly as a sort of temporary, morally myopic project which limits itself to meeting urgent physical needs before hurriedly abdicating in favour of development workers and their much grander ethic of social empowerment and transformation. Such conventional assumptions have often been most fervently encouraged by humanitarian workers themselves. But the stereotype helps no one in the long run.

Perpetuating a rigid distinction between humanitarian values and development values opens the door to absurd questions of comparison between the two. Is humanitarian work only about saving life? Is development work 'long term' and humanitarian work 'short term'? Is one apolitical and the other political? The answer is, of course, that both humanitarianism and development are concerned with saving life, both are short and long term, and both are political, in the proper sense of being concerned with the use and abuse of power in human relations. The idea that there is an implicit distinction in values between humanitarianism and development, which is encouraged by relief–development dualism, is misconceived. Poverty and violence both proceed from a common root in a human nature which finds sharing profoundly difficult, and a tendency to dehumanise the 'otherness' in potential rivals all too easy.

If the Arusha courtroom embodies a fledgling international justice system seeking to respond to inordinate violence and suffering with humanitarian and human-rights law, the pastoralist meeting witnessed the possible seeds of a struggle against sustained and iniquitous injustice which may yet produce political violence or war, which will demand a humanitarian response. The impoverishment and violence caused by political oppression and injustice which development seeks to prevent and transform is the same as that which humanitarianism seeks to restrain and abolish when it has overwhelmed a whole society. And the fundamental value that the humanitarian and the development worker bring to different manifestations of injustice is the same: the belief in human dignity and in the essential equality of all human beings.

Politically and legally, the dominant discourse for addressing equality and dignity is now voiced in terms of human rights. And it is in human rights that we can finally dissolve the unhelpful dualism between humanitarianism and development – a process which is already happening, as donors and NGOs alike become 'rights-based'. In doing so, we are really only making good another unfortunate fallout from the Cold War period, which for various reasons found it important to distinguish rigidly between humanitarianism, development, and human rights, so creating a widespread false consciousness on the subject.

In his detailed and very readable account of the five years of negotiations and diplomatic conferences that produced the Geneva Conventions of 1949, Geoffrey Best tells the intriguing story of the 'missing Preamble' (Best 1994). The post-war development of international humanitarian law under the auspices of the ICRC in Geneva took place in parallel with the development of human-rights law at the UN in New York. The UN Convention on the Prevention and Punishment of the Crime of Genocide and the Universal Declaration of Human Rights both appeared in December 1948 a few months before the four Geneva Conventions of August the following year. These two bodies of law emerged from rather different roots: human-rights law from the political tradition of 'the rights of man' (sic) and international humanitarian law from the military tradition of chivalry and the 'laws of war'. But in the heady days of the late 1940s, the values they had in common were obvious to all. Because of this, a Preamble to the IV Geneva Convention on the protection of civilians was drafted which 'would solemnise and strengthen it by explicitly proclaiming it to be a human rights instrument and in particular a protection of basic, minimal human rights' (Best 1994:70).

When the Preamble was brought to the final diplomatic conference in Geneva, no one objected to the reference to human rights, and it looked set to be agreed – until a group of countries working with the Holy See decided that the Preamble should affirm such universal principles of human rights still further by relating them directly to God as 'the divine source of human charity'. At the proposal of this amendment, a row ensued which saw the newly organised, and ardently atheist, communist bloc at odds with the religious alliance of key countries. To break the stalemate and move forward with the wider process, it was decided to drop the whole idea of a Preamble. Sadly, therefore, the opportunity to recognise international humanitarian law firmly and explicitly within the wider body of human rights was let slip, not because of a dispute about the affinity between the two bodies of law but as the collateral damage from a dispute about the existence of God!

In the decades that followed, there were those in the Red Cross movement in particular who were probably much relieved that the Preamble never materialised. As authoritarian régimes on both sides of the political spectrum increasingly equated human rights with subversive politics, many humanitarians capitalised on the lack of explicit human-rights discourse in their project and its Conventions and were able to distance themselves from human rights and so make their cause less politically charged. A distinction between human rights, humanitarianism, and development was allowed to emerge which had never really existed in the minds of those who produced the 1948 Universal Declaration or the 1949 Conventions. But this false distinction came to be corrected in the 1990s as human rights, humanitarian law, and rights-based development have made increasingly common cause. Indeed, the recent 'Humanitarian Charter', set forth by the many NGOs involved in the Sphere Project, could be seen as a second attempt at the missing Preamble (Sphere Project 2000: 6-10). Grounding humanitarian action firmly in a rights-based framework which takes account of international humanitarian law, human-rights law, and refugee law, this new charter serves to enfold humanitarian action and the laws of war within the embrace of human rights.

If humanitarianism is once again catching up with the idea of human rights, so too is development. In recent years, the dominant under-standing of poverty and suffering among 'thinking NGOs' has come to fix on power, its abuse and its imbalance, as the essential determinant in the construction of poverty and suffering. And as poverty and violence have become increasingly conceived of in terms of power, development has been re-framed – by NGOs and Western governments alike – in terms of human rights, which provide a countervailing force to challenge and make just demands of power. (See, for example, Oxfam GB's 1994 Basic Rights Campaign, of particular note in view of the fact that human-rights work as such is not regarded as a charitable activity under the law governing the behaviour of charities registered in England and Wales.) The development of universal human rights, whose fundamental value is a human dignity founded in individual equality, personal freedom, and social and economic justice, easily encompasses humanitarian and development activity and shows them to have common ends. The (re)discovery in the 1990s that both humanitarianism and development are 'rights-based' ended, once and for all, the distracting dichotomy set up between the two and it will, one hopes, silence the succession of debates about the differences or links between relief and development which have dominated so many conferences and occupied so much management time in agencies since the 1970s.

The schema of human rights, which development has found so late and which humanitarianism lost so early but has now rediscovered, is the common practical framework for elaborating values which underpin both humanitarian action and development work. Both ethics – the humanitarian ethic of restraint and protection, and the development ethic of empowerment and social justice – value the same common goods and embrace the same ideal of full human dignity. If, in the new century, humanitarians and development workers could both take the bold step of recognising that they are all human-rights workers, then the theory, management, and practice of relief and development work would be relieved of one of their most mesmerising and exhausting distractions – the false dichotomy between these two professions and their common values.

## References

Best, G. (1994) *War and Law Since 1945*, Oxford: Oxford University Press

Sphere Project (2000) *The Sphere Handbook: Humanitarian Charter and Minimum Standards in Disaster Response*, Geneva: The Sphere Project

# Should development agencies have Official Views?

## David Ellerman

## Introduction: a 'Church' or 'party' organisation versus a 'learning organisation'

In the world today, most organisations want to be seen as 'learning organisations' that emphasise the importance of the accumulation of 'intellectual capital' and 'knowledge management'. Yet many old habits persist that are in direct contradiction to learning and the advancement of knowledge. Church- or political party-like organisations proselytising their own dogmas apply the new rhetoric of 'learning' as a veneer. (Throughout this article, I use both the 'Church' and 'Communist Party' metaphors to indicate unitary organisations espousing certain 'truths' or messages instead of being engaged in an open-ended search for knowledge.)

Focusing on an organisation or agency involved in knowledge-based development assistance (such as the World Bank) operating as a 'knowledge bank', the main question I seek to address is: how can such an agency function as a learning organisation? I approach this question by first considering some of the major roadblocks in the way of organisational learning, before launching into a discussion of the open learning model and how development agencies can become learning organisations.

## Roadblock to learning No. 1: branded knowledge as dogma

To put it simply, the basic problem is that in spite of the espoused model of a 'learning organisation', the theory-in-use of a development agency is often a model of a 'development church' giving definitive *ex cathedra* 'views' on the substantive and controversial questions of development. As with the dogmas of a Church, the brand name of the organisation is invested with its views. Once an 'Official View' has been adopted, then to question it is to attack the agency itself and the value of its franchise. As a result, new learning at the expense of established Official Views is not encouraged. Thus when licensing an Official View, the authorities need to have what Milton called the 'grace of infallibility and incorruptibleness' (see Morley 1928:218), since any subsequent 'learning' is tantamount to disloyalty.

When an agency adopts Official Views, then discussions between the agency staff and its clients is a pseudo-dialogue, given that the former are not free unilaterally to change Official Views (just as missionaries are not free to approve local variations in Church dogmas) or to approve of a project that departs substantially from those views. The slogan is something like: 'Give the clients an inch of nuance, and they'll take a mile of status quo' (Kanbur and Vines 2000:101). Clients are like Henry Ford's Model T customers who were free to choose any colour car so long as it was black. The clients who wish to receive assistance are free to 'learn' and to 'make up their own minds' so long as they do so in conformity with Official Views.

There is little motivation for the staff actively to appropriate or understand any deeper rationale for the views, since they must espouse the Official Views *vis-à-vis* the clients in any case. The views are generally not those that individual staff members have decided upon personally, based on evidence or argumentation. In project design, the herd instinct takes over. If a manager designs a project in conformity with Official Views and the project fails, then those involved in the project can hardly be blamed for the outcome of their team efforts.

Publicly airing ambivalence or discontent about the Official Views outside the confines of the agency is frowned upon. The reasoning is standard: parents should not argue in front of the children; doctors should not debate in front of the patients. There can be debate inside the party but once a decision is made, then the members must publicly adhere to the party line. The Church or party model fits perfectly with the standard 'dissemination' or transmission-belt methodology of knowledge-based development assistance. The agency believes it holds the best 'knowledge for development' and is to transmit it to the recipients in the developing world through various forms of aid-baited proselytisation.

What is the alternative? The organisation of science provides the paradigm example of an 'ecology of knowledge' where the open and public contestation of ideas and criticism of conjectures is essential and actively encouraged:

*Criticism of our conjectures is of decisive importance: by bringing out our*
*mistakes it makes us understand the difficulties of the problem which we are*
*trying to solve. This is how we become better acquainted with our problems,*
*and able to propose more mature solutions: the very refutation of a theory –*
*that is, of any serious tentative solution to our problem – is always a step*
*forward that takes us nearer to the truth ... Since none of [the theories] can be*
*positively justified, it is essentially their critical and progressive character –*
*the fact that we can argue about their claim to solve our problems better than*
*their competitors – which constitutes the rationality of science.*
(Popper 1965:vii)

Another example of the 'ecology of knowledge' is provided by the modern Western university. The university does not set itself up as an arbiter of truth, but as an arena within which contrary theories can be examined and can collide in open debate. As Barrington Moore Jr has noted, 'among contemporary social arrangements the modern western university is the main one that has endeavoured to make intellectual criticism and innovation a legitimate and regular aspect of the prevailing social order' (Moore 1972:91). The organisation does not itself have Official Views or 'messages' on the questions of the day – and thus it does not need a public relations department to monitor and control the propagating of Official Views to the press.

When an agency takes Official Views on complex questions of development and considers its views as branded knowledge, then the genuine collision of adverse opinions and the rule of critical reasoning tend to give way to the rule of authority and bureaucratic reasoning within the hierarchy of the organisation (The 'Soviet Theory of Genetics' based on Trofim Denisovich Lysenko's work is a good example of this). While a sort-of-debate may be 'encouraged' within the agency, the perimeter of that discussion is framed, not coincidentally, by the jurisdiction of organisational authority. Debate should not stray beyond its pale into the public domain where the authorities have no writ. The authorities in the organisation determine 'the Official Views' and tend to shut off or 'embargo' any feedback loops that may call into question those views, thereby diminishing the 'franchise value' of the 'brand name' – not to mention reflecting poorly on the wisdom of the authorities who sanctioned the views in the first place. Learning from errors, which involves changing 'Official Views' and modifying 'branded knowledge', is minimised, so that the organisation tends to function more as a Church- or party-type organisation than as an open learning one – regardless of the espoused theory.

The Church/party model of proselytising directly contradicts autonomous or self-directed learning in the client countries (see below for more on the Socratic rationale for not having Official Views). The standard dissemination or transmission-belt methodology inhibits learning in a similar manner. The project manager from the agency wants the clients to 'learn', as long as they learn 'the right thing'. Any genuinely self-directed learning process in the client country may veer off in the 'wrong direction', which the project manager cannot withstand. The project manager would return to headquarters as a failure without a project. Therefore, the flow of knowledge must be carefully managed to prevent the clients from being distracted by alternative views.

## Roadblock to learning No. 2: funded assumptions as dogma

Why is it so necessary for a development agency to take an Official View on the 'One Best Way' to solve a development problem? One common answer is that a development agency is not a university; the agency puts money as loans or grants behind projects based on various assumptions. Since university professors do not 'put their money where their mouth is', they are free to debate questions for ever. Once an agency has committed significant resources to certain assumptions, then it becomes necessary to 'fall in line' and support the funded assumption.

But while there may be obvious bureaucratic reasons why individual project managers and their superiors would like a funded project assumption to be treated as 'gospel', that does not explain why the whole institution should take such a stand. The commitment of funds and prestige even seems to alter perceptions.[1] For instance, subjective assessments of winning probabilities tend to increase after the bets have been placed at a race track, but horses do not run faster when bets are riding on them. Theories are corroborated by evidence, not by funding commitments. Many businesses have come to grief because managers would not revisit strategies after initial costs were sunk. In view of the record of international development aid (see, for example, Easterly 2001), there is little support for the similar practice of hardening project assumptions into gospel simply because funds have been committed.

# Roadblock to learning No. 3: 'social science' as dogma

Today, 'science' has long since replaced religious authority as the source of dogmas that one can appeal to without further reasoning or corroboration, even though that line of argumentation completely misrepresents the scientific method, not to mention the role of critical thinking. But the all-too-human factors that previously made Church dogma appealing have not suddenly disappeared in today's scientific age, so one should expect the appeal to 'science' to be thoroughly abused. This is nowhere truer than in the social sciences (see Andreski 1972). Economics is the 'rooster who rules the roost' in the social sciences, so one should expect much to be passed off in the name of 'economics'. Yet many of the theses imposed by bureaucratic power as the 'Truths of Economics' would not pass without serious challenge in any open scientific forum – particularly when one goes beyond academic model building to policy applications. One example that springs to mind is the role in the Russian reform debacle played by Harvard economic geniuses and the Western agencies who tried to 'install' the institutions of a market economy (see Ellerman 2001).

It is particularly unfortunate when a Tayloristic 'One Best Way' (OBW) mentality creeps into development policy making in the name of 'science' (see Kanigel 1997). The problems of developing and transition countries are far too complex to yield to formulaic 'best practices' and 'magic bullets'. Many different approaches need to be tried on an experimental basis, so when a major development agency forsakes experimentalism to stake its reputation on the 'One Best Way', then the development effort as a whole is impoverished.

The idea that a development agency always has to have an Official View (rather than house competing views) is about as scientific as the 'scientific' socialism of the communist parties of the past. John Dewey quotes the English Communist John Strachey's statement that the communist parties' 'refusal to tolerate the existence of incompatible opinions ... [is] simply asserting the claim that Socialism is scientific'. Dewey goes on to comment that it 'would be difficult, probably impossible, to find a more direct and elegantly finished denial of all the qualities that make ideas and theories either scientific or democratic than is contained in this statement' (Dewey 1939:96). Critical reasoning and scientific methodology go in quite the opposite direction of fostering

*the willingness to hold belief in suspense, ability to doubt until evidence is*
*obtained; willingness to go where evidence points instead of putting first*
*a personally preferred conclusion; [and the] ability to hold ideas in*
*solution and use them as hypotheses to be tested instead of as dogmas*
*to be asserted ...*
(Dewey 1939:145)

This part of the scientific attitude is translated into the policy domain
with such suggestions as multiple advocacy (Haas 1990:210) and
double visioning (see Schön 1983:281). But it is not some wanton
perversity that prevents this scientific attitude from being implemented
in a large organisation such as a major development agency. There are
quiet human impulses that push for conformity and rigidity:

*To hold theories and principles in solution, awaiting confirmation, goes*
*contrary to the grain. Even today questioning a statement made by a person*
*is often taken by him as a reflection upon his integrity, and is resented.*
*For many millennia opposition to views widely held in a community was*
*intolerable. It called down the wrath of the deities who are in charge of the*
*group ... Baconian idols of the tribe, the cave, the theater, and den have*
*caused men to rush to conclusions, and then to use all their powers to*
*defend from criticism and change the conclusions arrived at.*
(Dewey 1939:146)

## Roadblock to learning No. 4: the rage to conclude

Albert O. Hirschman has often noted the problems created in
developing countries by the tendency that Flaubert ridiculed as
*la rage de vouloir conclure,* or the rage to conclude (see Hirschman
1973:238-40). The same attitude is rampant in development agencies.
Indeed, this is another self-reinforcing lock-in between development
agencies and their client countries.

*[Policy makers] will be supplied with a great many ideas, suggestions, plans,*
*and ideologies, frequently of foreign origin or based on foreign experience ...*
*Genuine learning about the problem will sometimes be prevented not only*
*by the local policy makers' eagerness to jump to a ready-made solution but*
*also by the insistent offer of help and advice on the part of powerful outsiders*
*... [S]uch practices [will] tend to cut short that 'long confrontation between*
*man and a situation' (Camus) so fruitful for the achievement of genuine*
*progress in problem-solving.*
(Hirschman 1973:239-40)

The puzzles that development agencies face about inducing economic and social development are perhaps the most complex and ill-defined questions confronting humankind. Donald Schön (1971, 1983) noted the novel complexity, genuine uncertainty, conflict of values, unique circumstances, and structural instabilities that plague problems of social transformation and preclude definitive blueprint solutions. Yet one must marvel at the tendency of the major development agencies to rush forward with universal 'best practices'[2] – a tendency based not on any methods resembling social science but on a bureaucratic need to maintain élite prestige by 'having an answer' for the client. In contrast, every field of science is populated by competing theories, and scientists do not feel the need to artificially rush to closure just to 'have an answer'.

Consider, for example, the complex problem of fighting corruption. Economists might approach the topic by trying to minimise government-imposed discretionary regulations which present rent-seeking opportunities to officials who might offer to relax a restriction for appropriate compensation. Accountants might emphasise transparency and uniformity of data and the independence of auditing. Civil servants might emphasise codes of ethics, organisational morale, and disclosure requirements. Lawyers might encourage civil discovery procedures and criminal sanctions. Others will promote a free and independent press, a high standard of public ethics, and a vigorous civil society. There are clearly many ways to approach the topic, and so a multi-pronged approach rather than a 'One Best Way' seems advisable. Yet the dogmatic mentality might express alarm and dismay when different groups from the same international development agency take different approaches to fighting corruption, and these different views are aired openly. Why can't the international agency 'get its act together' and tell the client the One Best Way to address the problem?

When journalists try to 'build a story' by pointing out differences within a development agency, then agency bureaucrats should point out the necessity of the open clash of adverse opinions to intellectual progress (perhaps with references to Mill's *On Liberty* or the history of science). They should point out that the real story is the intellectual honesty and integrity of an agency willing to have such open discussions, which are the lifeblood of intellectual and scientific progress. Instead, PR-oriented bureaucrats are more typically alarmed at the lack of 'coordination of messages' and re-dedicate themselves to better 'vetting' the public statements of agency officials and researchers, a tragi-comic effort usually carried out in the name of 'quality control'.

The Church/party approach has implications for the question of client-centred versus paternalistic approaches to client learning. What would be 'wrong' with an international development organisation acknowledging, and listeners or readers realising, that reasonable people within the same agency may differ on the remarkably complex questions of development? Indeed, such a realisation might have the rather positive effect of encouraging listeners or readers to reflect upon the matter more seriously and thereby take some responsibility in forming their own opinions.[3] In short, it would foster active learning rather than promoting passive acceptance of the 'truth' promulgated by a Church- or party-like organisation.

Often the argument is that 'Yes, there are doubts and differences within the agency, but the agency must show a united front in order to steel the resolve of the clients trying to implement a difficult programme of social and economic change.' Perhaps the clear resolve of the agency's Official View and the possibility of conditioning aid on the acceptance of that reform package will tip the domestic balance between reform and anti-reform coalitions in a developing country in favour of the former and bring the internal advocates of that view to power. But there are several problems with this line of argument. First, it implicitly assumes a Jacobinic (or market-Bolshevik) rather than an adaptive and experimentalist strategy of change. Indeed, a Jacobin-Bolshevik strategy does assume a fanatical resolve that cannot publicly entertain doubts, but that is one of the many problems with such a philosophy of social change. An adaptive, experimental, or pragmatic approach requires no such certitude and in fact welcomes a variety of parallel experiments in multiple regions or sectors to see what works (the social and economic reforms undertaken in China over the past two decades are a good example of this). Second, this argument assumes that the client is deriving its reform motivation from the agency, and not from within its ranks. Third, while Hirschman notes that this imagined sequence is not impossible, 'it is our conviction that this picture of program aid as a catalyst for virtuous policies belongs to the realm of rhapsodic phantasy' (1971:205).

## The open learning model and autonomy-compatible assistance

Surely much has been learned about economic development. What is wrong, one might ask, with espousing the best practices from successful development efforts as well as promoting underlying guiding principles? Should international development organisations just be agnostic on the questions of development and treat all opinions as having equal weight? To approach these questions, it is useful to consider the methodology of science. Science as a loosely structured international open learning organisation is hardly agnostic in any given area. All opinions are not given equal weight. Certain theories have so far run the gauntlet of criticism better than others, so they are accepted as the 'received' or current theories in a field. The difference from a more dogmatic Church- or party-type approach lies in the methodology used to sustain or overturn the hypotheses. In mathematics, it is inter-subjectively verifiable proof, not authority, that is the basis for theorems. In the empirical sciences, hypotheses are developed on the basis of intellectual coherence and factual cues, and are then openly subjected to experiments that can be inter-subjectively verified and reproduced (for example, as in the 'cold fusion' controversy). As long as inter-subjective verification remains the touchstone of any scientific theory, then no theory needs, in principle, to be accepted on the basis of authority. Science does not operate on the basis of brand names. Adding the brand name of an agency to a thesis in order to make it an Official View *adds nothing of scientific value* to the thesis. Indeed, the association of bureaucratic power with the thesis tends to corrupt the operation of critical thinking.

This methodology of science shows, at least in general terms, how an open learning model of a knowledge-based development agency might translate into assistance that is compatible with the autonomy of the client. The important thing is not to teach a client country the 'truth' but first to ensure that all major positions on a controversial question are presented, and second (and of greater long-term importance), to foster the active learning methodology within the country in order to find and corroborate or disprove the hypotheses and theories. That means capacity building in the knowledge institutions of the country.

When theories clash, then experiments should be encouraged to 'see what works'. Indeed, there are usually different decentralised experiments going on in a country (sometimes called 'moving trains') often unbeknownst to government officials. As Hirschman has noted, 'the hidden rationalities I was after were precisely and principally *processes of growth and change already under way* in the societies I studied, processes that were often unnoticed by the actors immediately involved, as well as by foreign experts and advisors' (Hirschman 1984:91-93). Where the train of reform is already moving on its own, then reformers can jump on board to attempt to help it run more smoothly. The 'moving trains' can be held up as models for other reform efforts in the country. Everett Rogers (1983:Chapter 9) describes decentralised diffusion systems for social innovations, with the primary example being the Chinese system of 'models' (e.g. model communes or enterprises) dating from the beginning of the modern reform period in the 1970s and forming an important part of the most remarkable growth episode in history (the 'Chinese economic miracle' of the 1980s and 1990s).

For instance, if a knowledge-based development agency wants to promote the OBW of reforming or changing certain institutions (e.g. the 'best' model for fighting corruption or the 'best' form of privatisation), then it should be willing to share the source of that 'knowledge', to promote experiments to corroborate hypotheses or to validate a local adaptation, and to encourage horizontal cross-learning from similar experiments documented in the organisation's knowledge management system – all before the reform is accepted as a 'blueprint' for any country as a whole. In short, the inter-subjectivity and reproducibility that are key to scientific knowledge translate into *local* experimentation and verification in the case of development knowledge. The message to policy makers should run along these lines:

> To the best of our accumulated experience (which we deem to call 'knowledge'), here is what works best in countries like yours. Why don't you study these principles together with their corroboration to date (best practice success stories), take a look at these case studies, contact the people who designed those reforms, set up horizontal learning programmes with those best practice cases, and try some experiments to see what works in various parts of your own country? After carrying out this learning process on your own, you might call us back if you feel we could help by partially but not wholly funding the reform programme you have decided upon.

The most important thing is to get away from a paternalistic model of 'teaching' as the transmission of knowledge from the development agency to the developing country. Using the slogan, 'Stop the teaching so that the learning can begin!', Ortegay Gasset suggested: 'He who wants to teach a truth should place us in the position to discover it ourselves' (1961:67). To impose a model without this local learning process would be to short-circuit and bypass the active learning capability of local policy makers, to substitute authority in its place, and thus to perpetuate the passivity of tutelage.[4]

If the development agency can move beyond the Church or party model to an open learning model, then it can also move from standard knowledge dissemination or transmission-belt methodology towards knowledge-based capacity building:

> The aim of teaching is not only to transmit information, but also to transform students from passive recipients of other people's knowledge into active constructors of their own and others' knowledge. The teacher cannot transform without the student's active participation, of course. Teaching is fundamentally about creating the pedagogical, social, and ethical conditions under which students agree to take charge of their own learning, individually and collectively.
>
> (Elmore 1991:xvi)

This form of activist pedagogy adapted to developing countries (as active learners) would constitute autonomy-enhancing knowledge-based development assistance.

## Competition and devil's advocacy in the open learning model

How can a large bureaucratic agency itself advance from the Church or party model towards an open learning model? One way is for the agency to foster competition in a market-place for ideas internally – something which requires an open ecology of knowledge and criticism, not the closed system of Official Views. This is expressed in the 'market-place of ideas concept – the proposition that truth naturally overcomes falsehood when they are allowed to compete ... The belief that competing voices produce superior conclusions [is] ... implicit in scientific reasoning, the practice of trial by jury, and the process of legislative debate' (Smith 1988:31). For instance, the defendant's right to an attorney in a US courtroom takes away from the prosecutor the monopoly right to present evidence and arguments. A judge may not go to the jury before both sides of the arguments have been heard, and a patient should not go to surgery before getting a second opinion. Even the Roman Catholic Church, when considering someone for sainthood, has a 'devil's advocate' (*Advocatus Diaboli*) to state the other side of the story. A development agency should not pretend to greater authority or infallibility when it canonises a good-practice success story as the OBW.

This idea of the constructive role of public criticism goes back at least to the time of Socrates in Athens:

> *For if you kill me you will not easily find a successor to me, who, if I may use*
> *such a ludicrous figure of speech, am a sort of gadfly, attached to the state by*
> *God; and the state is a great and noble horse who is rather sluggish owing to*
> *his very size, and requires to be stirred into life. I am that gadfly which God*
> *has attached to the state, and all day long and in all places am always*
> *fastening upon you, arousing and persuading and reproaching you.*
> (Plato 1997:30-31)

The penchant for competition seems to be one of the key features of Athenian Greece that distinguished it from other societies of antiquity, and Socrates represented the use of dialogue and contestation as the road to improving knowledge. 'The form Socrates' teaching took – intellectual duelling before a sportive audience – looks much odder to us than it did to Athenians, whose whole culture was based on the contest (*agon*), formal and informal, physical, intellectual, and legal' (Wills 1994:163). Immanuel Kant recognised that the 'means which nature employs to bring about the development of innate capacities is that of antagonism within society', and he portrayed the insight with the analogy of trees competing in a forest:

> *In the same way, trees in a forest, by seeking to deprive each other of air*
> *and sunlight, compel each other to find these by upward growth, so that they*
> *grow beautiful and straight – whereas those which put out branches at will,*
> *in freedom and in isolation from others, grow stunted, bent and twisted.*
> *All the culture and art which adorn mankind and the finest social order*
> *man creates are fruits of his unsociability.*
> (Kant 1991:46)

Of course, not all antagonism or unsociability is helpful, and Hirschman (1995) has investigated which forms of social conflict are more beneficial than others (see also Coser 1956), a question that also goes back to the contrast between Socrates' use of provocative dialogues to improve knowledge and the Sophists' eristic methods employed simply to defeat an opponent.

For our purposes, however, the focus is on the difference between an organisation that incorporates (one hopes, beneficial) antagonism and one that aims at a non-antagonistic idea of agreement, cooperation, and 'team play' – a small society like that dryly satirised by Kant as the Arcadian ideal where men would be 'as good-natured as the sheep they tended' (Kant 1991). Some modern research (Lloyd 1996) has used this contrast to address the question of why, after such promising beginnings in ancient China, science developed so strongly in ancient Greece did not develop further in China. The key feature in ancient China was the intermix of power with the desire to answer questions of empirical truth – a feature shared by the Church during the Middle Ages or by Lysenkoism (and the role of the party in general) in the Soviet Union. In ancient China, the emperor's Mandate of Heaven was based on a view of the world that pictured the emperor in the central role of maintaining harmony between heaven and earth, and the views of philosophers and scientists needed to accommodate that basic scheme. By contrast, Greek intellectual life exhibited 'radical revisability' (Lloyd 1996:216), where thinkers would offer theories completely at odds with those of their rivals. Chinese intellectual life emphasised accommodation and harmony, while the Greeks thrived on antagonism and adversarial clashes. The differences extended throughout social and legal affairs:

> Differences between individuals or groups that might well have been the subject of appeal to litigation in Greece were generally settled [in China] by discussion, by arbitration, or by the decision of the responsible officials. The Chinese had, to be sure, no experience that remotely resembled that of the Greek dicasts [large public juries], nor, come to that, that of Greek public participation in open debate of political issues in the Assemblies.
> (Lloyd 1996:109)

Given the rather clear historical verdict of the mixing of power and knowledge in ancient China, the medieval Church, and more recently the Communist Party, there seems to be little basis for a development agency dedicated to promoting development knowledge to adopt 'Official Views' on some of the most complex and subtle questions facing humankind.

Aside from not licensing Official Views, how might an agency promote internal adversarial engagement? Devil's advocacy is one practice that might be fostered in a development agency functioning as an open learning organisation.[5] The political scientist Alfred De Grazia recommends such a countervailing system as a part of any large bureaucracy: 'The countervailors would be a corps of professional critics of all aspects of bureaucracy who would be assigned by the representative council of an institution to specialise as critic of all the subinstitutions' (De Grazia 1975). Devil's advocacy might provide a constructive alternative in addition to negative criticism of the proposed policy. In economics, the opportunity-cost doctrine evaluates an option by comparing its value to the value of a best alternative. If plan B is the best alternative to plan A (and the plans are mutually exclusive), then the opportunity cost of choosing plan A is the value foregone by not choosing plan B. Plan A is preferable if its value exceeds its opportunity cost (assuming both can be quantitatively measured). The application of the opportunity-cost doctrine requires the analysis and evaluation of the best alternative – and that is the more general role of devil's advocacy even when quantitative values are not available. By eliciting plan B, devil's advocacy generalises the opportunity-cost doctrine from cost-benefit analysis to general policy analysis. Just as in an open market competition provides the B plans, organisational devil's advocacy could be seen as an attempt to provide benchmark competition within an organisation.

The general case for a more systematic devil's advocate or countervailing role in an organisation is much the same as the case for genuine debate and open discussion. One classic statement of that argument can be found in John Stuart Mill's 1859 essay *On Liberty*. If little is known on a question, then real debate and the 'clash of adverse opinions' are some of the best engines of discovery. If 'partial truths' are known, then the same is necessary to ferret out a clearer picture and to better adapt theories to new and different contexts. Mill argued that even in cases of settled opinions, debate and discussion serve to disturb the 'deep slumber of a decided opinion' so that it might be held more as a rational conviction than as an article of faith:

> So essential is this discipline to a real understanding of moral and human subjects, that if opponents of all important truths do not exist, it is indispensable to imagine them, and supply them with the strongest arguments which the most skilful devil's advocate can conjure up.
> (Mill 1972:105)

## Non-dogmatism and Socratic ignorance in organisations

I have argued that organisational learning can best take place if open competition, devil's advocacy, and the collision of ideas are fostered instead of being suppressed in favour of an outward show of allegiance to Official Views. This openness is now taken for granted in the institutions of higher learning as well as in the informal communities of the sciences, but many development agencies still operate on the basis of the Church or party model, regardless of the espoused theory.

I now turn from these competition- or rivalry-based arguments to a different type of argument against having Official Views in an organisation that aspires to be a learning organisation and to foster learning in its clients. How can the development agency help the client 'own' the knowledge being acquired? The helper needs to refrain from trying to teach or impose a certain representation or view on the doers.[6] That will call for the helper to display non-assertiveness, non-dogmatism, cognitive humility,[7] tolerance, 'egolessness' (Davenport and Prusak 1998:113), or Socratic ignorance.[8] This Socratic humility or ignorance is the cognitive counterpart to the forbearance of the type of material assistance that would create dependency and undercut the volition of self-help on the part of the doers. As George Bernard Shaw put it: 'if you teach a man anything he will never learn it' (Winsten 1962:174).

Thus even if an agency has the 'answer' (and that is a big 'if'), it should still refrain from 'teaching' it (not to mention enforce its 'learning' through aid conditionalities). It should engage in capacity building and facilitating the doers' own learning process, and not in trying to 'teach' or 'disseminate' what it takes to be the answers. Paulo Freire made this point about development professionals working with people in a community:

> *Whatever the specialty that brings [the professionals] into contact with the people, they are almost unshakably convinced that it is their mission to 'give' the latter their knowledge and techniques. They see themselves as 'promoters' of the people. Their programs of action ... include their own objectives, their own convictions, and their own preoccupations.*
> *They do not listen to the people, but instead plan to teach them how to 'cast off the laziness which creates underdevelopment' ... They feel that the ignorance of the people is so complete that they are unfit for anything except to receive the teachings of the professionals.*
> (Freire 1970:153-4)

For an example closer to home, upon seeing a child struggling with a homework problem parents may feel the urge to supply what they think is the answer, but parents also presumably know they should resist that urge, as it would undercut the learning process. Why do development agencies find it so difficult to apply the same principle?

---

## Disclaimer

# Notes

1   When predictions fail, then skewed perceptions and rationalisations are a likely outcome. See Festinger (1957) and Elster (1983). See Akerlof and Dickens (1982) for an economic treatment of cognitive dissonance.

2   The universal suggestion that everyone should wear a three-piece suit still requires local tailoring or adaptation to each person's size and shape. This illustrates the fallacy in the argument that an agency does not recommend a 'universal recipe' simply because it explicitly recognises the need for local adaptation.

3   Some of the best computer-based training programmes have 'experts' popping up on the screen giving contradictory advice. 'In other words, the program communicates that there's not always one right answer. It invites trainees to learn to use their own judgement rather than rely on someone else's – especially when the someone else isn't as close to the situation as you are. Organisations today are facing increasingly complex situations where there are many possible answers. Traditional training that insists on right and wrong answers disempowers the individual – it robs people of their decision-making ability' (Schank 1997:24).

4   In 1784, Immanuel Kant wrote a short but influential pamphlet *What is Enlightenment?* Enlightenment, he wrote, 'is man's release from his self-incurred tutelage. Tutelage is man's inability to make use of his understanding without direction from another. Self-incurred is this tutelage when its cause lies not in lack of reason but in lack of resolution and courage to use it without direction from another. *Sapere aude!* "Have the courage to use your own reason!" –

that is the motto of enlightenment' (see Schmidt 1996; see also Ellerman 1999 on these issues).

5   Devil's advocacy (see Schwenk 1984) is interpreted broadly to include a number of related techniques to better elicit the main policy alternatives. A *Cassandra's advocate* (Janis 1972:217) is a person who emphasises alternative interpretations of data and focuses on all the things that can go wrong ('Murphy's Law-yer'). The *Rashomon effect* (see Schön 1971:210) illustrates that the same set of circumstances and events can be interpreted very differently by different people.

6   The Socratic–Kantian Leonard Nelson emphasises this aspect of the Socratic process of instruction: 'Philosophical instruction fulfills its task when it systematically weakens the influences that obstruct the growth of philosophical comprehension and reinforces those that promote it. Without going into the question of other relevant influences, let us keep firmly in mind the one that must be excluded unconditionally: the influence that may emanate from the instructor's assertions. If this influence is not eliminated, all labor is vain. The instructor will have done everything possible to forestall the pupil's own judgement by offering him a ready-made judgement' (Nelson 1949:19).

7   'But all true effort to help begins with self-humiliation: the helper must first humble himself under him he would help, and therewith must understand that to help does not mean to be a sovereign but to be a servant, that to help does not mean to be ambitious but to be patient, that to help means to endure for the time being the imputation that one is in the wrong and does not understand what the other understands' (Kierkegaard, quoted in Bretall 1946:334).

8 'True Socraticism represents first and foremost an attitude of mind, an intellectual humility easily mistaken for arrogance, since the true Socratic is convinced of the ignorance not only of himself but of all mankind. This rather than any body of positive doctrine is the contribution of Socrates' (Guthrie 1960:75).

# References

Akerlof, George and William Dickens (1982) 'The economic consequences of cognitive dissonance', *American Economic Review* 72 (June):307-319.

Andreski, Stanislav (1972) *Social Sciences as Sorcery*, New York, NY: St. Martin's Press.

Bretall, Robert (ed.) (1946) *A Kierkegaard Anthology*, Princeton, NJ: Princeton University Press.

Coser, Lewis (1956) *The Functions of Social Conflict*, New York, NY: Free Press.

Davenport, Thomas and Laurence Prusak (1998) *Working Knowledge*, Boston, MA: Harvard Business School Press.

De Grazia, Alfred (1975) *Eight Bads – Eight Goods: The American Contradictions*, Garden City, NY: Anchor Books.

Dewey, John (1939) *Freedom and Culture*, New York, NY: Capricorn.

Easterly, William (2001) *The Elusive Quest for Growth: Economists' Adventures and Misadventures in the Tropics*, Cambridge, MA: MIT Press.

Ellerman, David (1999) 'Global institutions: transforming international development agencies into learning organisations', *Academy of Management Executives* 13(1):25-35.

Ellerman, David (2001) 'Lessons from East Europe's voucher privatisation', *Challenge: The Magazine of Economic Affairs* 44(4):14-37.

Elmore, R. (1991) Foreword, in C. R. Christensen, D. A. Garvin and A. Sweet (eds.) *Education for Judgement*, Boston, MA: Harvard Business School Press.

Elster, Jon (1983) *Sour Grapes: Studies in the Subversion of Rationality*, Cambridge: CUP.

Festinger, L. (1957) *A Theory of Cognitive Dissonance*, Stanford, CA: Stanford University Press.

Freire, Paulo (1970) *Pedagogy of the Oppressed*, New York, NY: Continuum.

Guthrie, W. K. C. (1960) *The Greek Philosophers: From Thales to Aristotle*, New York, NY: Harper & Row.

Haas, E. B. (1990) *When Knowledge is Power: Three Models of Change in International Organisations*, Berkeley, CA: University of California.

Hirschman, Albert O. (1971) *A Bias for Hope: Essays on Development and Latin America*, New Haven, CT: Yale University Press.

Hirschman, Albert O. (1973) *Journeys Toward Progress*, New York, NY: Norton.

Hirschman, Albert O. (1984) 'A dissenter's confession: "The Strategy of Economic Development" revisited', in G. Meier and D. Seers (eds.) *Pioneers in Development*, New York, NY: OUP.

Hirschman, Albert O. (1995) *Development Projects Observed*, Washington, DC: The Brookings Institution.

Janis, I. L. (1972) *Victims of Groupthink*, Boston, MA: Houghton Mifflin.

Kanbur, Ravi and David Vines (2000) 'The World Bank and poverty reduction: past, present and future', in C. Gilbert and D. Vines (eds.) *The World Bank: Structure and Policies*, Cambridge: CUP.

Kanigel, Robert (1997) *The One Best Way: Frederick Winslow Taylor and the Enigma of Efficiency*, New York, NY: Viking.

Kant, Immanuel (1991, orig. 1784) 'Idea for a Universal History with a Cosmopolitan Purpose', in H. Reiss, *Kant: Political Writings*, New York, NY: CUP.

Lloyd, Geoffrey Ernest Richard (1996) *Adversaries and Authorities: Investigations into Ancient Greek and Chinese Science*, Cambridge: CUP.

Mill, John Stuart (1972, orig. 1859) *On Liberty*, in H. B. Acton (ed.) *J.S. Mill: Utilitarianism, On Liberty and Considerations on Representative Government*, London: Dent.

Moore Jr, Barrington (1972) *Reflections on the Causes of Human Misery and upon Certain Proposals to Eliminate Them*, Boston, MA: Beacon Press.

Morley, John (1928) *On Compromise*, London: Macmillan.

Nelson, Leonard (1949) *Socratic Method and Critical Philosophy*, New York, NY: Dover.

Ortega y Gasset, Jos, (1961) *Meditations on Quixote*, New York, NY: Norton.

Plato (1997) *Apology of Socrates*, Warminster: Arias & Phillips.

Popper, Karl (1965) *Conjectures and Refutations: The Growth of Scientific Knowledge*, New York: Harper & Row.

Rogers, Everett (1983) *Diffusion of Innovations*, 3rd edn, New York, NY: Free Press.

Schank, Roger (1997) *Virtual Learning: A Revolutionary Approach to Building a Highly Skilled Workforce*, New York, NY: McGraw-Hill.

Schmidt, J. (ed.) (1996) *What is Enlightenment? Eighteenth-century Answers and Twentieth-century Questions*, Berkeley, CA: University of California Press.

Schön, Donald (1971) *Beyond the Stable State*, New York, NY: Norton.

Schön, Donald (1983) *The Reflective Practitioner: How Professionals Think in Action*, New York, NY: Basic Books.

Schwenk, C. R. (1984) 'Devil's advocacy in managerial decision making', *Journal of Management Studies* 21 (April):153-68.

Smith, Jeffery A. (1988) *Printers and Press Freedom: The Ideology of Early American Journalism*, New York, NY: OUP.

Wills, Garry (1994) *Certain Trumpets: The Call of Leaders*, New York, NY: Simon & Schuster.

Winsten, Stephen (ed.) (1962) *The Wit and Wisdom of Bernard Shaw*, New York, NY: Collier.

# Bridging the 'macro'–'micro' divide in policy-oriented research: two African experiences

## David Booth

## Introduction

The gap separating the concerns and activities of development practitioners from those of development researchers in academic institutions is no longer the yawning chasm that it once was. Though by no means universally accepted as desirable, closer collaborative relationships between academic researchers and those making decisions about policy and practice for development in official and non-government organisations are now a reality – including, and perhaps even especially, in the field of social development. Several intellectual and practical dimensions of this convergence have been explored from various angles in recent publications and workshops (Schuurman 1993, Booth 1994a, Edwards 1994b).

There remains, however, a need for discussion about the kinds of research that are effective in closing the gap between the worlds of academic analysis and practice. Relaxing the tensions between the practitioner's need for timely and up-to-date intelligence on key topics and the normal requirements of academic professionalism requires more than good will and imagination on both sides. It calls for different ways of working, combining both known and untried techniques in new ways, and the deliberate testing out of fresh approaches with a view to their improvement. It means going beyond general considerations concerning the requirements for academic research to be considered 'relevant' (Edwards 1994a, Booth 1994b) towards a critical discussion of specific experiences in non-conventional research design. This article is intended as a contribution to such a discussion.[1]

The article is based on the experience of two studies, both done on behalf of the Swedish official agency, SIDA. The first was carried out in Tanzania, by a team of Tanzanian and British researchers, in mid-1992. Its final report was published under SIDA's imprint as

*Social, Economic and Cultural Change in Contemporary Tanzania: A People-Oriented Focus* (Booth et al. 1993). The second was completed by another team, British and Zambian, during mid-1994. It is the subject of a draft report with the short title 'Coping with Cost Recovery', completed in November 1994. The present writer was the overall coordinator for both studies.[2]

## Orientations – objectives – conclusions

The Tanzanian study (hereafter 'Change in Tanzania') had very broad terms of reference. It was conceived as a means of addressing the lack of up-to-date information on the ways in which ordinary people have perceived, coped with, and been affected by major changes in the 'macro'-economy and national political system of one of the countries accorded priority for Swedish development cooperation. In other terms, the focus was on local-level change against a background of economic liberalisation, implementation of structural adjustment measures and initial steps towards multi-party politics. One of the objectives was to give a trial run to a possible methodology for addressing this kind of gap in donors' understanding of contemporary change in Africa. The basic design drew on a literature survey, combined with some 'rapid' interactive field-work in five regions of Tanzania.

The Zambian study, 'Coping with Cost Recovery', had a narrower focus. It was concerned with the social implications of the 'cost-recovery' or 'cost-sharing' measures adopted recently in the Zambian health and education sectors. Although the government of Zambia has been committed to cost-sharing policies since at least 1989, the concern was especially with those introduced as part of the Chiluba government's economic recovery programme since October 1991. The main focus was on the impact of the new charges for access to basic health and education services among the poorest sections of the urban and rural populations. The project was designed on the basis of experience with rapid interactive methods of research in other recent studies in Zambia and elsewhere, including 'Change in Tanzania'.

The conclusions of both studies have proved controversial. 'Change in Tanzania' found, among other things, that trade liberalisation seemed to have brought benefits to poor as well as better-off rural consumers and appeared to have been particularly appreciated by women. We also found that most people, especially rural women, were facing the prospect of multi-party democracy with trepidation and a strong sense of 'better the devil we know'. Within quite a short time, our report was being cited in World Bank circles as a new piece of evidence showing that structural adjustment was not invariably harmful to the poor. It was also criticised by socialist-inclined researchers in Sweden, who objected to the drawing of this sort of conclusion on the basis of the kind of field-work we had done.

'Coping with Cost Recovery' threatens to provoke similar controversy, although the ideological signs will probably be reversed. Despite our protestations that we are not opposed in principle to cost-sharing, the report is likely to be read as a damning indictment of a key aspect of the current reforms in Zambia. On the other hand, the recommendations are unlikely to offend anyone on the Left, and should be received enthusiastically by NGO activists inside and outside the country. This is in spite of the fact that the assumptions and style of research and analysis were essentially the same as those used in the Tanzanian study.

This observation could be the point of departure for a reflection on the rather simple polarities that tend to characterise many people's thinking about current policy issues in Africa, and the need for a more mature and even eclectic approach to such matters. However, this is not my concern here. The studies' conclusions and their reception are mentioned only to help give a rounded initial picture of the two experiences. The rest of the article focuses not on conclusions but on method, and in particular on some similarities and differences between the two studies, and the relevance of the experience as a whole for those interested in the interface between academics and practitioners.

## Tanzania 1992: a 'macro'–'micro' perspective on economic and political change

The starting point of 'Change in Tanzania' was the perception that most research available to the donor community focuses exclusively on 'macro' dimensions of change. Attempts to elucidate the situation prevailing at the community level often involve presumptuous statements, based on assumptions about the responses of rural inhabitants to 'macro'-economic and political processes. This represents a poor substitute for studies carried out with the explicit aim of understanding how ordinary people perceive, handle, and are affected by external forces and processes of change.

What is lacking is not community-based research *per se*. Although not as numerous as they might have been, a fair number of such studies have been carried out in Tanzania over the past 30 years by anthropologists, sociologists, historians, and geographers. However, anthropological monographs invariably adopt a narrow focus on a single ethnic group, village community, neighbourhood, or rural township. They also tend to be rather diverse, both thematically and in terms of the time-scales adopted.

One result is that it is usually difficult to draw together findings from such studies in a way that integrates the treatment of 'micro' and 'macro' issues, at a certain level of generality and over a definite period of time. Since the number of good field reports is comparatively small, it is difficult to get reasonably comprehensive information on *recent* changes, so as to begin to construct a picture of the local processes occurring in response to specified 'macro' events, such as a change of economic policy or a new political climate.

Thus there is a need for new styles of work that are capable of breaking out of these limitations and contributing to the development of a 'people-oriented focus' on contemporary change in rural Africa. It was with this methodological gap, as well as with the substantive issue of the nature of recent changes in Tanzanian communities, that the study was to be concerned.

## Approach

The research commissioned consisted of a desk study, followed by six weeks' field research in a variety of locations, involving a team of seven local and expatriate researchers, among whom were several students of Tanzanian rural conditions with many years' experience and one senior anthropologist (Dr Alison Redmayne) who had been in almost continuous contact with her research sites since the early 1960s.

We visited twelve carefully selected rural locations in different parts of the country in June–July 1992, drawing on our own experience in gathering and interpreting information. Thus, the findings emerged from a combination of three main elements: suggestions about broad tendencies derived from previous studies; general conclusions arising from the field study; and the team's assessments of the validity and reliability of the different pieces of available evidence.

The study had obvious limits. It deliberately concentrated on those dimensions of change that tend to escape the more usual country reports, survey-based enquiries, and sectoral evaluations. A 'people-oriented' focus on contemporary change was not seen as a substitute for ethnography. Not only was the time at our disposal extremely limited, judged by normal academic standards; but, as explained above, we were interested in specific issues which were only partly ethnographic in character.

The broad aim of the study was to provide a basis for provisional inferences about contemporary change and contemporary perceptions of longer-term processes, beginning with a survey of available documentation. In the event we found that previous studies provided a basis for certain suggestions about the way recent Tanzanian experience fitted into the 'structural adjustment controversy' in 'macro'-economic and sectoral terms. Earlier local studies also gave grounds for some worthwhile hypotheses about the direction of contemporary change at the community and household levels. But direct evidence on current responses to economic liberalisation at community level was still thin. There were also many unanswered questions about local responses to the arrival of 'multi-partyism'.

Twelve villages were visited, in eight Districts within five Regions of Tanzania. The areas for research had to be chosen partly with a view to feasible distances, and to the ethnographic knowledge and previous research experience of members of the research team; but the most important criterion was to provide a sufficient variety of socio-economic and ecological conditions. The field-work was carried out in six weeks. The research team included a core of two men and two women who were involved throughout the preparations as well as during the investigation and travelling. The others played leading roles in particular phases of the field-work, drawing on their previous knowledge of the sites and command of local languages.

We were able to spend about two-and-a-half days at each of the places we visited. The basic method was to arrange four to five group discussions with different kinds of representative of the village population, following as far as possible the 'focus-group discussion' approach. When feasible, the time before and after the group sessions was used for observing conditions and activities in the village, and for further conversations with individuals or small groups of villagers about the topics which interested us, so maximising opportunities for methodological 'triangulation' (cross-checking information in three different ways).

Generally, we sought to meet with one group of 'village leaders': a selection of members of the Village Government and some of the village-level technical specialists such as the agricultural assistant or primary school head teacher. Other groups consisted of villagers without leadership or technical responsibilities: one group of village women, one of young people of both sexes, and up to two other groups of ordinary villagers, male and female.

In all but a handful of groups, our promptings produced informative and often vigorous exchanges of views. Most group discussions yielded much information, including disagreements about facts, and controversy about their significance. Despite some team members' initial misgivings about raising the more sensitive issues relating to culture, ideology, and politics, we found there was little that could not be discussed in the groups.

The study had a frankly experimental character. The objective was both to make a substantive contribution to understanding what is currently happening in rural and peri-urban areas of mainland Tanzania, and to try out a methodology for doing so. To what extent was the experiment fruitful, in our view and that of other specialists?

## Assessment I

Our own assessment was fairly positive, but included some important reservations. Within the rather broad scope of a study of 'economic, social and cultural change', there was much about which we remained agnostic; but on a range of topics we felt confident enough to make definite claims. The study had relied a good deal on synthesising existing ideas and extrapolating from past investigations which employed more conventional methodologies. But it seemed clear that it could not have been done entirely on that basis. That is, the case for a combined methodology, drawing on documentary work *and* on a field-work basis, seemed to have been proved.

While the design of the study proved sufficient in terms of coverage of a range of rural and peri-urban conditions, it did not entirely resolve the difficulty of generating generalisable conclusions from location-specific material. Relatively little of the detailed material from the village studies could be included in the text of the report. In other words, the 'narrow focus' which we had described as a limitation of the traditional anthropological study was perhaps not so easy to overcome. In a similar vein, we were conscious that much less could be reported in general about 'culture' than we had hoped. This seemed partly due to the unsuitability of 'rapid' research techniques to the gathering of even moderately good ethnographic material, and partly to the difficulty of handling location-specific material within a general report about a country.

Use of focus-group work as a central technique, supplemented by observation and informal interviews, seemed to be fully justified by the results of the study. Those of us with experience of traditional anthropological methods but not of focus groups were impressed by the power of the method to generate large quantities of information, and even insights about process, in a very short time. We were also aware of various risks associated with rapid-research techniques, but had guarded against them in various ways.

However, while the focus-group method itself contains some internal checks on reliability of information, these had not been sufficient to prevent some things being said and agreed that we knew to be untrue. More generally, we often felt that certain discussion themes – such as the deplorable state of the roads or the constant rise in the cost of living – were being developed at least partly for effect; that is, despite their disclaimers, the researchers were being addressed as potential benefactors. We made appropriate adjustments before reaching conclusions.

The possibility of checking the results of the group discussions with a member of the team who had extensive knowledge of the field-work area was a very important feature of our approach. This was a key dimension of our triangulation in several cases, and it was especially valuable in the four sites that were familiar to Dr Redmayne. We felt that capitalising on this sort of expertise should be an integral component of the design of rapid studies of the type we were undertaking.

Last but not least, the fact that the work was commissioned not directly by SIDA but through a practice-oriented academic inter-mediary (the Development Studies Unit at the University of Stockholm) seemed to make a positive difference to the outcome in a number of ways. It gave us an additional source of specialist scrutiny in drafting our conclusions – professionally expert, but also attuned to what the sponsors did and did not want to know. At the same time, it provided us with a cushion against any over-simple or narrowly administrative interpretation of our terms of reference that might have arisen.

### Assessment II

Comments on our approach from other specialists were helpful and provoked further reflections in a number of respects. They concerned especially the scope and design of the study, and the appropriateness of field techniques selected.

Among academic commentators in general we found some impatience with the broad coverage of the study and more particularly with our failure to distinguish between those of our findings that were 'new' and those that were generally well known and understood among specialists. There is some justification for this point of view. On the other hand, the report was received warmly in donor-agency circles (as 'readable', 'informative', 'giving a real feel of rural life' etc.).[3] Unfortunately, we suspect that some of the features that commended the report to one set of readers were precisely those that worried the other set. This illustrates well one of the difficulties involved in crossing the divide between academics and practitioners.

In a sympathetic but challenging critique of our study, Peter Gibbon (1994) advanced a particular variant of the above argument. After commending the report as 'well-informed and extremely informative', he goes on to take issue with what he sees as two regrettable biases in our approach: towards 'average' or 'typical' rural conditions at the expense of various extremes; and, relatedly, towards elements of continuity at the expense of sources of change. Along with a correct emphasis on continuities in rural life before and after structural adjustment, Gibbon detects in the report 'a certain reluctance to identify and track down new elements in the picture, both positive and negative'. He would like to have seen more strategic sampling of areas of the country that are significant in relation to what are known to be factors of growing importance in the political economy of Tanzania.

These points should be carefully considered in the design of any future study on these lines. The brief for such a study should probably be clearer in this respect than ours was, since there undoubtedly is a tension between a strategy of portraying typical trends and one with a deliberate focus on change. This does not mean that systematic sampling to highlight novel or strategic factors is a bad idea; indeed this may be where the comparative advantage of rapid qualitative research as against 'proper' surveys lies. But there is clearly a choice to be made between prioritising that approach and taking the more obvious tack of focusing on 'typical' processes affecting large majorities of the population.

For many people, an obvious point of comparison was with 'rapid rural appraisal' (RRA) or 'participatory rural appraisal' (PRA).[4] In various forums we were accused both of committing the same errors as RRA/PRA practitioners and of not taking seriously enough the rigours and precautions that are now standard in PRA.[5]

The first was the less serious suggestion. It seems to be founded on two mistaken assumptions: (a) that our method rested wholly on the focus-group work, and (b) that it (therefore?) involved such fallacies as assuming that people do what they say they do, that observing behaviour and studying the wider context in which it occurs are unimportant, and so on. While obviously constrained by lack of time, our field-work approach had involved several methods, of which the group interviews was only one. Moreover, by placing the field-work rather firmly in the context of a literature-based analysis covering 'macro'-economic, institutional, and local-community studies over a decade or so, we had taken precautions to avoid the failing for which RRA practitioners among others have sometimes been criticised (cf. Bebbington 1994): that of detaching grassroots action from its 'macro' context. This could indeed be seen as the main objective and virtue of the design adopted.

The other type of criticism was more serious, being based on a full understanding of PRA techniques and some experience of their application under Tanzanian conditions. It pointed to one real limitation of our study. The heart of this objection was that in one important respect the study did not meet its terms of reference, and could not have been expected to do so, given the limited range of methods that we deployed.

Our terms of reference required us to give special consideration to SIDA's 'target groups', including 'the poorest' rural people. However, we did not make use of specific PRA techniques, notably wealth-ranking, which would have enabled us to identify the poorest people or households in the places we visited. Nor, on the other hand, had we been able to carry out any kind of rigorous sampling of richer and poorer villages, raising the possibility that our selection of sites reflected 'tarmac bias' as well as the almost inevitable 'dry-season bias' which Robert Chambers has warned against (Lindberg et al. 1993).

Our critics did us some injustices. On the basis of previous field-work in some of the locations (notably Redmayne's sites in Iringa), we are fairly confident that we did not 'miss' the poorest households entirely; and we would refute vigorously the suggestion that we were guilty of any of the grosser forms of tarmac bias. Also, the critics' suggestion that if rapid field-work is so rapid that it cannot employ wealth-ranking, then it is not worth having, seems a trifle inflexible. Nevertheless, they have a point. At the end of the day, we were not in a position to make any confident claims about 'the poorest'; we were compelled to formulate our findings in weaker (and, arguably, excessively vague) terms: 'poorer people', 'those locally regarded as relatively poor', and so on. It certainly bears consideration that if practitioners sponsoring rapid research are specifically interested in changes and responses to change among 'the poorest', they must allow for sufficiently intensive field-work, and insist on a research design tailored to this objective.

## Zambia 1994: an experience in rapid appraisal

The Zambia study was different in a number of respects. It aimed to cast fresh light on a relatively narrowly-defined issue of great concern among policy-makers and donor representatives in Zambia. It drew on the resources of a multi-disciplinary team which already had some training and experience in rapid-appraisal techniques. And the design of the work was able to reflect some of the lessons of the Tanzania study, as well as those of work of a similar kind done recently in Zambia.

The study originated from SIDA's concern, shared by UNICEF-Lusaka, about the implications for the urban and rural poor of the rapid extension of user charges in basic health services and education. The perceived dangers were of various sorts. The immediate danger was that the charges would contribute to a further deterioration in indices of morbidity, mortality and illiteracy following on a decade of declining social conditions. Less immediate, but no less important, was the danger of political backlash against the reform process in general, which would damage the chances of resolving these problems in the medium and long terms.

On both counts there was a need to increase the rate at which relevant data were being collected and fed into the policy process. In health there were plans to set up a regular monitoring system in the medium term; but the medium term might easily be too late. Therefore there was an urgent need both to summarise what was known already, albeit anecdotally, and to generate some 'rapid' results to flesh this out, to contribute to upcoming bilateral and multilateral discussions between Zambian and Swedish officials.

Apart from this substantive concern, there was interest at the SIDA Planning Secretariat in taking forward the methodological lessons of 'Change in Tanzania' and making connections with those of several studies recently completed in Zambia using rapid interactive methods. The key Zambian experiences were the *Participatory Poverty Assessment* (PPA) which formed part of the World Bank's Poverty Assessment for Zambia in 1993 (World Bank 1994), and three beneficiary assessments of social-rehabilitation projects carried out for different sponsors between 1992 and 1994. All of these studies had been coordinated by a senior Zambian anthropologist, Dr John Milimo, who now headed the local team for 'Coping with Cost Recovery'.

## Approach

A common feature of 'Change in Tanzania' and the Zambia Participatory Poverty Assessment was that they were based on a strategic sample of research sites treated as case studies, using rapid interactive techniques and methodological triangulation. There were also some significant differences. From the repertoire of RRA/PRA, the Tanzania study took only the overall methodological objective known as 'optimal ignorance'[6] and an essential research tool, focus-group work. This was backed up in *ad hoc* ways by anthropological insights from more traditional sources. The PPA, in contrast, employed a full range of PRA techniques and included a major training effort to familiarise the field researchers with their use.

'Coping with Cost Recovery' involved a blend of these approaches. A range of standard PRA techniques was deployed, though a major effort was needed to adapt these techniques to the specific requirements of the study. Also, as in the Tanzanian experience, it was found useful to leaven the findings of the rapid-appraisal work with evidence from longer-term anthropological field-work wherever possible. The main way this was achieved was by securing a significant input to the study from Ginny Bond, a leading researcher in an ambitious longitudinal study of community coping-capacity in Chiawa, a rural area in the south of Zambia.[7]

'Coping with Cost Recovery' had a relatively narrow focus, but had to be completed in less time than any of the previous studies in which we had been involved. At an early stage it was agreed that there would be much to be gained from selecting a smaller number of sites and spending more time in each place. The costs in representativeness would be more than repaid by the opportunities to explore a wider range of techniques and opportunities for triangulation. There would be further gains from choosing research sites in the same areas as those studied during the PPA or one of the beneficiary assessments. This would avoid the need to start by establishing baseline characteristics.

The terms of reference specified that the field-work should concentrate on poor communities. In view of the population distribution of Zambia, it was agreed to carry out studies in an equal number of urban and rural sites. Two of each were initially selected, with a view to maximising the range of locations within a practical itinerary for two field teams. An additional dimension of triangulation would come from commissioning some work on the themes of the study in Chiawa, where Ginny Bond was in a position to draw on a baseline survey and some intensive household studies carried out over several years. This was initially conceived as a means of 'piloting' some of the techniques of individual interviewing to be deployed. In practice, it produced sufficiently important results to be treated on a par with the other cases.

After an initial documentary search and a workshop for briefing and training in Lusaka, the teams carried out two weeks' field-work in each of the four main sites. Initially the teams – consisting of four local-language speakers, two men and two women – interviewed planners and staff at the provincial and district levels. They then took up residence in or close to the communities selected for intensive study, where they carried out individual and group interviews in fours and in pairs, and sometimes singly. Dr Milimo and the present writer accompanied the teams in different phases of the field-work.

Group interviews sometimes took the form of very loosely structured conversations; other times they were organised as focus-groups which followed a pre-determined interview route, usually including a mapping or ranking exercise. Specific techniques employed to facilitate the group interviews included social, institutional, and resource mapping; production of time-lines and seasonality charts; and pairwise and sequence ranking. Where possible these standard techniques were adapted to the particular purposes of a study of the social implications of cost-recovery, although in most cases they lent themselves 'merely' to setting a framework in which the topic of user charges could be approached concretely, in relation to specific aspects of the life-situation of the participants.

Individual interviews with community members, as distinct from 'key informants', were set up as far as possible on the basis of a wealth-ranking exercise which firstly indicated the extent and nature of social stratification in the area, and secondly allowed the interviewer to place the subject on a scale from 'very poor to not so poor' in local terms. Lines of questioning drew on the valuable experience of Chiawa study team in conducting household interviews on sensitive subjects such as illness and death.

### Assessment

At this point I can provide only a tentative assessment of the experience of 'Coping with Cost Recovery'. Naturally, also, the assessment is that of the study team itself; it has not yet benefited from the kinds of external critique that I was able to cite in regard to the Tanzanian report.

As in the Tanzanian experience, the team felt reasonably confident at the end of the field-work that the methods used had been sufficient to support some worthwhile findings, and that these could not have been inferred from a documentary survey alone. Once again, although less so thanks to the more closely defined terms of reference, the field-work had generated a good deal of interesting information that would not find a place in the report because it was too location-specific. The combination of group interviews, individual interviews, and observation, with careful use of internal consistency checks and triangulation, had proved again to be a powerful tool for shedding light quickly on a specific policy issue.

The deployment of a range of mapping and ranking exercises, which was an innovation in relation to the Tanzanian study, proved worthwhile, but not unreservedly so. As an aid to the conduct of a focus-group discussion, they served well in several instances, providing a helpful means of exploring issues related to the new user-charges concretely, in relation to everyday problems. The pairwise and sequence rankings were the most useful in this regard, whereas the mapping exercises and seasonality charting tended to reconfirm important findings already reported in the *Participatory Poverty Assessment*, rather than breaking fresh ground. Occasionally, mechanical deployment of the repertoire of PRA techniques threatened to be a distraction from the main tasks of the study.

The field-work findings included in the draft report drew significantly on the PRA-assisted group interviews. However, they also depended, perhaps to an equal extent, on each of the following: the key-informant interviews; quantitative data supplied by hospitals, clinics, and schools; direct observations recorded by members of the research team; and individual or household interviews. The most powerful single technique, given the questions that needed to be answered, was probably the use of wealth ranking to select households to be the subjects of semi-structured interviews. Somewhat to our surprise, it proved possible to do effective rankings of wealth or well-being in sections of poor urban neighbourhoods as well as in rural communities, and tracking down and interviewing some of those identified in this way as highly vulnerable was a productive, if personally rather harrowing, experience. This seems to confirm the good sense of allowing enough time to carry out wealth-ranking if the objectives of the study are focused on the poorest.

Special mention also needs to be made of the input from more conventional anthropological work. From the Chiawa study, Ginny Bond was able to contribute two key things. One was a body of observations and insights about one rural Zambian community, including its health and educational facilities, accumulated over a period of several years — a short period by the standards of Redmayne's Tanzanian field-work, but quite long for rapid-appraisal purposes, and long enough to include all the main steps in the implementation of the policies that were our concern.

The other was a set of interviews in households that were well known to the researcher, having been selected as case studies on the basis of a sample survey two years previously. These were a source of a kind of information about behaviour and behavioural change (or the lack of it) that was well-nigh impossible to obtain by the means at our disposal in the other study sites. The conclusions of our report would have been both less confident and more generalised without this input from outside the rapid-appraisal framework.

## Conclusion

This article has contributed material for a discussion about ways of working that are effective in closing the gap between academic research and development practice. An outline has been given of two recent experiences in which the author was involved that seem to provide one type of successful example of such bridging activity, involving different countries and somewhat different substantive issues. Both are instances of the use of local case studies based partly on rapid-appraisal techniques to highlight problems and issues arising from national policy measures. To this extent they are also efforts to bridge that other divide, high-lighted in the title of the article, between the 'macro' and the 'micro'.

The conclusions that it seems possible to draw from these two experiences, and others mentioned in the article, are necessarily provisional. Both of the studies described were learning processes, with one drawing substantially on the lessons of the other; and this type of continuous adjustment can and should continue. With this proviso, the following seem to be the suggestions that are worth making at this point:

- There clearly is scope for academic researchers to become involved in innovative research designs that meet the needs of practitioners concerned about social development issues without ceasing to be challenging, personally and intellectually, to those carrying them out.

- Combining rapid interactive field-work with documentary surveys seems to provide a way of bridging the 'macro' and the 'micro' that is both intellectually defensible and appealing to practitioners.

- The basic philosophy and technical repertoire of RRA/PRA represents a rich fund of thinking and experience in this sort of work. However, there is a very good case for combining PRA techniques flexibly with inputs from more conventional sources, including long-term ethnography, even when the time-scale is very short.

- Managing the balancing act that some of this involves may well be easier if the relationship between the sponsor and the research team is suitably mediated by a practice-oriented academic unit of some kind.

## Notes

1   Our views of appropriate methods for development workers, and background to some of the terms used in the article, are given by Rudqvist (1991), Pratt and Loizos (1992), and Moris and Copestake (1993).

2   I am grateful to my co-authors for the privilege of drawing on our joint work in this article, that is, to those named in the reference list below and to John Milimo, Ginny Bond, Silverio Chimuka, Mulako Nabanda, Kwibisa Liywalii, Monde Mwalusi, Mulako Mwanamwalye, Edward Mwanza, Lizzie Peme and Agatha Zulu.

3   The first type of reaction was among those recorded at the seminar organised by the Swedish Development Cooperation Office in Dar es Salaam to review the report and its findings. The second was more prevalent at the international seminar on the report organised by SIDA in Stockholm.

4   The most comprehensive introduction is Chambers (1992).

5   The former came from some Tanzanian academics at the Dar es Salaam seminar; the latter was made by the Swedish critics mentioned earlier, initially at the Stockholm seminar and subsequently in Lindberg et al. (1993).

6   A good brief account is given in Chambers (1993: 18-19).

7   This is being sponsored by SAREC and carried out jointly by IHCAR, a department of the Karolinska Institute, Stockholm; Hull University's Department of Sociology and Anthropology; and the Institute for African Studies, University of Zambia.

## References

Bebbington, A. (1994) 'Theory and relevance in indigenous agriculture: knowledge, agency and organization', in Booth (1994a).

Booth, D. (ed.) (1994a) *Rethinking Social Development: Theory, Research and Practice*, London: Longman.

Booth, D. (1994b) 'How far beyond the impasse? a provisional summing-up', in Booth (1994a).

Booth, D., F. Lugangira, P. Masanja, A. Mvungi, R. Mwaipopo, J. Mwami and A. Redmayne (1993) *Social, Economic and Cultural Change in Contemporary Tanzania: A People-Oriented Focus*, Stockholm: SIDA.

Chambers, R. (1992) *Rapid Appraisal: Rapid, Relaxed and Participatory*, Brighton: Institute of Development Studies, Discussion Paper 311.

Chambers, R. (1993) *Challenging the Professions: Frontiers for Rural Development*, London: Intermediate Technology.

Edwards, M. (1994a) 'Rethinking social development: the search for "relevance"', in Booth (1994a).

Edwards, M. (1994b) 'The Academic-Practitioner Interface: Report of a Workshop held in Manchester on 30 June 1994', London: Development Studies Association.

Gibbon, P. (1994) Review of Booth et al. (1993), *News from Nordiska Afrikainstitutet*, 1/94.

Lindberg, C., V.-M. Loiske, C. Mung'ong'o and W. Östberg (1993) *Handle with Care! Rapid Studies and the Poor*, Stockholm, Environment and Development Studies Unit, School of Geography, Stockholm University, Working Paper 24.

Moris, J. and J. Copestake (1993) *Qualitative Enquiry for Rural Development: A Review*, London: Intermediate Technology Publications for ODI.

Pratt, B. and P. Loizos (1992) *Choosing Research Methods: Data Collection for Development Workers*, Oxford: Oxfam.

Rudqvist, A. (1991) 'Field-work Methods for Consultations and Popular Participation', Stockholm University, Department of Social Anthropology, Popular Participation Programme, WP 9.

Schuurman, F. (ed.) (1993) *Beyond the Impasse: New Directions in Development Theory*, London: Zed.

World Bank (1994) 'Zambia Poverty Assessment, Volume 4: Participatory Poverty Assessment' (draft), Washington, DC: Population and Human Resources Division, Southern Africa Department.

# Capacity building: shifting the paradigms of practice

## Allan Kaplan

*' ... development must start in somebody's sense; development is not about things you see ... , it is about the way somebody is developed in their thinking'.*(Rural fieldworker, cited in Oliver 1996)

So here we are again, once more pursuing the elusive concept of capacity building with a dogged relentlessness which would be amusing, were it not charged with such a sense of responsibility and commitment. There is an image which comes to mind: the concept of capacity building as a captured member of a foreign people (perhaps called Development), about whom we would like to know more but who remain a strange and elusive tribe, forever beyond the borders of our realm. We have captured this one member called Capacity Building, we have thrown him into prison, interrogated him, starved and beaten and isolated him, cursed and abused and threatened him to find out what he knows; but he looks back at us, silent and resentful and unforthcoming. In his silence he remains beyond our abilities to bully, and the very flailings of our desperation seem to build rather than sap the strength of his resolve and the ramparts of his defence. He may lie naked and bleeding in the corner of his cell, but the very silence of his presence mocks and belittles us. After so much battering at the doors of his knowledge, still we seem to have gleaned very little.

What if we were to change tack, to alter our approach? What if we were to treat him with respect, even deference? What if we were to give him his freedom, to demand nothing from him, to release him from the burden of our despair and simply allow him to live among us, and to come and go as he would choose? Perhaps friendship and trust would allow his real self to emerge. Perhaps he might even allow us to walk beside him when he went back to visit his people. Perhaps, under these circumstances, a simple question would elicit an honest answer. And we might even discover that the answer was obvious from the beginning, that in fact it had been staring us in the face all the time, but that we had been unable to see it, because we had obscured our own vision through our desperate battering of the messenger. Is it possible that we are pushing the answers that we seek ever deeper into obscurity through the frantic complexity of our search? In our attempts to unravel the knot, are we in danger of drawing it ever tighter?

Is it possible that capacity building demands such a radically new form of practice, such a radically new form of thinking, that our current approaches are doomed to failure – not because we lack adequate models or 'technologies', but because our very approach to the issue is inadequate? The image presented above, of course, is pure fantasy, but the questions that it prompts are not. This paper is an attempt to outline some of the fundamental shifts that such a new form of approach would entail. It is an attempt to look honestly at the phenomena as they present themselves to us, without presupposition or assumption.

In a previous paper (CDRA 1995) the Community Development Resource Association (CDRA) described organisations as open systems, comprising a number of interlinking and interdependent elements. We noted that these elements form a hierarchy of importance, and that therefore certain elements are more central than others in the attainment of organisational capacity. Thus we noted the following.

## Elements of organisational life

### A conceptual framework

The first requirement for an organisation with capacity, the 'prerequisite' on which all other capacity is built, is the development of a conceptual framework which reflects the organisation's understanding of the world. This is a coherent frame of reference, a set of concepts which allows the organisation to make sense of the world around it, to locate itself within that world, and to make decisions in relation to it. This framework is not a particular ideology or theory, it is not necessarily correct, and it is not impervious to criticism and change. It is not a precious, fragile thing, but a robust attempt to keep pace conceptually with the (organisational and contextual) developments and challenges facing the organisation. The organisation which does not have a competent working understanding of its world can be said to be incapacitated, regardless of how many other skills and competencies it may have.

### Organisational 'attitude'

The second element concerns organisational 'attitude'. An organisation needs to build its confidence to act in and on the world in a way that it believes can be effective and have an impact. Put another way, it has to shift from 'playing the victim' to exerting some control, to believing in its own capacity to affect its circumstances. Another aspect of 'attitude' is accepting responsibility for the social and physical conditions 'out there', whatever the organisation faces in the world. This implies a shift from the politics of demand and protest to a more inclusive acceptance of the responsibilities which go with the recognition of human rights.

Whatever the history of oppression, marginalisation, or simply nasty circumstances that an individual or organisation has had to suffer, these 'attitudes' are the basis for effective action in the world. This is not a question of morality, or of fairness or justice; it is simply the way things work.

## Vision and strategy

With clarity of understanding and a sense of confidence and responsibility comes the possibility of developing organisational vision and strategy. Understanding and responsibility lead to a sense of purpose in which the organisation does not lurch from one problem to the next, but manages to plan and implement a programme of action, and is able to adapt this programme in a rational and considered manner.

## Organisational structure

Although these elements are not gained entirely sequentially, we may say that, once organisational aims and strategy are clear, it becomes possible to structure the organisation in such a way that roles and functions are clearly defined and differentiated, lines of communication and accountability untangled, and decision-making procedures transparent and functional. Put slightly differently, 'form follows function'; if one tries to do this the other way round, the organisation becomes incapacitated.

## Acquisition of skills

The next step in the march towards organisational capacity, in terms of priority and sequence, is the growth and extension of individual skills, abilities, and competencies — the traditional terrain of training courses. Of course, skills also feature earlier; they can, in and of themselves, generate confidence and a sense of control. Development cannot be viewed simplistically; these phases overlap. Yet what emerges clearly from extensive experience is that there is a sequence, a hierarchy, an order. Unless organisational capacity has been developed sufficiently to harness training and the acquisition of new skills, training courses do not 'take', and skills do not adhere. The organisation which does not know where it is going and why, which has a poorly developed sense of responsibility for itself, and which is inadequately structured cannot make use of training courses and skills-acquisition programmes.

## Material resources

Finally, an organisation needs material resources: finances, equipment, office space, and so on. Without an appropriate level of these, the organisation will always remain, in an important sense, incapacitated.

This perspective on what constitutes a capacitated organisation has been developed through years of reflection on the interventions that we have made to assist organisations, and through years of reflecting on the differences between those organisations which appear in some measure capable, and those which do not, or which appear less capable. But the most important insight it offers for capacity building is not simply a list of indicators which we can use as a framework for understanding capacity. Rather, it yields two far more radical insights with far-reaching consequences for practice.

# First paradigm shift: from the tangible to the intangible

If you look towards the bottom of the hierarchy, you will see those things which are quantifiable, measureable, elements of organisational life which can easily be grasped and worked with. Material and financial resources, skills, organisational structures and systems — all these are easily assessed and quantified. In a word, they belong to the realm of material and visible things. If, however, we turn our attention to the top of the hierarchy, we enter immediately an entirely different realm: the realm of the invisible. Sure, organisations may have written statements of vision, of strategy, and of value, but these written statements do not in any sense indicate whether an organisation actually has a working understanding of its world. They do not indicate the extent to which an organisation feels responsible for its circumstances, or capable of having an effect on them, or the degree to which an organisation is really striving to become a learning organisation, or to what extent it is developing its staff, or manifesting a team spirit or endeavour. Furthermore, they do not indicate the extent to which an organisation is reflective, non-defensive, and self-critical. In short, the elements at the top of the hierarchy of elements of organisational life are ephemeral, transitory, not easily assessed or weighed. They are observable only through the effects that they have, and largely invisible to the organisation itself as well as to those practitioners who would intervene to build organisational capacity.

We are saying, then, that the most important elements in organisational life, those which largely determine the functioning of the organisation, are of a nature which make them more or less impervious to conventional approaches to capacity building. Consider this from two angles.

First, from the point of view of the organisation itself. If you interview organisations which suffer from a lack of capacity, you will find that they complain readily about lack of resources, lack of skills, inappropriate structures, an unfavourable history or an impossible context. In other words, they place the blame for their circumstances 'out there', on others or on their situation which is beyond their control, and specifically on those visible elements which lie at the bottom of the hierarchy. But, as Stephen Covey once said, 'For those who think their problems are "out there", that thinking is the problem'. Interview organisations which have developed a certain strength, robustness, or resilience, and you will discover that they generally take responsibility for their lack of capacity, that they attribute it to their own struggles with organisational culture and value, with lack of vision, lack of leadership and management, and so on. In other words, they manifest self-understanding. Capacitated organisations will manifest both stronger invisible elements and an ability to reflect on these elements — which is itself a feature of these stronger invisible elements situated at the top of the hierarchy.

Second, from the point of view of the capacity builder. If we examine honestly the kinds of intervention that we perform, either as donors or as development practitioners, we have to recognise that most of these are concentrated on the lower end of the hierarchy. Mainly, our efforts consist in providing resources or training courses. These are sometimes accompanied by, or preceded by, 'needs assessments', or even 'audits', which themselves concentrate on the visible, more tangible, elements which have little impact if the top elements of the hierarchy are undeveloped. We also engage in advice-giving more than in facilitation; we try to get organisations to make changes which we think will be good for them, which in itself can diminish the robustness of those elements at the top, rather than strengthen them through a form of facilitation which enables organisations to come to grips with their own issues, thus developing those top elements. Finally, and more recently, we have begun to help organisations with 'strategic planning'. This in itself would be a step in the right direction, were we to include the conceptual construction of the organisation's world, as well as forays into organisational culture, in the process. Unfortunately many strategic-planning exercises consist of piecemeal attempts (that is, unrelated to other elements) which comprise the setting of goals and objectives, the 'material aspects' of planning, leaving the organisation pretty much as incapacitated as before, with a 'plan of action' but without the ability to innovate, reflect on, and adapt the plan as circumstances and time progress. (These latter abilities are what really constitute capacity, but —at the risk of repetition — they are 'invisible'.)

In other words, organisational life ranges from the visible, more tangible aspects to those which are less visible, more intangible. It is these latter aspects which by and large determine organisational functioning, yet it is on the former aspects that so-called capacity-building interventions tend to focus. To anyone who works intensively with organisations, this assertion should appear obvious, even 'common sense', or at the very least clearly observable. Why then do we not shift the focus of our interventions?

The answer is as obvious as the dilemma itself: because we do not see — have not been trained or conditioned to see — things in this way. Because it presents a radical challenge to our customary ways of seeing the world. Because our conventional packages and products, our short-term *ad hoc* responses and interventions, are what we have, are what we use, and we will resist the move away from them for as long as possible. Because we take comfort in what we can provide, rather than in what may be really necessary. Because these kinds of intervention are sanctioned by donors. Because organisations have learned to ask for them. Because they are tangible and quantifiable. Because they can be delivered. Because their delivery and assessment can be easily managed and monitored. Because our fieldworkers can be (relatively easily) trained to deliver them. Because they are hard-edged, unambiguous, and certain. Because they do not embroil us in the hazy shifting sands, in the uncertain worlds of fog and mirages which characterise the reality of organisational change processes. Because they do not challenge our certainties with the hazardous obstacles of organisational contradiction. Because they do not fundamentally challenge us.

Organisational change processes are contradictory, ambiguous, and obtuse. They are long-term and not easily observed. Most of all, they are unpredictable. Therefore, while they can be influenced, they lie forever beyond our control. The world of practice in the realm of the intangibles at the top of the organisational hierarchy of complexity is a world which is itself fraught with complexity. It demands constant self-reflection, reflection on practice, if practice is to be improved. It demands the exercise of facilitation skills which are labelled 'soft' but which are the most difficult, demanding, and challenging skills to master: skills of observation and listening, the ability to ask the right question, the holding of ambiguity, uncertainty, and contradiction, the ability to draw enthusiasm out of exhaustion and cynicism, overcoming resistance to change, empathy, and the tenacity to work over long periods with little direct product to show for it – to name but a few. In other words, it demands developmental skills; and, although we talk a lot about the development of capacity, we tend to concentrate on the delivery of 'product'. In short, we do not practise what the situation demands; rather, we produce what can most easily be delivered.

The paradigm shift that is demanded by the above argument is more than radical: it should shatter our complacency and throw the entire edifice of current development practice into doubt. Yet the ability to work with intangibles is only the first of the two paradigm shifts which loom across the boundaries of our practice. The second goes something like this.

## Second paradigm shift: from static model to developmental reading

While it may be true that organisations can be seen as systems of interlocking elements, arranged in a hierarchy of complexity from those which are less tangible to those which are more so, this perspective is not always real. It is not always the case that capacity-building interventions should begin with the intangible before they move on to the more visible. The reality is far more complex than any one theory or model can contain. It all depends on where a particular organisation is at a particular time, and on what kind of organisation it is.

A small, new NGO has a different level of impact and 'sophistication' from a large NGO which is established and effective. The larger NGO has more need of 'sophisticated organisational conditions', because development and growth in capacity implies greater sophistication of organisational processes, functions, and structures. While the new NGO will need clarity of vision, it may not yet have the problems which often accompany organisational vision-building activities within the older NGO. The needs of individual staff members in terms of skills — and therefore training courses — will differ at different stages of the organisation's life, as will material-resource constraints and assets. Similarly, with respect to structure, organisations will have different needs at different stages of their lives. At times, an increasingly complex structure will be called for; at other times, 'destructuring' will be required.

Or, for example, with regard to community-based organisations (CBOs), these can grow to become highly sophisticated organisations, but generally in southern Africa at present they are far less developed and sophisticated, in organisation terms, than their NGO counterparts. And within the organisational form of the CBO itself, a wide range of different capacities and competencies exists. There are communities which lack any organisational representation at all. There are embryonic CBOs, consisting of little more than a (theoretically) rotating committee, without a thought-through strategy, resources, or clarity of roles and functions. Then there is the CBO with employees, differentiated strategies, and office space and equipment.

All of these different stages of organisational development, from no organisation through organisation building through organisational differentiation to highly sophisticated national NGOs with mega-budgets, (theoretically) represent increasing capacity. And each of the elements of organisational life mentioned above recurs — with its different intervention demands — at different stages in the capacity-building game.

A CBO might be struggling with the transition in 'attitude' from resistance to responsibility, while an NGO is dealing with attitudinal issues which it refers to as organisational culture – issues of meaning, principle, and motivation. An NGO in its early phases may function healthily with a flat, informal structure; later, in order to maintain the same level of health, a more hierarchical structure may be called for. A CBO may have achieved greater organisational clarity through clarifying its constitutional or membership structures, only to discover that it degenerates into chaos and conflict when it begins to employ staff without clarifying the relationship between its operational structure (staff) and its constitutional structure.

The point is that, although there is a basic order in which competency in the elements is attained, and in which organisational capacity building occurs, needs change with respect to all these elements as the organisation develops. Even more importantly, although intervention or work done on any one of these elements will not prove effective unless sufficient work has been done on the preceding elements in the hierarchy — for example, training will not 'take' when organisational vision, culture, and structure are unresolved, and it does not help to secure resources when the organisation is not equipped to carry out its tasks — even so, these elements are interdependent, and one may have to work on a number of levels simultaneously in certain situations in order to be effective. And even more importantly — and perhaps paradoxically — while the concept of a hierarchy provides us with a guide, there are many times when one has to work on lower elements in the hierarchy in order to have an effect on higher elements. For example, there are times when the acquisition of an appropriate structure will have a beneficial effect on organisational culture where work on that culture alone has proved ineffective. Such organisational examples abound throughout the hierarchy.

What this means, in essence, is that although one may have an explanatory and sensible model of what constitutes organisational health, competence, and capacity, there are two aspects of organisational reality which confound simplistic attempts to impose this model on specific situations. The first is that, while every organisation may share similar features, nevertheless each is unique, both in itself and in terms of its stage of development, and this uniqueness demands unique, singular, and specifically different responses. Second, while the model may adequately describe the elements of organisational capacity and even the order of their acquisition, it cannot predict or determine organisational change processes, which are complex, ambiguous, and often contradictory. And organisational change, rather than a static model describing organisational elements, is the essence of capacity building.

In other words, being equipped with a perspective on how organisations function, while it is a prerequisite for effective capacity building, is no substitute for direct observation of particular organisational realities in which one is wishing to intervene. One needs the intelligence, acuity, mobility, and penetrating perception to be able to 'read' the particular nature of a specific situation if one hopes to be effective in organisational capacity building. It is all too easy to presume, to make judgements, to impose one's understanding, to compare one organisational situation with another. It is all too easy to base one's interventions on a theoretical model rather than on an accurate assessment of the situation at hand. It is all too easy to design general capacity-building interventions in the office, rather than make specific and individual interventions based on observations in the field. It is all too easy to design general capacity-building interventions for mass delivery, rather than individually specific and nuanced interventions. Once again, general capacity-building interventions, programmes, courses, mass-based delivery vehicles: all these are easy to manage, easy to quantify, to raise money for, to fund, to control. But they are all inadequate.

There are too few NGOs, too few donors, too few development practitioners, who take the time to read specific situations in order to design appropriate and necessarily transitory interventions based on an intelligent reading. (They are necessarily transitory, because the organisation being worked on will develop beyond a particular intervention as a result of the effectiveness of that intervention.) The radical nature of the paradigm shift we are suggesting here is that development practitioners are normally trained to deliver interventions — or packages or programmes — rather than to read the developmental phase at which a particular organisation may be and then to devise a response appropriate to that organisation at that particular time and to nothing else. The ability to read a developmental situation requires a background theory — which few practitioners employ — but it also requires an understanding of development; the ability to observe closely without judgement; sensitivity; empathy; an ability to penetrate to the essence of a situation, to separate the wheat from the chaff, so to speak; the ability to create an atmosphere of trust out of which an organisation may yield up the secrets that it will normally hold back (even from itself) in defensive reaction; the ability really to hear and listen and see; the ability to resist the short sharp expert response which is usually more gratifying to the practitioner than to the organisation; and then, out of an accurate reading, to bring (or arrange for) the appropriate response, one which may not even be within the ambit of the NGO's normal services.

This is a paradigm shift, a radically different approach, a far cry from the normal delivery mechanisms of NGOs, donors, and governments who hope to build capacity. It embraces the real meaning of 'people-centred development', to which we pay lip-service in terms of policy but hardly ever think through to its consequences in terms of practice. Perhaps such a paradigm shift deserves the coining of a new cliché: 'organisation-centred capacity building'. Yet it is precisely such phrases which confuse the issue: we are specifically saying that an adequate response to capacity building, albeit a complex one which turns all of our most cherished attitudes into disarray, is one which concentrates on the actual practice of the development practitioner, rather than on policy statements or well-worded programmes or well-designed courses.

## Some consequences

What are the skills which we normally think of as associated with development practice and capacity building? Whatever they are in specific detail, the generic sense of these skills is captured by the one phrase, the one concept, which always arises when talking about these issues — namely, 'train the trainers'. This is our conventional response when confronted with the demand for capacity-building skills. A wealth of implied meaning underlies this phrase. That what we require for capacity building is trainers. That these trainers can be trained — which implies that they are to 'deliver' specific and fixed 'products' (perhaps courses or programmes). And generally, training implies that the trainee is to learn the skills which are to be 'imparted' by the trainer; also that replication at an exponential rate is both desirable and attainable.

This is one response. The other is to concentrate on the setting up of structures or policies which create an environment through which capacity may be built. We know what is needed, and we must thus set the conditions in place that will allow its realisation.

Both of the above responses are valid and important, but they are not always appropriate, and we may undermine their effectiveness by the very strength of our focus on them. Besides, their danger lies in the fact that they are clearly a response which we can master relatively easily, and therefore they may ensnare us in the seduction of their appeal to our abilities, rather than challenge us by the relevance of their application. They are conventional responses, and their very conventionality should make us suspicious, because the success of our capacity-building efforts to date has been minimal.

The more radical response is to consider ourselves 'artists of the invisible', continually having to deal with ambiguity and paradox, uncertainty in the turbulence of change, new and unique situations coming to us from out of a future of which we have had as yet little experience. This more radical response would imply that we need to develop a resourcefulness out of which we can respond, rather than being trained in past solutions, in fixed mindsets, and trained behaviours which replicate particular patterns and understandings, instead of freeing us to respond uniquely to unique situations.

From the perspective of this paradigm shift there are new abilities which we as development practitioners need to develop — note, *abilities which we need to develop*, not skills in which we need to be trained. Some of these abilities may include the following:

- The ability to find the right question which may enable an organisation to take the next step on its path of development, and to hold a question so that it functions as a stimulus to exploration, rather than demanding an immediate solution, and to help organisations to do the same.
- The ability to hold the tension generated by ambiguity and uncertainty, rather than seek immediate resolution.
- The ability to observe accurately and objectively, to listen deeply, so that invisible realities of the organisation become manifest.
- The ability to use metaphor and imagination to overcome the resistance to change, to enable an organisation to see itself afresh, and to stimulate creativity.
- The ability to help others to overcome cynicism and despair and to kindle enthusiasm.
- Integrity, and the ability to generate the trust that will allow the organisation and its members to really 'speak' and reveal themselves.
- The ability to reflect honestly on one's own interventions, and to enable others to do the same.
- The ability to 'feel' into the 'essence' of a situation.
- The ability to empathise (not sympathise), so that both compassion and confrontation can be used with integrity in helping an organisation to become unstuck.
- The ability to conceptualise, and thus to analyse strategy with intelligence.

The list can go on, but such lists carry in themselves the dangers of new answers which become set routines and received methodologies. The true import of the paradigm shifts described in this paper is that we must remain awake, full of interest and wonder and awe, open and vulnerable, if we hope to find the resilience to respond to the diverse array of situations which challenge us as capacity builders. Above all, answers dampen our edge. It is living with questions that maintains the charge of our attention, and more than anything else we are called on to pay attention.

So, to conclude on a very open note, we include some questions which emerge for us if the perspective presented above is recognised as valid.

- With respect to government-sponsored, nationwide development initiatives which need to 'deliver' in the short term (and similar initiatives in the non-government sector): what needs to be in place so that they can really contribute to local-level capacity building?

- What are the implications for the way in which funding for capacity-building interventions is currently provided, and what needs to change in funding practice?

- What are the implications in respect of the current vogue for outcomes-based project planning, logical framework strategic documents, and 'business planning'?

- And what then are the implications for development management and leadership, monitoring and evaluation mechanisms, and the concept of the discrete 'development' project itself?

- Can the tendering process, with its rigid frames of reference, have any place in developmental interventions? Can it be adapted?

- Which kinds of organisations— with respect to both organisational type and organisational functioning — are capable of effectively deploying capacity-building practitioners?

- Who, of the organisations we know at present, is taking responsibility for developmental capacity-building interventions as described above? Who and where are the capacity builders?

- Who is, who could be, who should be performing developmental capacity building? And how would organisational conditions have to shift to allow them to perform effectively?

---

## Acknowledgement

This paper was initially prepared for the December 1996 NGO Week held in Johannesburg, and was distributed in South Africa by Olive in its MULBERRY (Mostly Unread Literature Bearing Extraordinarily Rich and Relevant Yields) Series, Number 1, 1997.

## References

Oliver, Di (1996) 'Capacity Building', unpublished MA thesis, University of Natal, Durban

CDRA (1995) *Annual Report 1994/95: Capacity Building: Myth or Reality?*, Woodstock: CDR

# Capacity building:
## the making of a curry

## William Postma

## Introduction

As Charles Handy once said, 'Life is understood backwards, but
unfortunately, it has to be lived forwards'.[1] Much the same can be said
for the capacity of a development organisation. When we look backwards in time, there are often significant events that indicate success
and achievement – periods when things seemed to have worked well.
We look back and see that, yes, there were times when the organisation's 'capacity' was high, or at least higher than at other times. In
reflecting on this, we may be able to uncover some of the reasons why.

When we approach the *area* of capacity building, however, we
approach something that suggests a thinking and looking forward.
That is not to say that we do not make plans without reference to some
*looking around* – reflecting on what other organisations have learned,
their experiences, their 'best practices'. Nor is it to be taken that we
approach capacity building without being shaped by past organisational
experience and events.

But, as this paper sets out to show, there is an insufficient amount
of *looking backwards* and *looking within* when it comes time to discussing
plans by which to enhance a given organisation's capacity. There seems
to be a disjuncture between an understanding of the lessons learned
from the life of one's own organisation, and the plans we set in place to
make organisational life more vibrant, more sustainable, and more
sustaining.

To paraphrase Charles Handy, this is unfortunate. Even more so
since this can serve as a detriment to good capacity building. There is
much to be gained, learned, affirmed, and celebrated when we draw
upon moments of organisational experience within which members
felt personal satisfaction, high levels of commitment, and excitement

because of their role in the organisation's work. When we do stop and reflect upon good things that have already happened in our organisation, we may very well uncover some powerful ingredients that can move us forward, in our planning, our doing, and even our defining of where we wish to go.

This paper describes a brief journey experienced by one organisation in seeking to come to a better understanding of capacity-building, and to be better equipped in assisting other partner organisations in building their capacity. With the support of the United States Agency for International Development (USAID), the Christian Reformed World Relief Committee (CRWRC), a small US NGO, has been undertaking a review of its organisational capacity-building measurement tools and methods, drawing upon innovative action-research methods as developed at Case Western Reserve University (CWRU) at Cleveland, Ohio.

The review over the 1994–1997 period has taken place at more or less the same time as a corporate initiative on CRWRC's part to re-allocate a larger share of its resources from sectoral areas of functional education, primary health care (PHC), agriculture and income-generation, to strengthening management and board functions, lending assistance in areas of policy and procedure development, monitoring and evaluation, grant-writing, resource development, and financial management. Such an attempt at re-allocation is not dissimilar from initiatives of other Northern development agencies[2] and reflects, among other factors, greater acknowledgement of sectoral skills already resident in developing countries, as well as the concerns of many in the development community for institutional viability and an embedding of transparent and effective policies and practices.

Historically, in its work with Southern partners, CRWRC has emphasised the importance of regularly assessing financial, technical, networking, resource development, and governance skills. Questions and a numerical sliding-scale system were used. Questions would ask, for example, about the levels of functionality, ownership, and transparency of a governing board and a Constitution, and about job descriptions, a training calendar, a clear book-keeping system, and so on. These series of questions would be asked every six months, with targets set for the following six-month period. The assessment and target-setting would form the basis for support by CRWRC to a Southern partner.

With the purpose of reviewing this system and suggesting possible changes, 'listening workshops' were arranged over a three-year period (1994–1997) in all four regions where CRWRC works (West Africa, East Africa, Latin America, and Asia). Over 120 national NGOs have now participated in about 50 different workshops, each of which lasted an average of two to three days. Workshops were framed so as to give space and significance to listening to one another and exploring dimensions of positive past experiences, which were shared through stories, songs, poems, and pictures. This, as well as the participation of a wide array of organisational members – Board and funding agency representatives and programme participants as well as staff – allowed for discussion to flow across a rich blend of interests and professional vocations including business persons, religious and community leaders, teachers, researchers, lawyers, and doctors.

## Appreciative Inquiry (AI)

An Appreciative Inquiry (AI) framework was used to guide the proceedings and frame the listening and review process. Appreciative Inquiry is a philosophy or an approach to organisational learning and analysis that seeks to evolve the vision and will of a collectivity, and to value and amplify the best of what already is practised.[3]

The inquiry dimension of AI affirms human beings' symbolic capacities of imagination and their social capacities for conscious choice and continuous willing. The 'appreciative' dimension seeks to celebrate and affirm that which works and has gone well. It seeks to locate and illuminate the reasons behind moments when, for example, commitment was exceptionally high; and to discover the factors and forces which allowed for that to be so.

Appreciative Inquiry suggests that any inquiry into the 'art of the possible' in organisational life needs to begin with an appreciation for those exceptional moments which have given life to the organisational system and activated members' competencies and energies. These resources – those actual, lived, personally satisfying moments when commitment and excitement were high – are powerful seeds and momentum-builders by which an organisation can grow and develop.

An AI approach suggests that organisations are made and imagined – not constructed in hard and fast ways. Organisations can be re-configured according to the wishes and hopes of their members. Habitual styles of thought and background assumptions by which we come to define our organisations in a particular way serve to constrain our imagination. Since organisations are human constructions, they are responsive to positive thought. Unlike a problem-solving approach whereby key problems are identified and prioritised, and solutions and an action plan developed to eliminate those problems, AI says that when there exists a foundation of mutual affirmation and organisation-wide appreciation, it will be that much easier to work towards a mutually desired future.

Moreover, when an organisation experiments with the conscious evolution of positive imagery and derives such an image for itself, organisational 'problems' will lose their daunting edge, and conditions will be much more amenable to resolving these problems. Organisations do not need 'fixing' but, rather, constant re-affirmation. Because organisations are socially constructed, patterns of action within them are also open to alteration. The largest obstacle in the way of organisational well-being is the absence of a positive image, an affirmative projection which would guide the organisation and draw it in the direction of the image of that future.

## AI and capacity building

An AI framework adapts well to objectives of a clearer and more contextual understanding of organisational capacity. Appreciative Inquiry methods, and what I shall call 'traditional' capacity-building plans, both seek and envision a better future. Whereas AI methods suggest that a future organisational state will draw upon the learnings and momentum of positive present and past experiences, most current capacity-building initiatives set out to follow well-considered and well-sequenced plans. Neither AI methods nor traditional capacity-building plans lay out a future on the basis of fancy whims or lofty hopes; rather, future hopes are earthed to real and firm ground – actual experiences in the case of AI, and clarity and sequence in the case of traditional capacity-building. Finally, AI methods profess openness and flexibility to varying symbolic and local media through which sharing and discovery can take place; this parallels the desire even in the most 'logically' developed capacity-building plan to give further value to culture and indigenous context.

The chorus of capacity-building enthusiasts is growing with each passing year. The World Bank recently announced a new and significant capacity-building thrust in Sub-Saharan Africa, one that would help to 'nurture the building and rational utilization of capacity' on the continent.[4] The Washington Microcredit Summit Declaration and Plan of Action, adopted in February 1997, noted that the single biggest constraint to expanding microcredit to 100 million of the world's poorest families – even more than mobilising support and seed funds – is the need to build local institutional capacity in communities around the world.[5] The International Training and Research Centre (INTRAC) has noted that, for an assortment of reasons, NGO capacity building, too, has moved to the 'top of the development agenda'.[6]

Appreciative Inquiry, meanwhile, is still a small and emergent stream among the many action-research and organisational trans-formation approaches. None the less, it has served to facilitate several significant learnings around capacity building.

## Learnings

Originally, back in 1994, we in CRWRC hoped that listening tours and appreciative methods would allow us to discern the real fundamentals – the nuts and bolts – of capacity. Southern partner perspectives. Attention to local culture. Being more attuned to local realities. Developmentally correct. With these, we thought, our understanding of capacity would become clearer.

Yet, if anything, our understanding of capacity and the issues around building capacity-building has become less crisp. Capacity, we are learning, is much more than the presence of good systems, well-trained staff, marketability, and resource-drawing capability. For example, we are learning that an organisation, in spite of demonstrating what is traditionally understood as capacity, may not have the wherewithal to weather crisis periods or assure that the working environment is encouraging and attractive enough to retain high-quality staff. Even in what may be perceived to be a 'high-capacity' organisation, it may be difficult when capable staff do leave, or there is a sudden shortfall in revenue, or a serious case of misappropriation, for example, to know whether the organisation will be able to bring in new people, pull itself together, and continue delivering services in a similarly satisfactory manner. Indeed, many developing countries face civil strife, and many national NGOs in the South operate in situations of resource constraints and high staff turnover.

Organisations with stellar management systems can fold rather quickly in the face of civil conflict or an abrupt funding cutback from donors. Others, for example, at the time of civil war in El Salvador in the 1980s and Sierra Leone in 1995, although admittedly weak in financial management and other technical skills, were able to bond closer together, hold fast, and serve as leavening influences among people in distress. Although they had not yet evolved good overall management systems, they were able to show empathy, and impart to local people significant messages of peace, solidarity, and reconciliation while also continuing – albeit at a temporarily reduced level – with health and education work.

We are also learning that there are important limitations in traditional capacity-assessment methods. Firstly, we have seen that although an ideal may very well be for an organisation to assemble every six months and assess its capacity, the process – a question-and-answer format for the most part, with varying degrees of discussion about what number from one to five to give, and what future numerical target to set – may not be a *significant* organisational event; and may not be sufficient to attract board members and staff to participate fully, enjoy what they are doing, or see it as important for their organisation or embrace the results in such a way as to build greater organisational commitment towards making their work more effective.

A second limitation is that traditional methods serve to set apart or demarcate capacity shortfalls or capacity gaps. By highlighting deficiencies and systematically setting out to eliminate weaknesses, traditional assessment methods can dampen or even extinguish joys that may have been ignited by successes in having attained new plateaux of, for example, resource development capacity, or a process by which a training programme has been put in place, or a Constitution amended. 'Capacity deficit reduction' does not necessarily arise out of malice or bad intent, but it can none the less dampen learnings and joys that, were they affirmed and celebrated, could motivate and energise an organisation towards further growth.

A third limitation is that traditional methods of planning and assessing capacity can reflect a Western conception of what an ideal organisation should be. A Western and uniform model may be a poor fit in the very heterogeneous cultures of Asia, Latin America, and Africa. Donor-required, pre-determined sets of assessment questions can serve to marginalise organisational qualities that are intrinsically desirable and valued by its members, and move such qualities out of the lived discourse of an organisation's reality – to the point where these are understood as being inessential to the viability and effectiveness of its work. Capacity-assessment questions have usually not sought to learn about levels of compassion, commitment, staff relationships, or shared hopes for the future. Although highly relevant, these values seem to be important outside the traditional boundaries and description of capacity.

Moreover, we are learning that good organisational capacity in one area of the world may be quite different from that in another region: a Cambodian organisation sees capacity as prioritising political awareness and advocacy among staff and board, while one from India sees empathy and solidarity with the Dalits as being most integral to their organisation's capacity, while yet another, in Mali, may value environmental justice and the building of vibrant communities as being of the highest importance. Over time, too, an understanding of capacity may evolve with a change in the working environment (say, a period of civil strife has come to an end) or a change in an organisation's maturity or mandate.

## Organisation as a car

An organisation has often been portrayed as a car. Invest an outlay of cash, add gas and oil, and out comes mileage: you move from point A to point B. You take good care of the car, ensure that it looks nice on the outside, and do preventive-type things – careful driving, and regular tune-ups and servicing – to make sure that the vehicle runs as well and for as long as possible. There will no doubt be maintenance work: new shock-absorbers, new tyres, changed gaskets. And the occasional accident may require body-work, putting the vehicle in the garage for a few days, perhaps a new windshield. But the car would get back on the road eventually and continue to run. Our definition of a good organisation, one with capacity, was that of a well-oiled machine, a smooth-riding car, one in which system inputs could be processed and transformed into system outputs.

A machine or vehicle metaphor of an organisation with capacity is valid up to a certain point, although it seems to suggest that capacity is fixed. Our use of a sliding scale, with a maximum number of five, seemed to suggest the same. Perhaps the terminology related to 'capacity', in the sense of industrial capacity or daily processing capacity of an oil refinery, for example, also encourages us to borrow factory analogies and apply fixed-type thinking into our understanding of capacity.

But organisational capacity is very different from industrial capacity. Whereas the daily processing capacity of an oil refinery can increase with more machinery or new and more efficient machinery, we are learning that organisational capacity is not proportionately linked to numbers of staff, or the quantities or even the qualities of trainings and policies in place. Organisational capacity incorporates quantity, quality, and efficiency dimensions – as would the oil refinery – but also more value-based, life-centric dimensions. Perhaps this is because development NGOs are service-oriented and people-focused. Both process and product are important.

## Capacity as ... capacity includes ...

Rather than wrangle over words and terminology about what capacity means – itself often a frustrating process when different languages are being used – more generative and enjoyable workshop time was spent telling stories, drawing pictures, and dreaming about what a good organisation is. Dom Helder Camara, the priest who laboured among the very poorest of the people of Brazil, once said that while dreaming alone may be a human reaction to tough day-to-day realities, dreaming together creates an unbreakable bond of commitment and a real hope that a better tomorrow will actually come. Appreciative Inquiry methods take his words one step further: when dreams are grounded on the already-lived and experienced 'ingredients' – as identified and affirmed from stories of an organisation's members – and shared out in full-system settings, they can become irresistible images of the future.

An AI approach suggests that organisations are essentially heliotropic, in that organisational actions have a largely automatic tendency to move in the direction of images of the future, much like a flower that grows towards its source of life or light. Organisations are drawn to images of the future that they themselves have chosen. The energy created in the process of constructing an image releases greater commitment and hope among those working towards it. Like the sunshine on a foggy morning, shared hope can dissolve rancour and burn away differences or apathy that, like the fog, hang over and impair even a short-term vision.

- Capacity includes commitment, compassion, connectedness. Members of an organisation in Bangladesh, when asked to give a metaphor for when they felt most satisfied and most committed to their work, chose almost matter-of-factly that of a family.

- A partner in the Dominican Republic shared a picture of a healthy organisation as a healthy human being in whom all the many miles of nerves and blood vessels are connected to such an extent that when one part of the body feels sensation of any sort, it is communicated instantaneously to the rest of the body and, in the event of pain in one part of the body, the rest of the body mobilises quickly to heal the part experiencing such weakness or pain.

- An Indonesian organisation pictured a coconut tree growing on the banks of a river as being a true symbol of themselves. The tree yields a harvest of coconuts each year, some of which are eaten, others of which fall into the river, only to be carried to another place, where the seeds will cause a new tree to come forth and continue the cycle of life and life-giving.

- A Honduran organisation suggested that a good organisation is not a smooth-running machine, but a winding river. It is a river that starts small and allows for other smaller streams to join with it. It develops strength along the way. The river gives nutrition, generates life, carries and deposits nutrients. It facilitates the regular acts of life, but is not the owner of them. Because the river accepts streams of water that have their origin elsewhere, it grows in strength. And because it grows in strength, it is able to nourish and carry life and joy to ever more people.

Like the river, growth in organisational capacity is not a straight path 'as the crow flies'. Capacity happens in fits and starts. A river meanders and winds with the lie of the land and the contours of the topography. Organisational capacity – happening at its best – may be two steps forward, one step back, perhaps not at all incrementally or in any sequential fashion, and perhaps in a timeframe that begs patience. 'Hardly a cut and dried affair', said one East African partner, 'building capacity can be a messy, up and down type business'.

Unlike the smooth-running vehicle, then, an organisation's life cycle is not linear, and its life not finite. There does not necessarily have to come a time when the costs of keeping the organisation going outweigh the benefits, where the inputs outweigh the outputs. Depreciation costs do not need to accumulate to the point where the vehicle – or the organisation – is written off.

## Capacity as a festive curry meal?

Today, capacity building seems 'a slippery concept', in description and in practice.[7] There are questions of semantics (to what extent does capacity-building overlap with institutional development?) and of definitional boundaries (can we talk about building the capacity of community groups, industries, sectors, and talk of extra-sectoral capacity building, *without* incurring some blurriness?). There may be an extra layer of slipperiness in seeking to carry out capacity building in the political unpredictability of those regions of the world where a range of contingencies and assumptions need to be factored in.

Trying to define capacity, we are learning, can become quite 'windy' when we seek to describe it and incorporate all its many angles. In a sense, capacity is like the wind. When we talk about wind, we talk about direction, velocity, consistency, a production of energy. It is essential and refreshing. Without wind, the air is stagnant. Yet, somewhat like the wind, organisational capacity is something that we will not be able to fully grasp, understand or predict.

There is an unfortunate disjuncture between *capacity building* and what Edwards has referred to as *institutional learning*: 'the process by which an organisation identifies key lessons of experience and uses them to improve the quality of its work'. Capacity building may be so programmed towards the attainment of an improved future that it unwittingly forgets key, past learnings. On the other hand, there may be a need to re-orient ourselves to how we perceive institutional learning: from a lessons-learned exercise to one of corporate valuation, validation, and appreciation of moments when satisfaction was personally felt; and where the reasons for this, when publicly shared, can ignite imagination and build momentum.

An organisation that reflects good capacity is somewhat like a festive curry meal. Making the meal requires skills, dedication, fresh ingredients, and good timing. There are staple ingredients that are understood as being essential – transparent management systems, clear communication, participatory work approaches – but there are also specific ingredients and spices that can only be selected by the people of that place. And, in the end, it is only they who will be able to put all the ingredients together in a recipe, select just the right cooking utensils, and make a curry that will truly reflect what they and their communities enjoy most.

Our listening has moved us to think through menu-driven approaches to capacity building and to adapt more inductive process templates that allow for flexibility, creativity, and learning. This aligns comfortably with an organisational shift away from grassroots implementation to a role of support and enabling – presenting partners with a menu of capacity areas (leadership development, human resources, gender participation, to name a few) from which they choose and within which they develop indicators that are meaningful to them and that are grounded in their own organisational experience and collective hopes.

One further avenue of exploration is to visualise a capacity-measurement tool as one of the growth-monitoring and promotion devices that are used in child health and survival. The idea originated from a discussion that took place in a village in Bangladesh, where several women participants, when asked about the 'capacity' of their community group, immediately compared it to their children's weight-for-age 'Road to Health' cards. They talked about their group's 'weight' – *shangstar ojone* – as increasing as the group became healthier over time, as they together learned new skills and, because of savings and profits earned, developed greater purchasing power. Table 1 develops the comparison between a proposed Road to Capacity card with the familiar Road to Health card.

| Table 1: Organisational capacity assessment compared with the monitoring of child development | |
|---|---|
| **Features of a Road to Health card** | **Features of a Road to Capacity card** |
| The growth or weight of the child is seen as a proxy indicator of the overall nutritional adequacy and the health of the child. Faltering growth - usually over two to three cycles of measurement - is the most sensitive indicator that all is not well with a child. | The capacity of an organisation is a measurement of its overall health and vitality. If 'capacity' swings downwards for any reason, this is not seen as a real concern, unless the downward swing persists over a longer period of time. |
| Weighing of under-5s is done regularly (monthly), and the child's weight is not compared with the weight or progress of other children. It is the child's own weight that is important. | Organisational capacity assessment is carried out regularly, but only in reference to itself and its own unique development and progress. |
| The parents can see (visualise) progress in a way that is simple but helpful. The mother or father usually weighs the child, records the weight, and draws the line from previous markings on the 'road to health' card. The card is designed to be used and fully and quickly understood by the parents and kept by them at home. The mother or father monitors and the field trainer or health worker observes and guides, if necessary. | Board members and all staff can visualise change and progress in an easily understood manner. Indeed, members of the organisation are the ones who carry out the assessment and the scoring. |
| | *continued ...* |

*Table 1 continued*

**Features of a Road to Health card**

Health workers or field trainers respond to each parent and child based on conversations with the parent and on the unique circumstances of that child. A key communication strategy in growth monitoring and promotion is listening and not talking, and giving prompt feedback that is easy to understand and implement. There is lots of learning in the interaction between the health worker and the parent. The health worker learns about the context and community, about what a particular set of parents have tried to do with a given child, what worked and what did not. There may be other social or economic factors that have affected or prevented growth from happening in a given couple of months. By using growth monitoring and promotion methods, the health worker becomes more productive and efficient.

Growth monitoring and promotion is a preventative strategy, in that it seeks to identify problems before malnutrition occurs. It also promotes good nutritional health. For the child, it seeks to achieve and maintain a state of nourishment. The preventative and promotional aspects need to begin within the first few months of the first year.

A child's growth is indicative of well-nourishment but also overall community well-being (quality of the physical environment, economic opportunities, income distribution, community education).

Growth monitoring and promotion is not one of many health-related interventions but is rather a basket into which all interventions can be put (immunisations, vitamin A treatment, oral-rehydration therapy, breastfeeding, etc.) and taken out as needed or required. The intervention used in given contexts (say, iodine supplements or Vitamin E) can vary, but the desired result is the same: growth. Growth monitoring and promotion is a framework, an operational strategy for the entire range of PHC and educational inputs.

**Features of a Road to Capacity card**

The emphasis on the input of a partner organisation is to listen, learn, discern the broader and deeper circumstances, and be ready to offer prompt feedback. Such feedback requires a thorough knowledge and background experience. Moreover, there needs to be a good working relationship within which discussion takes place and any advice is offered.

Mapping that is carried out on a Road to Capacity card is done with both prevention and promotion in mind, with the goal being overall organisational health and growth, and a receptiveness to learn and embrace new ideas, through which further growth and continued good health can be assured.

Organisational capacity needs to be understood in relation to the organisational environment and the development of civil society.

Organisational capacity-building is an over-arching and all-encompassing framework within which work is carried out. It includes many things, but depending on context and situation, responsiveness (which ingredient to use) can vary.

There is an undoubted need to build capacity, embed effective policies and practices, and work towards goals where streams of benefits do not dry up once external support comes to an end but, rather, continue to flow, nourish, and sustain. However, as we have learned, there is a similarly pressing need to see the methods and tools of capacity building capture the imagination of an organisation's members, lending focus to their dreams, and building energy and momentum for seeing these dreams realised.

## Notes

1 Charles Handy (1995), interview by Joel Kurtzman with Charles Handy, *Strategy and Business*, 4th Quarter, p. 5.

2 Overseas Development Institute (1996): 'The Impact of Development Projects', Briefing Paper 2. Presenting a review of policy shifts in Norwegian, Danish, and US official aid allocations, the ODI paper concludes that there appears to be a 'recent shift in debate, and in some cases, in practice away from funding projects for the poor to work involving capacity building and support for processes of democratization'.

3 The discussion of Appreciative Inquiry draws on material produced by the Department of Organisational Behaviour, the Weatherhead School of Management, Case Western Reserve, Cleveland, Ohio, and in particular, *Appreciative Inquiry: A Constructive Approach to Organisation Capacity Building* (1993) by Jim Ludema, Charlie Pratt, Suresh Srivastva, and Craig Wishart.

4 World Bank Press Release, World Bank Supports New Partnership for Capacity Building in Africa, 28 September 1996.

5 Article 13.1 in the Declaration.

6 *ON-TRAC*, the newsletter of the International Training and Research Centre, No. 2, March 1995, p. 4.

7 J. Bossuyt (1994) *Capacity Development: How Can Donors Do It Better?*, Policy Management Brief No. 5, Maastricht, European Centre for Development Policy Management (ECDPM), p. 2. Bossuyt's comments about a 'slippery concept' actually apply to what he called 'capacity development'. Capacity development, he noted, 'remains a rather obscure concept. It lacks an agreed definition, a clear analytical framework, and related *modus operandi*. This is reflected, for instance, in the indiscriminate use of similar concepts such as "institution-building", "institutional development", and "capacity building".'

8 Michael Edwards (1994): 'NGOs in the age of information', *IDS Bulletin* 25/2, p. 119.

# Operationalising bottom–up learning in international NGOs:
## barriers and alternatives

## Grant Power, Matthew Maury, and Susan Maury

---

### What's wrong with this picture?

In 1995, a leading international NGO (INGO) fielded two community organisers in Harare, Zimbabwe, to live and work with residents of two different urban poor areas.[1] In the ensuing months, the organisers unhurriedly tried to encourage 'bottom–up' development: understand the local situation, build on the local people's material resources, creativity, knowledge, and views, strengthen local collective action, and facilitate a process in which the communities propose and pursue ideas that are organic to them. The workers did not put any funding into the communities for over a year. However, funds for the projects had been raised from private sources under the banner of community-based, sustainable development.

In 1996, the organisers were told by their regional programme manager that they were behind schedule in producing results. The programme director stressed that INGO performance criteria required that communities show progress on specific material improvements within one year. Further delays could result in a cut-off of funds, as donors might think the projects were going nowhere.

The organisers, hoping their bosses would come to understand the communities' perspectives and adjust their expectations, resisted pressure from headquarters to spend money. They believed their work would be undermined if the communities realigned their activities to receive outside funds, rather than rallying around a shared vision of a preferred future relying primarily on their own resources. In the end, under pressure to spend the funds and in danger of losing their jobs, the organisers finally relented. The funding tap was turned on, and the INGO reported to donors in 1997 that the projects were reaching their targeted benchmarks.

# Do INGOs have a learning disorder?

The Harare case reflects a tendency in INGO operations to resist allowing communities to lead the development process. Given the choice, many of us in the INGO world still are opting for fast results on the ground while only rhetorically embracing community-based self-development. Producing visible results validates the INGO's activities and secures ongoing funding. Facing uncertainty and rapid change, we tend to make decisions that privilege our organisations' self-preservation. However, the emphasis on achieving rapid, visible results often backfires. While we can 'see' development happening, the less photogenic, but ultimately longer lasting aspects of development, such as local initiative, community cohesion, resilience, self-reliance, and resourcefulness – leading ultimately to self-determination – take a back seat. In other words, INGOs tend to set up internal but largely unrecognised barriers to their own values-driven goals. Observers in the early 1990s attributed this problem to a state of confusion among INGOs regarding their purpose, direction, and identity. However, we believe this incongruity of behaviour to be rooted in a failure to translate new knowledge gained from development experience into changed organisational behaviour. As Edwards (1997) notes, INGOs tend to have difficulty with organisational learning because it requires humility, honesty, openness, and the ability to welcome error. Development institutions, like other organisations, have a natural propensity not to dwell on the past (that is, on mistakes) and to move forward without the painful self-scrutiny necessary to learn from experience.

On the other hand, many INGOs have eagerly embraced organisational learning in principle, following the lead of commercial businesses. This appears to be a step in the right direction, but can in fact be problematic. Although many businesses are developing models of learning practice, neither the for-profit environment nor its corporate structures fit well with the environment and organisational forms needed for grassroots development. Have INGOs mimicked a for-profit model of organisation too closely?

INGOs differ from their for-profit counterparts in important ways. One is the values-driven approach to attaining justice, equity, and empowerment for the poor that most international non-profits share (Hailey 2000). Often these goals are accompanied by the promotion of full stakeholder participation, mutual learning, accountability and transparency, local self-governance, long-term sustainability, and, perhaps above all, a people-centred approach (Korten 1990; Hailey 2000). Much development theory focuses on the benefits of building on these values, and many practitioners develop, test, and share various processes that can be used to promote and further their use.

## An alien-hand syndrome

This leads to a second key difference between for-profit and non-profit organisations. From a values-based paradigm, the notion of 'organisation', as borrowed from the for-profit world, can be argued to work against responsiveness to the poor.[2] In a traditional for-profit organisation, there is a direct link between the customer and the success of the business. In general, the business must be responsive to customer needs, or sales will decline and the company will be in danger of liquidation. INGOs and other non-profits, on the other hand, are usually set up to serve marginalised communities that are generally without voice. Whether or not an INGO adequately understands and responds to their needs seldom has an impact on the solvency of the organisation.

In order to remain solvent, the INGO must be responsive to its *donor base* – a group that is neither receiving the organisation's primary services, nor is generally capable of monitoring and ensuring that the INGO is adequately responding to the needs of the poor. While the for-profit world has built-in accountability structures between customer and company, there is a 'disconnect' between the 'customer' and organisation for most non-profits which is inadequately bridged by the donor community. This is a symptom of the *alien-hand syndrome*, an organisational learning disorder which ' ... involves a disconnection between organisation intentions and actions ... Organisations may have clear goals and well-defined routines, yet lack adequate incentives to ensure that actions are consistent with intentions' (Snyder and Cummings 1998). An alien-hand syndrome afflicting INGOs has its origins in a model of organisation and learning borrowed from the for-profit world that is inappropriate to the goals and outcomes of development initiatives, but that is nonetheless beneficial to the INGOs' survivability.

What are the practical implications? An INGO may provide inadequate and at times appalling 'service' to marginalised individuals and communities without any repercussions. As long as the donors are satisfied, the organisation can continue not only to operate but also to grow, thrive, and expand. 'Success' in a developmental sense – that is, empowering poor communities, giving them voice, and developing self-governance skills – may in fact be detrimental to the success of the organisation for two reasons. First, it creates a direct accountability link, which may threaten the organisation's method of operations, focus, mission, and vision. Once the community has voice, it can question or reject the organisation's operational choices. In other words, the INGO faces a conflict of interests – succeeding at its mission could threaten its existence. Therefore, most INGOs, from a self-preservation perspective, prefer to keep accountability links solely with donors and perpetuate the *status quo*, even though this may fail to empower targeted communities.

Second, donors are generally unenthusiastic about supporting a long, iterative, people-centred process, because it may not produce an immediately measurable impact, or may not accomplish the original intention of the intervention. Funding agencies tend to prefer short-term, measurable outputs, which demand a high level of control over decisions and the conditions in which projects are implemented.

This is not to imply that INGOs are conspiring to subvert their own values. But they have significant, unrecognised barriers to aligning behaviour with those values, particularly through learning that comes from communities. Perhaps this is because 'members may see only what the strong culture of the organisation permits them to see' (Snyder and Cummings 1998). Perhaps there has been no push to look for more appropriate models, because the sense of self-preservation is strong in any human system. Few have dared to question the system, because those who have the ability to do so benefit from the current structure, and those who suffer most from failures in the system do not have a voice adequate to challenge it. To the degree that a conflict persists between an INGO's mission and self-preservation, the former is often, unconsciously, sacrificed. The INGO may not recognise negative consequences, because it lacks an effective feedback mechanism and accountability link to communities where the effects are felt.

We are not advocating that INGOs close down or that one type of unidirectional accountability replace another. But we believe INGOs can do better in bringing their practices in line with their core values. For this, INGOs must recognise and correct the power asymmetries embedded within them so that both sustainable development *and* organisational sustainability are possible.

Some INGOs, seeking a solution, are institutionalising a corrective kind of organisational practice – bottom–up learning (BUL). This is a process of comprehensively (re)orienting their operations to the concrete realities of people living in poverty and injustice in vastly diverse local contexts worldwide, and allowing those realities to form the basis for programme designs, fundraising targets and methods, and management policies, plans, and budgets. In a 'bottom–up' approach to learning, organisations strive sensitively to understand people's needs and conditions in each area where they are working, and to allow each community's priorities to determine (not just inform) organisational objectives, methods, timetables, benchmarks, and funding.

## Bottom–up organisational learning

Bottom–up organisational learning is a sub-discipline of organisational learning (OL). OL has been defined as a process of developing new knowledge that changes an organisation's behaviour to improve future performance (Garvin 1993).

Such learning is not simply about making better decisions but also about making sense of our perceptions and interpretations of our environment. Organisational learning may be either adaptive (questioning the basic assumptions an organisation holds about itself and the environment) or generative (questioning an organisation's perceptions of both its internal and external relationships) (Barker and Camarata 1998).

The agenda of the 'learning organisation' has likewise been described as a challenge 'to explore ... how we can create organisational structures which are meaningful to people so they can assist, participate and more meaningfully control their own destiny in an unhampered way' (Jones and Hendry 1994:160). In practising bottom–up learning, an organisation makes a moral choice to draw insights and feedback from people at the low end of a socially constructed hierarchy (that is, from those who are most vulnerable in the system). It then refocuses and redefines itself, its operational choices, and its performance measures in light of its accountability to the poor. This is not the only type of learning in which an organisation can, and should, engage, but it provides a counterbalance to other types of learning that may fall short of addressing the alien-hand syndrome. BUL assumes that an organisation sees the most vulnerable part of its constituency as its primary source of legitimacy. A BUL organisation commits itself to work for the liberation of those at the bottom by drawing its own sense of direction and priorities from this group, rather than 'developing' them. As those at the bottom are given a voice and enabled to develop themselves on their own terms, most other stakeholders (including donors, managers, and staff) may also find greater freedom, as they no longer need to control development outcomes in an effort to sustain the life of their organisation. They are instead incorporating the massive resource represented in the partner community.

BUL asks organisations to adapt their internal *structure, systems,* and *culture* to the complex and evolving struggles of those in poverty, including even the choice not to be 'developed'. INGO operations following BUL are comprehensively recalibrated to let go of the controls in community development. They recognise that they need to adapt themselves to environments that are chaotic, uncertain, fraught with risk, unpredictable, not conducive to being standardised, often hard to fund, and which defy linear, quantifiable models for project planning and evaluation. While BUL organisations' roles become pliable and versatile, their mission of strengthening the poor and increasing social justice remains at the forefront. They situate their work inside a broader context of serving and advancing the agendas of organised grassroots social movements, and thus work as often as possible in situations where they can work alongside partners. This partnership helps further the struggle of an established, indigenous, local organisation (or network of organisations) that is embarking on social change, based on the wishes of the local people. Over time, new initiatives may be carved out through mutual agreement and increasing trust.

BUL is contrasted with *organisational pragmatism* in which the primary agenda is to 'adjust' the poor to fit in (and thus benefit from) standardised INGO programmes, usually through the promise or provision of material assistance. Making constituents adjust to an existing programme suggests that the INGO may not acknowledge the uniqueness of the needs and conditions in each new community, preferring (even with the best intentions) to find an 'easier fix', based on time and budget constraints. This is often driven by an overarching premium in INGOs on utilitarian thinking and practice, which states that *'what is useful is true, and what works is good'*. It is based on the false objectivity of a cost–benefit calculation that, while claiming to benefit the poor, in the end works more to protect the interests of employees who benefit most from maintaining the *status quo* (Murphy 2000). A decision by the newly selected president of a major INGO in 1997 to retain child sponsorship as the organisation's primary (and lucrative) funding vehicle for the sake of financial stability, despite emerging evidence that development outcomes implemented under the sponsorship system were not self-sustaining, is a clear example of such pragmatism.

BUL does not romanticise the poor or suggest that their interests can be easily defined or treated as an unfragmented whole. On the contrary, a core strength of BUL is precisely that it is grounded and realistic in approaching the complexities of poverty and development 'from below'. In short, BUL rejects top–down development programmes, and promotes the interests and priorities of marginalised individuals and groups, so that their voices are not only heard, but can exercise a discrete and overriding influence not only on the actions of INGOs on the ground, but in their internal operations as well.

## Theoretical underpinnings

BUL is grounded in a convergence of theories within the disciplines of development studies and organisational psychology. From development theory, we draw from the framework of alternative development, or *democratic development*, depicted by Friedmann (1992), among others. Poverty here is understood mainly as *disempowerment*. Development is a process of vision-driven organising, initially at the local level, which 'focuses explicitly on the moral relations of persons and households, and it draws its values from that sphere rather than from any desire to satisfy material wants, important as these may be' (Friedmann 1992:33).

People's active participation in identifying and addressing forces that marginalise them leads to respect for the diversity and complexity of local communities, and is the most effective and lasting way to remove structural constraints on their development at national and global levels.

This perspective moves development out of the realm of charity and into a moral framework of justice and rights. For development workers, an alternative development commends a position of *solidarity* with the poor. Advocacy with the poor in defence of their rights (to land, capital, and other productive assets) can go hand in hand with sensitive, tailored support for local people's self-development, self-reliance, and increased ability to sustain their own desired improvements. The fundamental questions to be answered in any initiative are 'In whose interest? In whose voice?' (Murphy 2000).

Even when we embrace an alternative, democratic development paradigm, we still need further conceptual tools to undertake BUL. In this regard, the theoretical literature on organisational learning in the NGO sector is thin, but initial inroads have been made. Korten (1990), building on people-centred development theory, offers an organisational typology in which young NGOs tend to focus on charity but mature (fourth-generation) NGOs on solidarity. Coopey (1995) and Snell and Chak (1998) build an argument for 'learning empowerment' in organisations through constitutionally protected democratic rights and obligations for all members, coupled with a culture of developmental leadership. In this connection, Srivastva *et al.* (1995:44) look to INGOs to initiate 'the discovery and mobilisation of innovative social/organisational architectures that make possible human cooperation across previously polarising or arbitrary constraining boundaries'. Presumably, organisations advocating such broad participation by societies' members in the face of the 'stark legislative pressure of governments' would themselves be bottom–up learners. Elliott (1999) begins to address this issue by arguing that NGOs themselves are most likely to become effective learners through a broadly authentically participative process of appreciative inquiry, similar to the process now being used to facilitate change in some 'flat' corporations.

The ambitious changes implied by BUL may seem utopian to seasoned INGO workers. However, a movement among some INGOs in this direction (described below) suggests there is interest and the possibility of making real and lasting change. We believe that by recognising and directly addressing the built-in barriers many INGOs have to utilising BUL principles fully, great strides can be made in increasing INGO impact. To this end, we now look at some hopeful alternatives and discuss how barriers can be minimised or eliminated, leading to successful community empowerment.

## Signs of mission-centred thinking – and practice

Development practice has come a long way since the 1940s, when many INGOs were first formed. From an initial focus on providing immediate needs, development theory and practice have matured to include such considerations as community empowerment and self-governance, gender equality and opportunity, solidarity and voice, advocacy issues, economic advancement, and political recognition and participation. Most development practitioners express an understanding of and commitment to the importance of helping communities to self-develop, and they recognise the danger of providing goods and services without some sort of community input or response (note the proliferation of food-for-work or labour-for-development models in the past decade or so). The principles are known and understood, and attempts have been made to put them into practice.

Specifically, research and practice in the sub-fields of community research and evaluation have tended to reflect progressive thinking. The development and wide dissemination of tools used in Participatory Rural Appraisal and Participatory Learning and Action (PRA and PLA) methods show a hunger for appropriate tools and methodologies for engaging local communities in the development process. Programme evaluation increasingly draws on participatory techniques and processes as well, with many organisations reporting positive results. Additionally, new breakthroughs in organisational theory are helping development organisations rethink their internal processes and external delivery systems from top to bottom.

The evolution of theory and practice has been rapid, and many organisations report positive results in using these methods. Yet, despite the practical application of BUL principles, many of the same problems stemming from values conflicts continue to afflict INGOs. Why is this? We argue that good practice at the field level is not sufficient where organisational practice inhibits or retards learning from field outcomes. Organisational structure and practice is seldom in alignment with development principles, but rather adheres to principles which ensure self-preservation and perpetuation, as reflected in policies and procedures, reporting practices, and relationships with communities of need as well as donors and the general public. Development practice is compartmentalised to *field* practice, and is not allowed to permeate the organisation as a whole. Assumptions about what is good for the organisation as an institution lead to stability and self-perpetuation, but also shut out the potential learning and change that adopting BUL principles offers as reward. Not only do these operating principles restrict institutional development: organisational practice at times reaches down and inhibits the implementation of good field practice (as the Harare case illustrates). Often, tools such as PRA or participatory evaluation methods may be employed but are not allowed to inform fully what occurs in the community, or else community members are given the promise of self-determination, only to have it pulled away when their outcomes conflict with organisational priorities. The following section will briefly outline areas where barriers tend to exist, and some suggestions for removing or minimising them.

## Barriers and alternatives

### Community interaction

*Barrier:* most INGO interactions with community groups can be defined by a single input: money. While there are often attempts to build a more holistic partnership, once funds are introduced the relationship becomes one of power held by the INGO, with the community often forced to respond 'appropriately' to the INGO's real or perceived wishes in order to secure the elusive funds. Some INGOs have sought to mitigate this effect by working through local community organisations or local NGOs. However, the unequal power relationship generally is transferred to this relationship as well. Ashman (2000) observes that formal agreements as written by INGOs (a) almost always ensure upward (rather than mutual) accountability; (b) are bounded by timelines too short for effective development (usually three years); and (c) suffer from a lack of mutual agreement on the terms for ending funding (tending to be INGO driven).

*Potential alternatives:* it is difficult to separate the link between funding and power. One radical but seriously proposed solution is to redirect the attention currently placed on funding towards organisational autonomy. For example, in working directly with communities, more INGOs are providing training in the skills required for self-governance. The aim is to enable communities to use appropriate methods to self-assess their current situation, develop a vision for their desired future, develop a plan *for themselves* (and not reliant on an external agency) and move towards that vision, self-monitor progress, and finally evaluate the results and adjust future plans as necessary. In this scenario, the power lies not in the funds but in the skills and self-knowledge that are developed *and remain* in the community, including appropriate methods for guiding and directing action and reflection.

If an INGO's primary input to communities is the ability to govern the process of self-development, an implication is that the INGO also changes *as an organisation,* including administration, fundraising, and management. In practice, INGOs might still introduce funding, but mainly to promote communities' self-development plans by linking them to other organisations or perhaps offering small grants or low-interest loans to finance planned activities. Other concepts that have been tried and have met with success include teaching small-business and budgeting skills for locally based enterprises, or providing scholarships for specialised schooling that result in stronger local leadership. These approaches de-emphasise the receipt of a large cheque and instead look at building skills that lead to autonomy and independence.

Because such intensive, hands-on activities often demand a deep sensitivity and familiarity with local needs and conditions, we believe it may be most effective if INGOs go beyond decentralising their operations and *cease being operational* in the field. This can be done by forging ties with autonomous local NGOs that have a proven commitment and track record in handing over controls in the development process to the communities where they are working. To the degree that terms for partnership can be negotiated equitably, the imperative for standardised and impersonal mass reproduction of one strategy, which ironically is often only magnified (rather than adapted) in the process of decentralisation, can be significantly curtailed.

## Systems and procedures

*Barrier:* organisational systems and procedures are too often excused as a 'necessary evil' in meeting bureaucratic requirements. We contend that many systems and procedures are inappropriate for attaining the goals of most INGOs and may work to limit their effectiveness and impact. For example, standard INGO accounting and management information systems (MIS) are complex and require individuals in the field who have specialised training to operate them effectively. It can be difficult to find accountants who are adequately trained in computer skills (much less a specific accounting or MIS package), and INGOs often find they spend excessive resources recruiting, training, and then losing these individuals (who, once trained, are valuable to other INGOs). Additionally, the reporting required for these systems often forces accommodation at all levels of the organisation, reaching to the community level. At times this may require field staff to be hired and trained simply to fill and submit reports to the INGO national office on behalf of the community.

Programme planning and reporting are another key barrier. Instruments now widely used by INGOs, such as the logical framework approach (LogFrame), were originally developed by and for engineers and planners in heavy industry. LogFrame models fit with the way that INGOs and donors typically budget and package projects, but they are alien to community processes and understanding, and can prevent communities from driving the development process. A few years ago, a staff member from one large INGO sat down with community representatives from a historically nomadic tribe in Botswana to discuss the annual INGO planning and budgeting forms. When she posed the question, 'What would you like to see accomplished and funded by the end of next year?' she was met with silence. After several minutes of dialogue in the local dialect, someone responded, 'How can we plan for the next year when we do not know if we will be alive tomorrow?'. INGO planning and reporting procedures usually cannot accommodate people with such vastly different worldviews, even though these procedures are sometimes claimed to be necessary to empower communities.

*Potential alternatives:* the goal here is not to require the *programme* to accommodate the systems, but rather the other way around. It is important to build systems and procedures starting from the community's needs and abilities, rather than expecting communities to conform to organisational or donor requirements. Appropriate methods of accounting, planning, and reporting would allow community groups to self-report back to the INGO. This not only frees valuable staff time, it also puts the responsibility for action where it should be – on the community. As long as staff members are responsible for reporting on the 'INGO's projects', they will remain the INGO's projects in the eyes of the community. This means that reporting systems and procedures need to be appropriate for community use – ideally that community groups actually use the information and processes for their self-development, and not merely to meet reporting requirements. By developing systems in response to community needs, it probably means that INGOs would need to abandon their high dependency on computer-based reports, graphs, and charts, and replace them with methods and processes that are meaningful to local people in vastly diverse settings. Examples include plans, accounts, and reports developed using pictures, graphics, or narrative stories which are appropriate to communities and to BUL.

### Donor and public relations

*Barriers:* in the late 1970s, as he was about to retire, the founder and president of one large INGO looked back over the organisation's history. In considering its past and present difficulties, he reflected in a moment of unusual candour that the organisation had erred when it began to believe what it was telling donors about itself. Today, we might add that

INGOs err to the degree they believe what they are telling donors about poverty and development. Educating constituents and donors about the complexity of international development seems largely out of fashion among INGOs. What passes for public education tends to be slanted towards child sponsorship and emergency appeals. Public relations systems rely on a continuous stream of uncomplicated success stories (Edwards 1997) that not only obscure community realities but skip over problems in the performance of the organisations themselves. While there are notable exceptions, the central tendency, with scale, is for INGOs to increase gloss and decrease substance in donor communications. The reason, INGO resource-development personnel argue, is that donors will not fund complexity, process, and ambiguity. Like business investors, they want clear results, now. INGOs give donors what donors are saying they want. As discussed earlier, this creates barriers to development by the poor: first, it unduly restricts the focus of accountability to donor expectations, which do not adequately address the aspirations of marginalised people in distant lands. Second, it may create long-term barriers to complex, messy, but potentially much more long-lasting and far-reaching development efforts.

*Potential alternatives:* admittedly, it can be difficult for large INGOs to make the time and effort necessary to educate a populace on the complexities of international development. However, some organisations have taken on the task as part of their call to advocacy. One Australian development organisation, for example, employs staff to work with their base of church supporters to provide seminars and workshops to explore difficult development issues, thus providing individuals and the church as an institution with a deeper understanding of and commitment to international work. Fundraising is an opportunity to advocate for people's rights with a particular audience. INGOs using a rights-based framework are able to facilitate a process of mutual transformation (involving both donors and communities) as donors (both institutional and individual) respect communities' discretion over their own future and learn from them as partners on a common journey, rather than 'helping' them meet externally imposed criteria. Ultimately, a donor who is involved in this deeper way will prove more beneficial to communities, and may in turn be more enriched personally, than one who is fed success stories and quantitative data showing community improvement.

In our experience, INGOs' failure to restrain the level of controls on development in order to 'protect' their funds has the effect of further crippling the poor. Because accountability for genuine self-policing in INGO funding policies is almost totally lacking right now, one alternative is to establish a global funding 'watchdog' organisation modelled on the National Committee for Responsive Philanthropy (NCRP) in the USA. The NCRP educates US donor publics on the practices of various funding organisations and related government policies, rating them on the basis of their degree of respect for community self-determination and commitment to empowerment.

## Feedback loops

*Barriers:* perhaps the most challenging aspect of organisational learning is to develop the feedback loops that allow for bottom–up transformation and mutual accountability. Some of the barriers to establishing effective feedback loops have already been mentioned, such as reporting systems. Elsewhere, INGOs will conduct extensive evaluations and collect information from their beneficiaries, only to have the report sit on a shelf, with no realistic way to act on the findings. The beneficiaries themselves are sometimes blamed for their unhappiness with the programme, often linked to their 'unwillingness' to conform to programme requirements. Field staff are generally the best conduit of information and impressions from the beneficiaries to upper management levels – but they may carry biases of their own, selectively hearing and interpreting what is communicated from the communities. This information may or may not be passed back up the chain, or it may be misrepresented in some way. Without a direct link to the beneficiaries, impressions and informal reports of this kind are seldom triangulated and verified but often have a powerful impact on organisational attitude and practice. Even where field staff have excellent relations with communities, field positions are often considered 'entry level', and good fieldworkers are quickly promoted up the ladder and away from direct contact with the local population. The ultimate barrier is the lack of direct contact or practical formal feedback flows from the communities to the INGO (although, interestingly, communication is often solid in the other direction). This barrier is just as serious for non-operational INGOs, who may not bother to investigate directly the realities they are seeking to address and are wary of offending their local NGO partners if they appear to be 'going around' them.

*Potential alternatives:* if an organisation truly is embracing BUL as a critical foundation of good development practice, it must find viable ways *as an organisation* to listen and respond to the concerns and perceptions of its host communities. Recent breakthroughs in organisational theory are helping INGOs rethink their internal processes and external delivery systems from top to bottom. A key example may be the tools of appreciative inquiry, which in some cases can lead INGOs to make radical, organisation-wide changes based on a participatory process. All stakeholder groups are invited to consider the possibilities of strategic change based on both a desired future and a 'positive present'.

Some INGOs are experimenting with governance structures that include formal feedback loops. For example, representatives of the INGO's target population are elected to a General Assembly which meets once yearly at the Annual General Meeting. During this time, they confirm and retire board members, hear a report on the organisation's activities over the past year, review budget-to-actual information, and confirm the coming year's plan and budget. This builds a direct accountability structure between the beneficiaries and the organisation's activities and expenditures, while also modelling and providing experience in genuine self-governance. Does a model of this nature complicate things for the organisation? Most certainly! But it also seeks to model principles of development *throughout the entire organisation* which are more consistent with its mission than a more pragmatic approach.

## The way forward

The alien-hand syndrome in INGOs raises uncomfortable questions. Whose needs (and interests) have we privileged in the past, and why? How can those at the bottom of society gain a decisive voice in INGO planning and operations? How do strategies for re-tooling operations for downward accountability become adopted by an entire organisation, rather than a small group of thoughtful individuals within it – especially in an organisation as departmentally fragmented as most INGOs are? How can we find courage to face our collective and unconscious resistance to change? What is blocking us from respectfully engaging the community in a partnership of negotiation that leads to *mutual* use of pertinent information – collection, analysis, and interpretation – and to decisions that are made jointly, implemented jointly, and evaluated and adjusted jointly?

We have proposed BUL as a normative framework for INGOs as they confront an alien-hand syndrome in their operations, replacing systems of control with tools for facilitating mutual learning and community-based sustainable development that can have an impact throughout the entire organisation. Our discussion of INGO barriers to learning, and of current experiments in institutionalising BUL, presupposes the existence of a *process of learning* in organisations that is understood, accepted, and accessible. In reality, our understanding of how organisations learn is still in its infancy. Recent studies on this subject in the government and business sectors may be helpful to INGOs, as they work through the questions posed above. In addition, we believe two process-related steps may be helpful as INGOs begin to put BUL into practice.

First, INGOs might begin by engaging in *second-order learning*, or *learning how they learn*. Here, INGOs focus on their inward process of developing and spreading new understandings across their departments and programme sites. They also might consider ways in which they may be resisting change that is needed in order to align their practices with their core values. Is it possible that INGOs do not want to know about some hidden dimension of themselves, or might have to un-learn something, or change what they are doing even to the point of reducing budgets or losing employment? Is it possible that communities we have tried to help have in fact been harmed because we chose not to assess critically the outcomes of our actions? Will we have to redirect ourselves radically? Are we allowing our fear of the implications of such learning to make us block needed change?

Second, INGOs in this process will need to face up to the political implications of becoming downwardly accountable. This could mean opening more space for equal exchange with local partner organisations and grassroots communities in their operations. Internal champions of such steps may not be enough. BUL may only come about if INGOs move towards adopting flatter, more democratic structures and dramatically revamping administrative, fundraising, and staffing systems and policies to let communities take control of their own development. In addition, BUL promotes partnerships with local NGOs that are autonomous, or without any dependent linkages to an INGO. In short, INGOs will need to move towards truly participatory management in an open system, tying sustainability of their operations to authentic sustainable development on the ground (Johnson and Wilson 1999). In this regard, the meanings, processes, and output of development become a matter to be negotiated between equals, with no predetermined outcomes, and involving INGOs, local partner organisations, and their constituent communities.

In the short term, BUL organisations may find it necessary to make some painful changes, and possibly shrink their operations as they redirect and retool themselves for less controlling and fewer hands-on roles in development. However, it is noteworthy that those INGOs already putting the interests of poor communities ahead of other interests, with a clear commitment to downward accountability, are increasingly able to operate with moral and structural integrity, gain deeper respect and trust with the communities where they work, and see those communities empowered. *These* invisible assets are the surest indicators of their viability and effectiveness, whatever their other stakeholders' interests may be.

## Notes

1   We define international NGO (INGO) as a non-profit development agency with global operations whose mission is (among other things) to assist the poor through community development. Examples include CARE, Oxfam, Save the Children, World Vision, and other similar groups. The names of INGOs have been omitted from our examples to avoid unfairly singling out specific organisations that are facing problems or challenges endemic to the INGO sector as a whole.

2   It is difficult to find a phrase that adequately captures the intended target population of most INGOs without sounding over-simplistic. We use the term 'poverty' to indicate disempowerment, and the term 'poor' to indicate lack of choice and marginalisation from formal political and social institutions. Many within this population also fall within the lower fortieth percentile of the GNP within their respective countries. Having said this, we realise the terms used here do not adequately to reflect the diversity in terms of gender, urban versus rural settings, working poor versus the unemployed, issues of stigma, and vast socio-cultural differences found throughout the world.

## References

Ashman, Darcy (2000) 'Strengthening north-south partnerships: addressing structural barriers to mutual influence', *IDR Reports* 16(4).

Barker, Randolph T. and Martin R. Camarata (1998) 'The role of communication in creating and maintaining a learning organisation: preconditions, indicators, and disciplines', *Journal of Business Communication* 35(4):443-67.

Coopey, John (1995) 'The learning organisation, power, politics, and ideology', *Management Learning* 26(2):193-213.

Edwards, Michael (1997) 'Organisational learning in non-governmental organisations: what have we learned?', *Public Administration and Development* 17:235-50.

Elliott, Charles (1999) *Locating the Energy for Change: An Introduction to Appreciative Inquiry*, Winnipeg: International Institute for Sustainable Development.

Friedmann, John (1992) *Empowerment: The Politics of Alternative Development*, Cambridge, MA: Blackwell.

Garvin, David A. (1993) 'Building a learning organization', *Harvard Business Review* July-August:78-91.

Hailey, John (2000) 'Indicators of identity: NGOs and the strategic imperative of assessing core values', *Development in Practice* 10(3&4):402-7.

Johnson, Hazel and Gordon Wilson (1999) 'Institutional sustainability as learning', *Development in Practice* 9(1&2):43-55.

Jones, Alan M. and Chris Hendry (1994) 'The learning organisation: adult learning and organisational transformation', *British Journal of Management* 5:153-62.

Korten, David (1990) *Getting to the Twenty-first Century: Voluntary Action and the Global Agenda*, West Hartford, CT: Kumarian.

Murphy, Brian K. (2000) 'International NGOs and the challenge of modernity', *Development in Practice* 10(3&4):330-47.

Snell, Robin and Almaz Man-Kuen Chak (1998) 'The Learning Organisation: learning and empowerment for whom?', *Management Learning* 29(3):337-64.

Snyder, William and Thomas Cummings (1998) 'Organisation learning disorders: conceptual model and intervention hypotheses', *Human Relations* 51(7):873-95.

Srivastva, Suresh, Diana Bilimoria and David Cooperrider (1995) 'Management and organisation learning for positive global change', *Management Learning* 26(1):37-54.

# Organisational change from two perspectives: gender and organisational development

## Penny Plowman

## Introduction

How do you develop an organisational change process which has gender inequalities at its heart? That is the focus of this article. Organisational change has for many years been informed by organisational development (OD) theory and practice which have traditionally been 'gender blind'. Within the development sector, this gender blindness is increasingly under the spotlight from practitioners or change agents who come with a gender perspective, such as Anne Marie Goetz, Aruna Rao, Rieky Stuart, and Michelle Friedman. As a result, OD practice is being challenged and new ways of addressing organisational change processes are being developed.

OD theory and practice fail to address the impact of unequal gender relations both within organisations and in their programmes. At best, gender issues are addressed as part of a wider package, commonly referred to as 'diversity' issues. Here 'gender' is placed alongside differences of race, ethnicity, religion, age, disability, and so on, and is therefore easily and often conveniently lost in the diversity melting pot. Feminists and gender activists take a different approach. From the outset, the key area for analysis is power; women and men experience power differently and unequally. Unequal power relations are, of course, just one of many gender dynamics that come under scrutiny, but are critical in the area of personal and organisational change. At the same time, gender inequalities are understood in a context where other inequalities are interlinked and are of equal importance, notably race and class. However, experience has shown that unless there is a specific focus on gender, it is easily subsumed under these other 'cross-cutting' issues. It is with this understanding that this article focuses on gender.

Gender inequalities obviously need to be out in the open if they are to be addressed, challenged, and changed. 'Gender' can no longer be viewed as an optional topic, a soft or women-only issue relegated to a second or third level in OD theory. We do not need to search hard for what we are talking about. Gender inequalities are all around us, we face them every day of our lives. We just need the courage to open our eyes and ears, face reality – and act.

The shift in Gender and Development (GAD) theory and practice, from a focus on external programme policy and planning (Moser 1993) to getting one's own house in order, is critical in the change process. It is no longer acceptable for Northern donor agencies to raise concerns about gender inequalities in the South if they are doing nothing about gender inequalities in their own organisations (Macdonald et al. 1997). This shift presents new and potentially exciting challenges. How do you get your own house in order, and how do you manage resistance to change, whether this comes from management or from field workers? Unlike OD, there are no neat theories to draw from, no simple steps. The work is new, the terrain is complex and meets with much resistance; and yet we are slowly breaking new ground.

It is therefore not a question about tampering with OD to make it better, but rather acknowledging the need to look for new approaches to organisational change, that will benefit women and men equally. OD is not the answer.

This article thus begins to explore what motivates and informs gender and OD as two different approaches to organisational change. It presents a new model, drawing on my work as a gender and development consultant working with NGOs in South Africa.

## Background

My work as a gender consultant began in 1994, just after the first democratic elections in South Africa. In the context of a country going through total transformation, space opened up for a range of organisational change interventions, including gender and OD. The gender interventions can broadly be described as 'raising gender awareness' and 'institutionalising' a gender perspective.

In the case of gender and OD, organisations have found themselves involved in parallel change processes. In practice, this can result in both processes addressing very similar aspects of the organisation but coming up with different analyses of what needs to be changed. For example, a gender analysis of an organisation's organogram will look at where women are in relation to men in terms of access to information, decision making, and power (and link this with race and class). An OD approach is more likely to analyse the functioning of the hierarchy of the organisation but not to raise consciousness about gender or other cross-cutting differences. The gender approach therefore deepens the analysis of how organisations work from the outset by acknowledging that unequal gender relations have a profound impact on their efficiency and effectiveness.

The links between gender and OD were the focus of a workshop held in Zimbabwe in August 1997, attended by practitioners from both disciplines who were working in Southern and East Africa. The aim was to explore the dual agenda of gender and OD in making organisations efficient, effective, and equitable, both in terms of their internal structures and systems and in relation to their 'end users' (Made and Maramba 1997). What was striking was the similarity in how we describe what we do as gender and OD practitioners. For example, both engage in processes of strategic planning, leadership and team building, management training, skills development, and monitoring and evaluation. However, it became apparent that these activities are often conceptualised in different ways. Looking at what informs the interventions, techniques, and tools shows that the starting points for gender and OD are distinct.

The debates at the Zimbabwe workshop highlighted the need to re-examine OD practice in the light of gender inequalities and to address organisational change in the context of the growing demand for gender equality.

It is not within the scope of this paper to carry out a comprehensive review of both disciplines, but rather to highlight key aspects of how gender and OD approach organisational change. Before doing so, it is useful to clarify what I understand by these approaches and where they come from.

## Gender: meaning and roots

'Gender' means different things to different people and is often used synonymously with 'women'. Here I use the term to mean the unequal social relations between women and men in which unequal access to power and resources ensures that women are kept in a subservient position to men. These inequalities are not natural but are constructed and perpetuated by society. Powerful forces like culture, tradition, and religion ensure that such unjust gender relations are maintained. However, just as society has constructed gender inequalities, so they can also be dismantled; they are not set in stone and they can be changed.

Theorists and practitioners from all over the world have influenced the links between gender and organisational change within the development sector. The first feminist critiques of organisational theory were developed in the mid-1970s. At the heart of the analysis was the need to understand that organisations are not gender-neutral, but mirror gender differences to be found in the external environment. A number of fundamental inequalities were highlighted for examination with a 'gender lens', starting out with a gender analysis of power. Women and men experience power differently and unequally. Just as in the broader society, power and authority within organisations lie with men, as do access to and control over resources (Mills and Tancred 1992).

Other areas for examination include the positions of women in organisations. Women are in general still in the lower echelons of the organisational hierarchy, fulfilling traditional caring and nurturing roles such as administration and personnel. It is well documented that even when women do reach senior management positions, mechanisms are found to keep them in their place, so that they lack the real power to facilitate change.

While this kind of organisational analysis has had an impact in the development sector, the analysis of unequal gender relations began by looking at the position of women outside specific organisations and in the broader society.

At first, the focus was on exclusively on women; it is encapsulated in the Women in Development (WID) approach from the 1970s. Here, women were viewed as an untapped resource in the economy, and it was this aspect of their lives which was targeted for change. Income-generating projects (IGPs) for women are one notable outcome. The analytical framework, however, did nothing to try and shift the position of women in relation to men. For example, IGPs could well result in women having more money but lacking the power within their families to make any decisions about how that money is used. WID did not set out to change unequal gender relations but rather to try and improve women's lot within these.

In response to the limitations of WID, there was a conceptual shift in which it was argued that in order really to empower women, their position needed to be understood in relation to men – the Gender and Development approach (GAD). A key to the GAD approach, as already stated, is the importance of analysing where power lies between women and men. GAD theory and practice are committed to the redistribution of power in order to bring about gender equality (Razavi and Miller 1995).

These unequal power relations are rooted in the different roles and responsibilities that society prescribes for women and men. Caroline Moser's 24-hour-day exercise, developed as step one of a gender planning framework, is a powerful tool in this regard. By analysing separately what a wife and husband do in the course of 24 hours, the stark differences between the roles and responsibilities of women and men are exposed. Typically, women fulfil the caring, nurturing, and family responsibilities and spend more time in the privacy of the home. In contrast, men have fewer responsibilities in the home and have greater access and connections to the wider world. This translates into more men being in decision-making roles at all levels in society as well as in the home. Men generally have more access to power and control of resources both inside and outside the home. The unequal relationship to power emerges as a fundamental area for change in order to bring about gender equality (Moser 1993).

The analysis of the individual is interlinked with an analysis of the external context, since it is society that shapes who we are. The ways in which culture, tradition, and religion determine how we shall be as women and men all need to be examined. These are not easy areas to explore, let alone change, since they represent powerful sites of learning from the cradle to the grave. However, adherents to the GAD approach believe that changes are possible over time. Unlike the biologically determined fact that you are either female or male, gender refers to relationships between women and men, which can be changed. The concept of a GAD approach was therefore first used in relation to development planning – 'based on the premise that the major issue is one of subordination and inequality, its purpose is that women through empowerment achieve equality and equity with men in society' (Moser 1993:4).

The analysis of what needs to be changed continues to be developed by practitioners and theorists. For example, the Social Relations Framework (Kabeer 1994) identifies five main areas for analysis, including institutions and the application of gender policies. In the case of the institutional analysis, there are five distinct but interrelated dimensions of social relationships that need to be addressed in terms of understanding how gender inequalities persist: rules, resources, people, activities, and power. For each there are new kinds of question that need to be asked, to tease out how women and men are affected differently, so that the appropriate strategies can be developed to bring about the necessary changes.

Organisations also have a number of choices about how they can address gender inequalities. Kabeer (1994:307) identifies three different kinds of policy options in terms of gender-sensitive policies for external programme development, which I believe are also helpful and relevant to internal organisational policy, namely:

- 'gender-neutral' policies, in which interventions are intended to leave the unequal distribution of resources and responsibilities as they are;
- 'gender-specific' policies, which target the specific needs of women or men within existing unequal relations; and
- 'gender-redistributive' policies, which aim to transform the existing distributions in a more egalitarian direction.

The latter could refer to a less hierarchical decision-making structure and a shift towards a more collective responsibility for the development of internal organisational policies.

While much of the thinking on gender has been in relation to planning a given organisation's external programmes, it is increasingly clear that there is a need to bring a gender analysis into the organisation itself. This requires a shift in understanding about what needs to be changed and how. It is always much easier to raise questions of gender differences in an organisation's programmes 'out there' in the field, than it is to get your own house in order first.

As the links are made between the need to address internal organisational gender inequalities, as well as those found in external programmes, it becomes evident that there is no quick fix. The process of change in the context of the need for gender equality has to be approached with a long-term vision. In this regard it is helpful to think about the steps involved, in order to be clear about target areas and to generate a sense of progress. There are any number of points of departure, but an analysis of the external environment is often a good place to start. Identifying where women and men are situated in the broader political, social, and economic spheres immediately raises consciousness about the institutionalised and structured nature of unequal gender relations. It also makes very clear what it is that we are up against. The analysis can then shift from the bigger picture to the level of the organisation, which is, of course, shaped in so many ways by the external environment, unequal gender relations included.

Of course, the way in which gender is understood and experienced in terms of women's and men's roles and responsibilities is different in different cultures and societies. There cannot be any blueprint for change. Each individual and every organisation will have its own specific needs, for which tailor-made strategies will be needed. In view of its personal nature, the process of change has to be handled sensitively. Unless these fundamental principles are understood, the process becomes confused and frustrating for everyone.

## OD: meaning and roots

In contrast to gender, OD comes out of a framework in which gender differences are inconsequential. Traditionally, OD has been developed as an approach to assist organisations to improve how they function in order to help them be more effective and efficient. The following description provides the key:

> Organisational development is an effort (1) planned, (2) organisation-wide, and (3) managed from the top, to (4) increase an organisation's effectiveness and health through (5) planned interventions in the organisation's 'processes', using behavioural-science knowledge.
> (Beckhard 1969:9)

The OD process is characterised by a number of processes, which include the emphasis on team and group effort and the analysis of systems and structures. Typically, the intervention is carried out with the assistance of an external change agent, a consultant who facilitates the process of change.

The study of what makes organisations more effective, efficient, and competitive began at the turn of the century in the industrialised North. Scientific management made the links between financial incentives and productivity and continues to be enormously influential in mainstream thinking about the world of work. However, as the name implies, the scientific approach neglected to see people as human beings, as distinct from machines. As a result, new thinking developed in which the need for communication and consultative workplace processes were highlighted (Human Relations School). These shifts in thinking took time. By the 1960s, there was recognition of the place of conflict in organisational change, and the need to make work more meaningful and participatory (Sitas 1997).

The concept of OD therefore emerged from a process of thinking in a specific context over a period of time. It is clear that the dominant theory and practice have been informed by and developed from within the private business sector and in the context of the North. This has raised questions about how OD can be transported into the non-profit development sector in the South.

The introduction of OD into the development sector is relatively recent (in the last ten years or so). After many years of a training-dominated approach to capacity building, NGOs and donors alike have recognised that this has limited impact in terms of improving organisational effectiveness. Hence a need was identified for a different kind of intervention (Fowler and Waithaka 1995). International donors and NGOs have taken OD to be more appropriate.

There are a number of fundamental differences in terms of approach between gender and OD (see Table 1). At the very core of the gender approach is an understanding that both the internal and external aspects of any organisation are negatively affected by gender inequalities. To build healthy, effective, and efficient organisations, women and men need to be able to play their different parts in full. The gender perspective allows gender inequalities to be seen and understood and so gives space for different needs to be addressed in order to bring about long-lasting change. While OD shares a commitment to helping organisations become more efficient and effective, the approach limits the possibility of real growth and personal development by not acknowledging the negative impact of gender inequality from the outset. An organisation may become more effective and efficient, but the failure to address the disempowerment of women severely diminishes the extent of change achieved.

The differences emerge at various levels. The following section considers what informs these differences and begs the question: is it possible to merge the two disciplines, or are we looking for a new approach?

## Values and practice

The critical area for examination is what informs OD and gender approaches in terms of values and practice. The values are very clearly linked with the analysis of what needs to be changed. Both approaches are working towards the same goal, in the sense that both want to assist organisations to become more effective and efficient. However, the gender approach starts with the recognition that gender inequalities affect how an organisation functions, so that the links between gender equality, efficiency, and effectiveness are made from the outset.

A healthy organisation is one in which both women and men play equal parts. This analysis and the values that inform it reflect an understanding that such gender differences matter and need to be radically changed. The focus is on changing discriminatory attitudes, behaviours, and beliefs in the context of unequal gender relations.

Gender and OD approaches share many of the more general values, including being respectful, non-judgemental, open, and sensitive. There is also a strong commitment in both to raising awareness about the needs of the individual and supporting self-development. However, by analysing an organisation through a gender lens, the gender approach identifies and exposes the needs and differences for women and men, and helps to identify different strategies and support mechanisms to bring about effective change. For example, this analysis might lead to women attending a women-only management course.

In terms of practice, both gender and OD practitioners are usually involved in a process of engagement with a client before the intended work begins. In most cases this means the practitioner is an external consultant (sometimes a team) who is requested by the client organisation to carry out a set of tasks. The 'pre-engagement' process involves clarifying the actual request, ensuring that there is a close fit between what the organisation wants and what the consultant can offer, agreeing on areas of responsibility (terms of reference), methodology, and the implementation programme.

It is in these first communications and negotiations – before, for example, the strategic planning or organisational audit begins – that both organisation and consultant can share invaluable information about values, beliefs, and what they hope to achieve through the process. In all cases, this is a critical time as both sides lay down their cards. However, whatever their respective agendas, the process is never cut and dried. In the case of gender, there are particular sensitivities and the consultant needs to be conscious of several possible intervention strategies. For example, organisations are seldom likely to 'jump up and down' and ask for work on gender issues if they have requested strategic planning. Nevertheless, the consultant might well see an opportunity to work with the organisation and use it to raise gender issues.

On the one hand, if the organisation shares the consultant's views on the need for a gender perspective or is at least open to exploring what it means, there is a basis from which to proceed. On the other, however, if there is no shared view on the need to address gender inequalities, the consultant may withdraw. It is, therefore, important to be open and transparent about values at this early stage even before the process gets underway.

In general, the value given to the OD intervention appears still to outweigh by far that given to gender. Gender is typically seen as something that can be addressed in a one-off workshop and as an intervention that falls outside the organisation's mainstream business. However, this is changing, and I have witnessed examples of organisations which are beginning to see the need for a holistic approach to change in which a gender perspective is critical from the outset. There is clearly a need for a long-term vision and support and, as already noted, there is no instant solution.

## Recognising fundamental differences: a way forward

The analysis has shown that there are fundamental differences in approach between OD and gender. While the two approaches may use similar activities and tools as highlighted in the Zimbabwe workshop referred to above – strategic planning, organisational audits, developing missions and visions, etc. – the analysis of what needs to be changed in the first place is different.

Many of us involved in the gender approach are thinking about how we can develop new ways of working, drawing on theory and practice from both gender and OD. The following case study describes the ways in which an organisational change process can be approached with a gender perspective from the outset.

### Background

My first contact with the client organisation, a South African NGO working in youth and career development, was at a gender-training workshop. The workshop was at the invitation of a donor and aimed to raise awareness and understanding about gender issues and to look at the implications at personal, organisational, and programme levels. The NGO's Director and Deputy Director attended and were obviously very committed and open to the issues being raised.

Following the gender-training workshop, the NGO was invited to participate in a 'sustainability' programme (set up by the same donor) of which one component was an organisational audit. As a result, a number of issues were raised, including a need to re-examine the organisation's mission and vision.

It was at this point that the NGO requested my services to facilitate a process to help them look at their mission and vision. As a 'gender consultant', I was excited about this offer, because for many in the NGO sector such a task is normally the terrain of an OD consultant. I therefore seized the opportunity to take the organisation through a process of analysis which would lead to a revised vision and mission by putting gender differences at the heart.

The first step was to look at the external environment. The task was to identify key events which had affected the lives of South Africans since 1994, and to look ahead to 2002. The events were linked to different spheres of life – political, economic, social, the NGO sector in general, and in terms of funding. The result was a complex table of information.

At this stage there was little or no distinction made about how these events had affected women and men differently. The following question was then posed, with the aim of confronting the 'gender-blind' analysis: *'What has been the impact on girls and women in the past, and how will the environment look in the future?'* This immediately raised awareness about how women and men are affected differently by broad political, social, and economic events and trends. By naming girls and women separately from men, the organisation was able to see that there were specific activities and trends that affected women. (It also opened up gaps in organisational knowledge about girls' and women's lives.)

In a similar way the NGO was asked to analyse the main problem that it is trying to address, incorporating a gender perspective, by answering *'What are the causes and effects of this problem for women and men?'* This led to an analysis of the impact of culture, tradition, and religion on gender roles and responsibilities, and how these limit choices for both sexes, but in particular for women.

In addressing both sets of questions, issues of race and class were also made explicit. The organisation was able to name its target group as black, rural, and working-class young women. Gender was therefore understood as a concept that is interlinked with race and class.

It became clear that if this NGO was going to redress some of these gender imbalances, it had to revise its vision and mission. Previously neither had included any gender analysis, but talked about young people as one, not recognising the different needs of women and men. The inclusion in the new vision statement of the NGO's intention to 'increase the career and life-choices available to disadvantaged South Africans, particularly young women in rural areas' embodied a new way of thinking. Similarly, in the mission statement which emerged from the gender analysis of the main problem, the inclusion of young women was added: the NGO 'aims to equip young people for the world of work, focusing especially on young women in rural areas'. The previous vision and mission statements had no overt reference to the position of young women.

These important first steps in gender analysis have led the NGO to develop appropriate strategies to meet the specific needs of young women who are disadvantaged in relation to men. The Director claims that, since the workshop, the commitment to raising gender issues, and in particular to focusing on rural young women, has been profound. In all areas of training the NGO is insisting on a 60 per cent quota for female participants, whereas before the workshop, 75 per cent of participants were men. Staff are actively pursing what has become a gender-specific policy for the organisation.

At the same time, the staff recognise that the quota system in favour of women will not work by itself. Other strategies are needed. These include the development of materials to encourage women to explore a wider range of careers and the identification of working women who have successfully challenged existing gender stereotypes, thus providing new role models for younger women. While the impact of these different strategies is as yet unknown, it is possible that more will be developed – for example, training courses for girls. What has changed is that there is now the basis from which this NGO can develop its work within a gender justice framework.

### Lessons

What are the lessons that can be drawn from this case study? The first relates to the choice of consultant and role of the Director. In this case, the Director was already aware of the perspective that I would bring to the workshop, from our meeting at the first gender-training event. Her decision to invite me to facilitate this organisational change workshop was therefore strategic, since she knew that I would work with a gender perspective. By the same token, I was aware of the Director's commitment and openness to a gender approach, which was invaluable. I knew I could open up new ways of approaching the questions of vision and mission from a gender perspective.

The Director also believed that attention to gender issues could not be imposed by management, but rather needed to evolve from a participatory process among staff. In this way, she anticipated that there would be less resistance and a greater acceptance of a gender perspective as integral to the NGO's development. I also made a conscious decision not to use the word gender initially, but rather to talk about the differences for women and men. (In South Africa, 'gender' has become a very loaded term and often meets with resistance before one gets a chance to start working.) This allowed a way into other cross-cutting issues, namely race and class.

It is also clear that just as inequalities of race and class need to be addressed at different levels – personal, organisational, and programme – the same attention needs to be given to inequalities based on gender. While there was little opportunity to delve very deeply into the personal level in this workshop, the process started with the analysis and discussion of the main problem. The links between the external environment and the NGO's strategies for career development and training were more clearly made.

## Developing models for appropriate organisational change

New ideas are emerging out of a range of innovative and exciting practices. However, much of this is being carried out by individuals and is not commonly shared, documented, or institutionalised. There is now a need to stop and reflect on practice and situate it within new theoretical frameworks.

While it is increasingly recognised by GAD theorists and practitioners that many of the gender frameworks and tools are limited when it comes to thinking about organisational change within a broad transformation agenda, there are also other issues at stake. As already noted, gender does not stand alone; it is intrinsically connected to other inequalities, all too easily referred to as 'cross-cutting' issues in current development jargon. However, while there is acknowledgement that such inequalities need to be addressed, there is often a lack of any meaningful commitment, at both personal and organisational levels, to developing change strategies that seriously take these dynamics into account. The 'cross-cutting' issues remain outside mainstream approaches to change and the *status quo* prevails.

All of the above raises critical questions that are linked to our conceptual thinking about organisational change: what exactly needs to change, and how is this going to be done?

## Table 1: Key differences between gender approach and OD approach

| | Gender approach to organisational change | OD approach to organisational change |
|---|---|---|
| **Goal** | Goal of organisational change is to build equitable, efficient, and effective organisations. Gender equality is at the forefront of organisational understanding and change. Gender is one of a number of unequal social relations and is interlinked with race and class, amongst others. | Goal of OD is to build efficient and effective organisations that can survive in the wider world. |
| **Starting-point** | Starts with an analysis of the individual, highlighting gender differences for women and links the 'I' with the external context, before coming to the organisation. | Starts with the organisation's systems and structures and links to the external context. |
| **Analysis of organisations** | Organisations are like people – they need to be understood in terms of thoughts and feelings as well as intellect and action. Organisations have their own gender dynamics and can be described as exhibiting masculine or feminine traits. | Analysis starts from mission, vision, structures and adds in issues of gender difference later on. |
| **Analysis of power** | Gender inequalities in the broader environment, in terms of power, access to, and control over resources are mirrored in organisations which then perpetuate those inequalities. Men continue to dominate in every sphere of political, social, and economic life and women are second class citizens. | Analysis of power relations, access to, and control of resources but not situated within a gender framework. |
| **Analysis of the individual** | Analysis of the individual is key to the gender approach which recognises gender differences. This leads to an understanding that self-development for women and men is different and we need different kinds of support and development, e.g. women may need assertiveness training while men require training in listening skills. | Individual development is addressed, but gender differences are not overtly examined. |

*continued ... .*

*Table 1 continued*

| | Gender approach to organisational change | OD approach to organisational change |
|---|---|---|
| **Analysis of the external environment** | Gender analysis, first developed in relation to external development programmes, works from the premise that gender roles and responsibilities are shaped by society – culture, tradition and religion – and can be changed. | Scan of external environment but not carried out with a gender perspective. |
| **Gender and diversity** | The need for gender justice shapes internal and external change process and is interlinked with other issues including race and class. | Gender is one of many 'diversity' issues to be addressed, e.g. age, religion, disability, sexuality, and economic status. |
| **Values** | Values are shaped by commitment to gender justice. Recognising differences in the way women and men experience life informs the organisational change process. Belief that effective and efficient organisations can only be developed if women and men are involved in equal part. | Values are shaped by commitment to organisational change processes in which people are critical and gender relations and differences are not highlighted. |
| **Culture** | Processes of change focuses on organisational culture in which differences in the way women and men are socialised and behave are challenged. Begins with changing discriminatory beliefs, attitudes, and stereotypes based on gender. | Process looks at organisational culture without highlighting differences for women and men. |

For far too long, gender frameworks have been perceived as limited and concerned only with what are mistakenly referred to as 'soft issues', i.e. to do with women's emotions and feelings. The links with and need to build a gender perspective into broader organisational change processes have only been made more recently. However, OD, in part because of its roots and longer history, is accepted more easily and is clearly perceived to be less threatening since it does not set out to change the *status quo* in terms of gender, race, and class.

## Can gender justice and organisational change agendas be linked?

From my experience, there has to be commitment from every level in an organisation – in particular senior management – to the goal of eradicating gender inequality. The enormous challenge is, of course, how to get this. It appears that for some organisations this is not so difficult, because their analysis of the problem they are trying to solve has a gender dimension. For example, a women's organisation working on violence against women already has a commitment to gender justice. While working with women separately as a strategic policy choice, they may well be working with men too. On the other hand, there are many organisations that have no overt commitment to changing unequal gender relations because their main mission is, for instance, to build houses or help to redistribute land for the poor.

How can we help to make the link between organisations' work and gender inequalities? As I have argued, I believe the starting point has to be with an examination of both the internal and external contexts. Friedman and Rao (1998) have recently introduced a conceptual framework which does just this, and only then moves on to questions of vision and transformation, and how organisations can ensure sustainability and also monitor and evaluate progress.

The importance of this and other frameworks is to understand how organisational change can take place in a sustainable and gender-equitable way. The new ways of thinking come out of the frustrations and limitations of the conventional intervention strategies, which are only beginning to scratch the surface of what needs to change.

### Dealing with resistance

The gender approach to organisational change inevitably raises fear and resistance, just like any other change process. However, 'gender and change' have a particular dynamic, which makes dealing with conflict essential. Why? In part it forces us to reassess who we are as individual women and men, a level at which the work is immediately personal and can be frightening. Another critical factor is power. Men feel threatened and want to hold on to power, and as such 'it is likely to be in men's strategic interests to resist the idea that gender inequalities exist, that such inequalities might be socially constructed, rather than naturally given, and that they can consequently be challenged and transformed' (Kabeer 1994). This is understood in the context of prevailing gender relations that embody male privilege. Denial of the root causes of gender inequality is an ever-present challenge and block to change:

- 'Why rock the boat?'
- 'No one has ever said anything is wrong in our organisation. We have just had an organisational audit, and nothing came up about gender problems.'
- 'How will you control the outcomes once you have opened up the can of worms?'

These questions reflect common concerns when trying to raise a gender perspective. To address them is a complex task but not impossible. The overall aim is to bring organisations to a point whereby they can share in a vision of the world in which they are situated in an environment characterised by enabling and enriching values and practices for women as well as men. At the same time, the change agent has to acknowledge that the concerns are shaped by a reality that is going to take time to evolve. There is no simple cure, no magic medicine to make organisations and individual staff feel better quickly. It is indeed a change process.

For this reason, practitioners need to draw on a range of skills, including conflict management. Dealing with resistance should not be seen as proof of failure by the change agent leading the process, but rather an indication that real change is starting to happen and can therefore be embraced and skilfully managed.

### Who should be the change agent/s?

One key issue concerns who should be carrying out this kind of work. It is extremely challenging and complex. Practical experience suggests that a team of practitioners may well be needed to assist organisations. The challenge here is that everyone involved shares the common goal that transformation needs a gender as well as a race and class perspective and that these cross-cutting issues need to be addressed at every level.

In Southern Africa today, an NGO may well have a number of external consultants working with it to help bring about change and yet there is often little or no serious attempt to bring these individuals together to discuss and agree on a comprehensive change process. The result is a number of isolated interventions that are unable to build on each other. The idea of a team is appealing, since no one person can offer everything that is needed. In terms of race and gender it may well be that a mixed team is the most effective, but the critical aspect is that people share the same fundamental values. The commitment to ending discrimination on the basis of race, gender, and sexuality – among other diversity issues – is the essential criterion.

Developing a shared team approach is not easy, especially when so many practitioners work as individual consultants. This links closely to ideas shared at the Zimbabwe workshop referred to above, about the need for more openness about their practice between and among consultants. This discussion also raised issues about a code of ethics for practitioners.

The desire for a shared commitment and common understanding about gender often emerges as a strong need among those of us working in the field, because there is so much resistance to what we are doing. However, a common language about women's empowerment and gender policies can often mask different interpretations for different ends. Research has shown a lack of consensus about the objectives of gender equality and transformation, reflecting different ideological standpoints (Jahan 1995).

## Gender and organisational culture

A critical area that has come under the spotlight in terms of the analysis of the internal workings of an organisation is organisational culture. While attention is given to this in OD practice, the difference once again is the way in which the gender approach addresses these questions.

Organisational culture goes far deeper than any formal statement of organisational principles. It is best thought about in terms of how values, beliefs, and attitudes are played out in practice. An organisation may be committed to full participation by its entire staff, while in practice this is rarely experienced. Men participate in full and women remain on the sidelines. There are many reasons why this is so. However, we come back to the fundamental understanding that organisations are not gender-neutral but mirror all the gender inequalities to be found in the external environment.

Questions of where power lies and where women are situated in relation to the seats of power are, therefore, critical. This links into the need to find new ways of understanding what power means. The idea that power is something that we can create as a source of positive energy distributed to everyone challenges traditional notions of power being about control of people (Rao and Stuart 1997). It is only when this kind of analysis has been carried out that appropriate strategies can be developed for real change; changes that will affect both sexes positively.

Another indicator of gender and organisational culture is how time works in organisations. It is common for NGOs to operate flexi-time. Some organisations have two distinct shifts, e.g. 8 a.m–4 p.m. and 10 a.m–6 p.m. It is not unsurprising that women tend to dominate the first shift and men the second, for powerful gender inequalities persist. Women have to accommodate a whole range of childcare and domestic activities in addition to what they get paid to do at work. Such constraints do not affect men to the same degree.

By bringing a gender perspective to the analysis of organisational culture, it is evident that change has to take place at many levels. For example, once an awareness of the two-shift system is raised, it can be further analysed in terms of when key decisions are made and by whom. When are the meetings scheduled? Who attends? And does it matter if these meetings go on beyond 4 p.m. – if so, for whom? It is this kind of detailed analysis that is needed in order to expose the complexity of what it is that we are trying to change.

Many of the areas for organisational change were identified in feminist theory long ago. For example, the links between the private and public spheres of women's and men's lives. The critical gap in terms of organisational change processes in the development sector is that while the theoretical importance of these issues is acknowledged by some, it is not emerging as a mainstream concern in practice. Rather, mainstream thinking tends to ignore unequal gender relations.

## Conclusion

While large amounts of money, time, and other resources are being poured into OD, as an approach to organisational change OD clearly fails to address gender inequality. In stark contrast, the gender approach opens up a very different way of analysing organisations and provides an opportunity to bring to the surface other kinds of inequality. The gender approach to organisational change gets right to the heart of what is fundamentally wrong, namely that power is unequal and remains firmly in the hands of men. From this point of departure, everything else flows. Since the gender approach is breaking new ground, every organisational experience based on using a gender perspective needs to be documented and analysed. Obviously, there is no blueprint for change but important lessons are being learned that can help us in developing new theoretical frameworks and practice.

Building gender awareness is just the beginning; the challenge continues way beyond and takes us deep into organisational culture, systems, structures, and programmes in order to bring about long-lasting change for the benefit of women and men. Breaking new ground requires vision, commitment, risks, and the belief that real change and development is only possible when women and men can be involved and benefit equally.

## References

Beckhard, R. (1969) *Organisation Development: Strategies and Models*, Reading, MA: Addison-Wesley.

Fowler, A. and D. Waithaka (1995) 'NGO-PODS programme proposal Kenya: Matrix', cited in R. James (1997) 'Organisation development and NGOs in Africa', *OD Debate* 4(5):3-6.

Friedman, M. and A. Rao (1998) 'Gender Justice and Organisational Change: Questions and Issues', paper prepared for conference on Gender Justice and Organisational Change held in Cape Town, South Africa.

Jahan, R. (1995) *The Elusive Agenda: Mainstreaming Women in Development*, London: Zed Books.

Kabeer, Naila (1994) *Reversed Realities: Gender Hierarchies in Development Thought*, London: Verso.

Macdonald, Mandy, Ellen Sprenger and Ireen Dubel (1997) *Gender and Organisational Change: Bridging the Gap between Policy and Practice*, Amsterdam: KIT Press.

Made, P. and P. Maramba (1997) 'Workshop on Organisation Development and Gender', unpublished report, Hivos, Novib and ZWRCN.

Mills, A. J. and P. Tancred (eds.) (1992) *Gendering Organisational Analysis*, London: Sage.

Moser, C. O. N. (1993) *Gender Planning and Development Theory, Practice and Training*, London: Routledge.

Rao, A. and R. Stuart (1997) 'Rethinking organisations: a feminist perspective', *Gender and Development* 5(1):10-16.

Razavi, Shahra and Carol Miller (1995) cited in Anne Marie Goetz (1997) *Getting Institutions Right for Women in Development*, London: Zed Books.

Sitas, A. (1997) 'Senge's learning orgworld', *OD Debate* 4(3):13-14.

# Beyond the 'grim resisters':

## towards more effective gender mainstreaming through stakeholder participation

## Patricia L. Howard

## Introduction

Substantial consensus has emerged in the literature with regard to some of the 'minimum requirements' for gender mainstreaming within organisations (e.g. Kardam 1991; Hannan-Anderson 1992; Jahan 1995; Macdonald 1994):

- a positive policy commitment to gender and development, with management support;
- gender experts acting as focal points with a catalytic role;
- awareness- and skills-raising for all relevant personnel through gender training;
- incorporation of gender objectives into planning and implementation procedures;
- a clear identification of who has responsibility for implementation and a system of accountability.

Many of these requirements have been recognised and at least partially implemented in international development organisations and NGOs over the past decade or so. The ongoing discussion on gender mainstreaming has reached the 'lessons learned' stage, and is achieving sophistication and refinement. There are two main bodies of literature on gender and mainstreaming in complex organisations.[1] The first presents frameworks for gender planning that are meant to provide means to define goals and relate these to strategies and instruments (e.g. Moser 1993; Young 1993; Kabeer and Subrahmanian 1996). The second consists of organisational case study analyses of practical gender mainstreaming experiences that benefit from a longitudinal perspective (e.g. Kardam 1991; Jahan 1995; Macdonald et al. 1997; Ravazi and Miller 1995; Wallace 1998). It is driven by the desire to explain the continued frustration of attempts to mainstream gender in development policy, planning, and programmes, in spite of much progress achieved in implementing, at least partially, the 'pre-requisites' mentioned above.

While all of the above literature provides substantial insights into the needs, complexity, and potentials for effective gender mainstreaming, it also presents a series of conceptual and methodological shortcomings that inhibit our abilities to come to grips with both the impediments to mainstreaming and the means to make it more effective. In this paper, I focus on the critical issue of stakeholder involvement in gender mainstreaming. Stakeholder involvement refers to 'who' should be involved in the mainstreaming process, the nature of their involvement, and the means to make their involvement work in favour of women. I illustrate the importance of this issue through three practical experiences within the UN system.

## Conceptual frameworks for gender mainstreaming: who are the stakeholders?

Conceptual frameworks for gender planning have evolved in part due to a shift towards greater emphasis on women's participation, empowerment, and diversity. In comparison with the project frameworks available in the 1980s, these newer planning frameworks seek to address gender policy at an organisational level; to deal with causes rather than merely symptoms of women's subordination; and to incorporate the multiple dimensions of power, consciousness, position, and interests that differentiate women. These newer frameworks stress the need to involve women beneficiaries as stakeholders in the planning process, regardless of the level at which planning occurs (e.g. policy planning or grassroots project development). Moser (1993) argues that this is needed to give a direct voice to and empower women. She also sees it as a means to deal with 'women's diversity' and to bring pressure to bear upon, and raise consciousness among, (male) planners and policy makers. For Kabeer and Subrahmanian, 'participation of the excluded in the process of policy design is not only critical to ensure policy goals which respond to their priorities but is also a strategic means for overcoming social exclusion' (1996:27). For Young, 'involving women at all levels of development thinking, planning and implementation will make a world of difference' (1993:147). However, as Young points out, it will be a long time before women at the grassroots are systematically involved in the planning process in most large bureaucratic organisations.

The obstacles to grassroots women's involvement in planning and the obstacles to mainstreaming in policy-making organisations in general stem from the same sources. Drawing from gender and organisational theory, the planning frameworks are analysing some of these 'structural blockages' and providing tools to diagnose gender power relations within organisations, including organisational cultures and management styles as well as psychological and structural conditions. Kabeer and Subrahmanian, for example, discuss methodologies to identify institutional barriers to change, and highlight conceptual and technical biases, errors, resistance tactics, rules, and practices which work against a 'new, human-oriented approach' (1996:47). Power remains in the hands of non-gender-expert (male) policy makers and planners whose belief systems, culture, and procedures preclude gender mainstreaming and women's participation.

Gender planning frameworks are clearly written for gender experts to help them guide the process of institutional change. The gender planner is *the* major stakeholder—the person who is expected to carry out the diagnoses, mobilise the women, implement the framework, etc. Besides involving grassroots women, all of these conceptual frameworks point to the need to involve policy makers, planners, and implementers who are clearly key participants. However, the discussion about this last group is generally quite vague, in terms of both their roles and contributions. Generally, policy makers and planners are characterised either as active resisters or, at best, passive implementers of gender planning. If they have anything to contribute to the process, it is resistance or simply compliance. Where there is detailed discussion of the non-expert (male) planners, it is in relation to them as obstacles, and hence, to what must be done to overcome their resistance so that the gender planners and their allies can get the job done. In fact, it seems that the more emphasis there is on incorporating insights from organisational theory regarding the gendered nature of institutions, the more the discussion focuses on planners as obstacles. For example, Kabeer and Subrahmanian disaggregate the category 'people' within development organisations as 'innovators, loyal bureaucrats, hesitators, and hardliners' (1996:49). These being fairly typical epithets, there are numerous prescriptions offered to deal with the resistance or passivity that planners present.

# Lessons learned from mainstreaming experiences

The growing body of literature documenting institutional experiences with gender mainstreaming is oriented both towards attaining a better understanding of organisational conditions and impediments, and to drawing lessons on strategies at a number of levels. This literature has provided a great deal of food for thought in relation to specific types of organisation, strategies, and 'stages' of evolution in the mainstreaming process. Here the analysis with respect to the stakeholders, and the strategies to overcome 'structural blockages' to gender mainstreaming, tend to be more pragmatic and nuanced in comparison with the gender planning literature.

The analysis naturally tends to focus on who *has been* involved in the mainstreaming process and how, rather than who *should be* involved and how. The discussion of change agents is often very concrete. For example, there are careful assessments of the pros and cons of particular roles and organisational locations for gender experts or of the efficacy of particular strategies to sensitise planners or convince managers. In fact, non-expert (male) planners are implicitly a central focus of this literature insofar as it seeks to diagnose how to be more effective in convincing them to implement gender-sensitive policies and procedures.

There are two tendencies with regard to the conceptualisation of stakeholders, and they are often mixed. On the one hand, the language often reflects the negative assessment of planners as active resisters: policies need to be 'enforced'; implementers should be 'policed'; managers should be 'made accountable' through various types of top-down administrative procedures (e.g. Berg 1993). The characteristics of the 'grim resisters' (following Staudt 1990:10), their degree of resistance, the amount of power they wield, and the means to pressure, lobby, and persuade them to change, are standard fare. On the other hand, there is a tendency to see non-expert planners as passive recipients rather than active resisters, and as such they must be properly sensitised and equipped through gender training, data, studies, guidelines, and procedures. If backed by the encouragement of management and the support of gender experts or consultants, they can be expected to at least implement what they have learned. Frequently, those who characterise planners as passive recipients also note that they are not all the same: they work in different sectors and with different procedures and target groups, so that gender planners need to develop specific tools that meet their needs.

The degree of success of the mainstreaming approaches used to date varies substantially depending upon the strategies used, the resources allocated, the type of organisation, the commitment of management, etc., so that it is difficult to generalise. To the extent that generalisations are made, however, it is with respect to the conclusion that not nearly as much progress has been made as could be expected, or certainly as is desired.[2] In terms of diagnosing why this is the case, the literature most frequently focuses on factors 'out there'—that is, on external or organisational constraints limiting the implementation of mainstream strategies (e.g. resistance)—and, somewhat less frequently, on problems with the strategies themselves. Only rarely are the assumptions underlying the strategies questioned. In particular, the assumptions about planners-as-stakeholders go unquestioned and, therefore, strategies are usually evaluated in terms of how well they either (a) overcome resistance, or (b) develop, adapt, and diffuse the necessary knowledge, skills, and tools.

The analysis of the gendered nature of organisations illuminates a series of inter-related factors which, taken together, present very serious problems to be resolved before gender mainstreaming can be made effective. However, there is much that is unproductive in the characterisation of (most) planners as resisters, which implies that people (both men and women) and organisations are resistant, static, tradition- and interest-bound, and inherently and unconsciously (structurally) biased. These characterisations, no matter how well founded, tend to lead to prescriptions that are top–down, based upon ('correct') expert input, and managerial and administrative coercion. On the other hand, the characterisation of planners as passive recipients leads to somewhat different strategies, where at least it is recognised that, in an enabling environment, they have the capacity to learn, understand the need for change, and implement procedures that will improve the outcomes for women. However, such a characterisation is also in many ways top–down and static, since the involvement of non-expert planners is as implementers rather than as innovators or even planners. The strategies are often reinforced by measures that are used when planners are seen as resisters. In fact, both conceptualisations of planners as stakeholders are contradicted by most contemporary approaches to participatory development. I argue that the conceptualisation and characterisation of non-expert planners that prevails, in the literature and in practice, presents an important obstacle to gender mainstreaming.

Most participatory approaches to development start with assumptions that are quite different from those which many gender specialists use to characterise non-expert planners, such as: everyone has knowledge, can learn, and can take responsibility for change, if they are provided with the opportunity. In stakeholder approaches, experts have knowledge to share, but are only one part of the equation—they have as much to learn from other stakeholders as other stakeholders have to learn from them. Often, the expert's role must be to facilitate the process whereby the diverse stakeholders diagnose their problems and discover and negotiate their own solutions. The expert's role is to provide information, ensure that the enabling resources and environment exist, and represent their own 'stake' in the process. With stakeholder participation, it is assumed that one has to begin with conditions as they are (including knowledge, consciousness, interests, etc.). It is also assumed that conditions can change. Finally, it is assumed that the process is as important as the outcome, and that the outcome is innovative (not the one predicted or desired by any particular stakeholder). The process moves in the only direction in which it could have moved—that is, it moves both towards mutual learning, and towards the best *possible* outcome, given the real starting point (the information, knowledge, interests, and power relations entailed). Gender experts have promoted this approach at the grass-roots level, but have been hesitant to try it as a strategy for gender planning and mainstreaming.

## Mainstreaming gender through stakeholders: a pilot experience in Honduras

The experience with gender mainstreaming at the Food and Agriculture Organization (FAO) that I present below was influenced by an exercise I carried out in Honduras in my junior years as a gender planner. The UNDP asked me to review all UN projects in Honduras to determine how they could better meet women's needs. Three outputs were sought: (1) sensitisation of project managers; (2) a prioritisation of the most strategic projects that would receive my direct inputs to improve their design and implementation; and (3) an assessment of global constraints of projects and lessons learned that could be addressed by system-wide activities (at government or UNDP level). With more than 30 projects to address in less than three months, we decided that the most efficient way to proceed would be to hold a workshop with the project directors, to sensitise them, and carry out a joint analysis of their achievements and constraints. Having had little practical experience, we had little idea that such an exercise would meet with substantial resistance on the part of these nearly all-male, all-Honduran planners.

To prepare, I developed a background paper using national-level data to illustrate some of the main problems that Honduran women confront. This was accompanied by a questionnaire for project heads to hand in prior to the workshop, in which they were to relate some of the main issues presented in the paper to the specific projects that they were managing. At this point, some coercion and support was required: some of the project heads had to be repeatedly requested to hand in the questionnaires, and some needed my support to fill them in. During the one-day workshop, I presented a summary of the issues in the paper. Project heads then met in small sectoral groups to discuss questions related to the 'gender biases' they encountered in their project. In plenary, groups reported their conclusions and held further discussion. A second small group plenary session focused on what project heads saw as constraints to working more effectively with women; and a third focused on what needed to be done to overcome the constraints.

Everyone who participated estimated that the outcome of the workshop was very positive, insofar as project heads had clearly identified a common set of constraints as well as a series of activities that they themselves, the UNDP, and the government of Honduras could implement to begin to overcome these constraints. The major constraints identified related to (a) a lack of information at project and national level on gender relations and women; (b) a lack of sensitivity of project staff and target groups to gender issues; (c) a lack of research on women in specific sectors (e.g. reproductive health); and (d) a lack of access to gender expertise. After the workshop, the list of 30 projects was reviewed in order to identify the five most strategic projects, which I would then help to redesign to ensure more gender-sensitive outcomes. The criteria used to select these projects centred on their potential impact at national level, including their potential for providing new models or instruments for gender-sensitive outcomes applicable to wider governmental programmes; their potential to benefit a large number of women living in poverty; and the economic importance of the sector in which they were located. I then studied the respective project documents and developed a series of recommendations for the project heads. I was concerned that the project teams would resent someone from outside attempting to redesign their projects, all of which were in the implementation stage. However, when I met with the individual project teams about two months after the workshop, on each occasion the project team *informed me* about what was needed to redesign their projects. In four out of five of the cases, the project teams' recommendations were nearly identical to my own recommendations; in three of the five cases, the project heads had already contacted the donors to request additional resources in order to implement their recommendations. In only one case did I find that the project team was unable to identify the steps that would be necessary to redesign their project. Follow-up on three of the projects some two years later showed that two of the three indeed implemented the recommendations made by the project teams, whereas the other only partially implemented its ideas since the additional resources requested had not been forthcoming from the donor.

The other outcome of the experience was the development of an 'umbrella project' that contained five separate modules to respond to global-level constraints and needs. Only one module was financed and implemented—that which was designed to improve national-level information on women (statistics)—where ILO, UNFPA, and the Honduran government, with the support of gender experts, undertook major efforts to improve the gender sensitivity of the national labour force survey and the population census.

## Learning from stakeholders: the experience with gender training at FAO

Beginning with where people are at (ideologically, substantively) and realising that they can learn represent the fundamentals of traditional (passive) training. Participatory training further assumes that people have knowledge and experience that they can bring into the change process, and that can lead to substantively different and new knowledge for all those involved, including the trainer. Participatory methods in gender training have been used mainly to overcome resistance on the part of planners to permit gender experts to do their work. However, they have not generally been used to generate innovations in the gender planning process itself, or seen as an opportunity for the trainer *qua* gender expert to learn. Generally, training has been seen to be effective in improving receptivity and understanding of gender issues among a majority of those trained. However, it has not proved to be as effective in terms of operationalising gender goals; in and of itself, training has not usually led to gender mainstreaming.

I spent two years at FAO as the officer responsible for gender training within the WID unit (Women in Agricultural Production and Rural Development Service—SDWW), and trained some 750 professional staff at regional and headquarters level, 80 per cent of whom were male, and 85 per cent of whom were not social scientists. I evaluated the training exercise with participants at least six months after they received their training. From this evaluation, I learned that the majority of people who were trained were 'ready, willing, but unable' to deal with gender issues in their daily work. When asked to explain why, a majority of these infrequent users indicated that they didn't see the connection between gender issues and their own specific field of work or, if they did see the relevance, they lacked the skills and tools to permit them to address gender in their specific tasks. Gender training was too 'generic' to address the wide range of activities, processes, and subject areas that were represented within the organisation.

I was unhappy with the conceptual framework used in the training (an adaptation of the Harvard Framework), since it perpetuated non-participatory approaches to planning. It envisioned the planning exercise as a technical rather than a technical–political process entailing power relations and interests; it focused on gender while ignoring all other types of social differentiation. It focused exclusively on projects and paid no attention to policy, programming, monitoring, and evaluation or other tasks in the workplace, and it left aside environmental issues. I took a small step forward by introducing participation in the project design process. Trainees had to role-play different stakeholder groups (e.g. peasant women, peasant men, donor and government representatives) and the overall outcomes began to improve. When playing roles, barriers to discussion of gender power relations began to tumble down, and the outcomes of project planning processes visibly began to change as the different 'stakeholders' became more demanding and began to negotiate. Another step forward came when I introduced a training module which asked trainees to identify procedural problems that acted as impediments to the implementation of gender planning, and, afterwards, to identify solutions to the problems that they had found. That is when my attitude towards the trainees began to change, and I began to learn from them. I learned that men in traditionally male-dominated technical fields were far more open to discussing issues of equity, equality, and power than had been contemplated in the training package developed by the gender experts. I learned that real resistance was far less common than we had imagined (but nearly impossible to overcome when genuinely strong). I learned that I could challenge assumptions and ideas in a respectful and intelligent way and find the overall outcome improved; that people wanted to be convinced but were also willing to convince each other. I also learned that these 'resistant' or 'passive' trainees, when properly stimulated, often knew more about problem identification and potential solutions than I, as a specialist in my own field, could ever have known.

I incorporated what I learned as a gender trainer into an effort, which is now called SEAGA—Socio-economic and Gender Analysis—to develop a new conceptual framework for gender training that parallels the efforts to develop new conceptual frameworks for gender planning, and SEAGA introduces a much more holistic framework containing overall socio-economic assessment and, within this, gender as an ever-present dimension. Further, it envisions programme formulation as a political–technical process involving stakeholders, power relations, and potential for conflict, where environmental problems are generally also ever present. One of the provisions that I built into the SEAGA programme is that the main training materials would be complemented by a continually expanding and evolving set of interactive materials and manuals that are sector- and task-specific, which will meet the express needs of planners, and which will be designed and improved by planners themselves. The SEAGA conceptual framework was further developed by a team at Clark University (Thomas-Slayter et al. 1995), and the training-of-trainers programme is now in implementation phase (FAO 2000).

## Developing the Second FAO Plan of Action for Women and Development

The first FAO Plan of Action for Women and Development was formulated for the period 1989–1995, in accordance with the request of the FAO Conference (its governing body). A consultant was hired to draft the Plan in two months, with supervision from the WID unit (SDWW). This document was then sent to the departmental level for approval, but was rejected. A new Plan was formulated in four days by one WID officer and a non-WID department manager, and sent up the hierarchy for approval. After some going back and forth, the Plan was approved and presented to the next FAO Conference, where it was ratified. For the next five years, SDWW oversaw implementation of the Plan. Progress on implementation was reported every two years at the

FAO governing bodies. Having participated in these reporting exercises, I recognised, as did everyone else in SDWW, that the Plan was barely being implemented. Most implementation was being done by SDWW itself. Very little progress was evident within the organisation—what progress was being made was *ad hoc*, and depended largely on the 'innovators' in other units who happened to take gender issues seriously for one reason or another.

In 1994 SDWW began preparations to develop the next FAO Plan of Action (1996–2001), which would take effect after the first Plan expired. Seeing this as an opportunity to make amends for a poorly formulated First Plan of Action, we began to discuss ways to ensure that the Plan would be implemented organisation-wide. My previous experiences led me to suggest that, this time, non-expert FAO planners should formulate the Plan. These people, I suggested, had participated in gender training. They knew better than we did what their work programmes would be over the next five years. If they didn't formulate the Plan themselves, they certainly wouldn't be likely to implement it. The then Chief of SDWW, Leena Kirjavainen, fully supported the idea; we proceeded to develop a methodology and convince management.

A presentation was made to the Director General and top management to obtain their approval and support for the 'strategic' planning process. A 'strategic planning method' together with a manual and set of supporting materials were presented to represent-atives of each of 65 Services (technical units) grouped into 25 Divisional (sectoral) workshops that SDWW facilitated, to familiarise the planners with the procedures and stimulate the generation of ideas about medium-term goals. These planners then worked over a six-month period to develop their 'strategic plans', which included a background, a justification, a statement of the development objectives, a description of the activities, inputs, outputs, and monitoring indicators to be used, and a budget and calendar of implementation. The Service plans were reviewed and eventually approved by all Service staff. The draft plans were commented on by SDWW and by the FAO Evaluation Service. Comments focused only on technical questions such as 'Are the objectives attainable? Are the inputs appropriate?' With rare exceptions, there were no normative judgements made regarding the gender content of the plans. The support of gender experts was requested on only two or three occasions, when the respective Services were unable to formulate their own plans due to lack of knowledge.

In these cases, SDWW staff or a gender consultant provided the expertise, working directly with the staff of these Services and their work programmes.

The 65 individual Service plans were consolidated into 25 Divisional plans by divisional staff (usually they were not gender experts). These were then consolidated into five Departmental plans, which were then consolidated by SDWW into a single FAO Plan of Action that was presented to the FAO Conference in 1995 and approved (FAO 1997). Follow-up to the Plan's implementation was meant to be done in the same fashion in which it had been formulated: Services are responsible for implementing and monitoring their own Plans; Divisions monitor and evaluate their Services; Departments monitor and evaluate their Divisions, and SDWW, together with the Service responsible for overall planning, would monitor and evaluate the Departments.

The Plan had many unique features:

- All activities foreseen in the plan fit carefully within the 'normal' working programmes of the various units.

- Responsibility for implementation of the plans lies with the staff of these units who are aware of, and generally in agreement with, what they are supposed to do.

- All activities foreseen are budgeted.

- All development goals have specific monitoring indicators.

- Almost all units in the organisation, irrespective of their areas of activity, have WID plans— including 100 per cent of all technical units, but also many administrative and service units—for example, Personnel, the document and photo libraries, the press service (several of these were at first excluded from the planning process, but later *they asked* to be included).

- Some of the technical units are concerned exclusively with developing and implementing operational procedures, such as planning, reporting, and monitoring. These units also developed their strategic WID plans, which, unsurprisingly, contemplate ways to make these procedures more gender sensitive.

- With respect to Personnel, the development objectives were to improve the overall hiring, retention, and promotion of women professional staff. Personnel couldn't achieve this alone—the support of all technical units was required. Therefore, all Divisions set targets for hiring and promotion.

How do I explain the fact that, while staff indicated that gender training had left them 'ready, willing and unable' to deal with gender in their work, they were in fact able to develop strategic WID plans? First, many of the plans devised anticipate the means to enable staff to better incorporate gender dimensions in the future—such as guidelines, evaluations, and even specific training. Second, the strategic planning process was an 'action-research' and 'action-learning' process where staff worked together, with gender experts as facilitators and resource persons, to formulate plans. Therefore, the participatory planning exercise should be evaluated not only in terms of its outcomes (the plans themselves), but also in terms of the learning processes that were generated throughout the organisation.

An undertaking of this magnitude was not simple. The main problems encountered during plan formulation can be summarised as follows:

- Due to unevenness in the gender training process, a few Services lacked properly qualified or motivated staff and were unable to formulate plans on their own.

- Lack of familiarity with strategic planning and formulating plans on the part of staff meant that many plans had to be reformulated several times, generating resistance due to excessive workload.

- The concern about lack of funds to implement the plans was present at the time the plans were being formulated, since many Services considered that their funds were too low even to implement their 'normal' programme of work. Therefore we encouraged the development of activities that would require no additional funding, and we encouraged people to seek external funding where necessary. However, some two months after the Plan was approved, FAO was forced to cut its budget by about 20 per cent, which was followed by additional severe budget reductions. In these circumstances, many staff reported that the WID plans would not be fully implemented without these required additional resources.

Three years after the Plan was adopted, an evaluation of gender mainstreaming at FAO, carried out for the Norwegian government, had this to say about its implementation:

> Even though divisions have been mandated to write their contribution to the Plan of Action, not every division represented in the plan has adopted mainstreaming ideals. It seems that divisions that have always been active

*in integrating gender concerns have been encouraged by the Plan of Action
and the process of drawing up the activities has been a participatory process.
For other divisions, writing the Plan of Action contribution has been a
necessary evil, with which nobody identified and which some staff member
had to comply with for form's sake. Others hired outside consultants to
write the divisions' contribution. Obviously in such cases there is no
ownership or commitment. Thus, a member of one division included in the
Plan of Action and operative in a field where gender issues are of
considerable importance, plainly rejected the thought that the operations of
his service had any bearing on gender whatsoever.* (Geisler et al. 1999)

This generally negative assessment of the plan's methodology is valid
to a certain degree, since staff members were indeed 'forced' to
contribute to plans. But 65 Services and 25 Divisions developed plans,
and it is perhaps not reasonable to expect that *all* would 'adopt
mainstreaming ideals', particularly when gender considerations are
not equally relevant to all Services and Divisions (e.g. to the Service
dealing with international trade in products such as oil seed). It is also
not necessarily the case that, if a consultant is hired to formulate the
plan together with the Service involved, there will be no 'ownership'.
The provision of gender expertise to support a Service's staff can work
very well, as was the case with the Statistics Division at FAO which is
cited as a 'success story' in the same Norwegian review. The Statistics
Division, known as one of the most conservative at FAO, began
seriously to mainstream gender issues and change its work methods
and plans after a gender statistics consultant worked directly with and
for its staff (Perucci 1992).

The Norwegian government report went on to note:

*The overall impression still was that nobody followed up on the
implementation of the Plan of Action . . . the gender focal points who should
be doing the monitoring have neither the skills, tools nor the time and
money to comply with this task. Since . . . there is no ownership of the plan
in senior management this situation is not going to change until incentives
are built into the structures. This might also mean that the gender
mainstreaming activities that are happening, might remain unnoticed,
unrecorded and unmonitored.* (Geisler et al.)

Senior management, indeed, authorised but was barely involved in the
planning process. Unfortunately, owing to the lack of effective
monitoring, it is not possible to assess the actual impact of the planning
process on the organisation's work. Setting up a participatory planning

process is one thing, but getting top managers to participate actively, and replicating the process continuously in order to monitor implementation is quite another. Stakeholder participation is time-, energy-, and financial resource-intensive. What was clear to me, however, was that the non-expert planners in general responded well; they were capable in most instances of carrying out their own planning, and had the knowledge about their programmes and needs to permit realistic and relevant mainstreaming to occur. They were generally pleased with the fact that they were considered as stakeholders, were treated with respect, and weren't being forced to implement someone else's ideas (although a minority did resent having to develop a WID plan at all). In fact, the strategic planning exercise itself was appreciated so much that several Services began to apply the process to create their own five-year Service work plans.

## Conclusions: stakeholders as an impediment, or an opportunity?

In this paper, I have presented two types of mainstreaming experiences. One was at field level, with UN project heads who had no previous gender training and who had no clear mandate to deal with gender in their work, other than a request from UNDP that they participate in a workshop. The other was at headquarters level, with staff who had received gender training, and where there was a clear policy mandate and a top–down instruction for people to participate in the mainstreaming exercise. Both exercises were premised on the idea that meaningful planning can occur through dialogue in an environment of mutual respect and mutual learning. Both exercises depended upon the knowledge and experience of the different stakeholders in the process. In both experiences, the immediate outcomes expected by the different stakeholders were not those that actually materialised—they represented in some instances a compromise, and in most a distinct improvement over the pre-existing situation, but in no instance were they less than what those involved anticipated. As gender experts, we were pleasantly surprised by the outcomes, since we, like most others, had learned to have low expectations—to encounter perhaps insurmountable resistance, incomprehension, and lack of skills. Stakeholder participation is not a 'magic bullet'. It is difficult, it has certain prerequisites, and its results are still subject to external limitations and to internal problems related to lack of follow-up and institutionalisation of democratic procedures. Whether the ultimate outcome in implementation fulfils everyone's newly created expectations or not, one thing seems fairly certain—the direction is the right one.

Drawing upon these experiences, and reflecting on the gender mainstreaming literature, I am led to conclude that there is as yet great inconsistency in both analysis and recommendations in terms of: who precisely the stakeholders are in gender mainstreaming efforts; how these stakeholders should be characterised; how the stakeholders should be involved in the process of organisational change; and how the *process* of gender mainstreaming affects the *outcomes*. A tentative summary of the different approaches to these questions is presented in Table 1. In general it can be said that the literature on gender mainstreaming is beginning to place greater emphasis on trans-formative processes throughout organisations that are expected to be mainstreaming agents (e.g. planning agencies). A small body of literature is beginning to emerge that documents strategies to achieve more far-reaching changes in work relationships between gender experts and other stakeholders within organisations. For example, Rao and Kelleher (1998) report on the BRAC Gender Quality Action-Learning experience and methodology that improved these working relationships, although it has not yet achieved gender mainstreaming. This experience is informed both by participatory planning methodologies, and concepts from gender and organisational change, focusing on how organisations in general are gendered, how women within organisations are disempowered, and how male management cultures function. Rao and Stuart are among the few who advocate a 'stakeholders' approach to gender planning. They are concerned that the tendency of gender planners is to focus on outcomes, 'not recognising that process itself may be an outcome' (1997:16).

> We must negotiate with members of the organisations, and discover what they see the issues to be regarding gender . . . [N]egotiation is not simply a tactic to increase the enthusiasm of those with whom one is engaging in the organisations, the ideas of the change agent are also a subject for negotiation. (Rao and Stuart 1997: 14–15)

The room that I leave for sceptics is very great indeed. It will, for many, be incomprehensible that I could suggest that those who should be responsible for empowering women are precisely those who do the most to disempower them; that we should place such a critical task in the hands of those who are the most unaware and bound by tradition,

**Table 1: Mainstreaming approaches based upon characterisation of planners as stakeholders**

| Strategies | Active resisters | Passive targets | Active change agents |
|---|---|---|---|
| Sensitisation | *Emphasis on outcomes* | *Emphasis on outcomes* | *Emphasis on process* |
| | • Participatory gender training with or without follow-up.<br>• Studies and data incorporated in main policy documents.<br>• Pressure from outside groups on management. | • Participatory gender training to reduce resistance, with or without follow-up.<br>• Studies and data created for specific units and tasks.<br>• Persuasion of management. | • Gender training followed by:<br>- action-learning processes on an ongoing basis;<br>- trainer learns together with trainees. |
| Planning tools | • Pre-formulated global plans, guidelines, monitoring indicators, etc. with mandate from above for adherence. | • Increasingly sector-specific and task-specific guidelines created by gender experts.<br>• Gender support provided to specific units. | • Activity-specific<br>• Devised jointly with change agents at level of specific work programmes/sectors. |
| Gender experts | • High-level management positions or input.<br>• Gender units formulate policies, procedures, targets, and instruments.<br>• Build alliances within and outside organisations.<br>• Mobilise pressure groups. | • Gender units and focal points.<br>• Dissemination of information.<br>• Participation in teams of non-experts providing gender input. | • Facilitators.<br>• Prioritisation of strategic interventions.<br>• Consensus building.<br>• Mobilisation of resources for action-learning.<br>• Participatory organisational change. |
| Accountability | • Centrally-managed monitoring.<br>• Personnel performance assessments.<br>• Organisation-wide evaluations. | • Reporting procedures | • Developed on a participatory basis.<br>• Voluntary adherence.<br>• Incorporation in lessons learned experiences . |

procedure, and bureaucratic systems of rewards. But this I do not argue. The gender 'expert', 'entrepreneur', or 'advocate' has a crucial role. In a 'stakeholders' approach this role is, in fact, greater and more difficult than in a more conventional planning process. The 'gender expert' is the catalyst *par excellence*. The gender expert also bears a great deal of the blame if the process does not work—rather than pointing the finger at the institutional, psychological, and cultural barriers, the finger gets pointed right back at oneself. The process focuses not on barriers, but on releasing potential. If it didn't work, one didn't deal adequately with the potential, or there was something wrong with the process. The process itself is risky, the outcomes are uncertain, the transformative potential as yet unknown. However, I would suggest that we already know the risks, uncertainties, and transformative potential of continuing to see the majority of the stakeholders in the process either as active resisters or passive implementers. We know that it is time to try something new.

## Notes

1 The discussion in this paper is restricted to gender mainstreaming in complex organisations. It does not pretend to broach the broad and much more diverse literature that deals with grassroots or project-level experience, or that dealing with women-only organisations.

2 There are notable exceptions, for example with respect to the Ford Foundation (Kardam 1991).

## References

Berg, Gitte (1994) 'Structures to promote gender within MS', in M. Macdonald (ed.).

FAO (1997) 'Gender: key to sustainability and food security. FAO Plan of Action for Women in Development, 1996–2001', Rome: FAO.

FAO (2000) 'SEAGA: the Socio-economic and Gender Analysis Programme', updated September 2000, available at http://www.fao.org/sd/seaga/default. htm.

Geisler, Gisela, Bonnie Keller and Anne-Lene Norman (1999) *WID/Gender Units and the Experience of Gender Mainstreaming in Multilateral Organisations: 'Knights on White Horses'?*, Report submitted to the Norwegian Ministry of Foreign Affairs by the Chr. Michelsen Institute, available at http://odin.dep.no/ud/engelsk/publ/ rapporter/ 032001–990250/index-hovo10-b-n-a.html.

Hannan-Anderson, Carolyn (1992) 'Gender planning methodology. Three papers incorporating the gender approach in development cooperation programmes', Rapporter Och Notiser 109, Institutionen for kulturgeografi och ekonomisk geografi vid Lunds Universitet.

Jahan, Rounaq (1995) *The Elusive Agenda: Mainstreaming Women in Development*, Dhaka: University Press, and London and New Jersey: Zed Books.

Kabeer, Naila and Ramya Subrahmanian (1996) 'Institutions, Relations and Outcomes: Framework and Tools for

Gender-aware Planning', *IDS Discussion Paper 357*, September.

Kardam, Nuket (1991) *Bringing Women In: Women's Issues in International Development Programs*, Boulder: Lynne Reinner.

Macdonald, Mandy (ed.) (1994) *Gender Planning in Development Agencies: Meeting the Challenge*, Oxfam: Oxford.

Macdonald, Mandy, Ellen Sprenger and Irene Dubel (1997) *Gender and Organisational Change: Bridging the Gap between Policy and Practice*, Amsterdam: Royal Tropical Institute.

Moser, Caroline O. N. (1993) *Gender Planning and Development: Theory, Practice and Training*, London: Routledge.

Perucci, Francesca (1992) *Improving Gender Disaggregated Data on Human Resources through Agricultural Censuses*, Rome: Statistical Development Service and Women in Agricultural Production and Rural Development Service, FAO.

Rao, Aruna and David Kelleher (1998) 'Gender lost and gender found: BRAC's gender quality action-learning programme', *Development in Practice* 8(2):173–85.

Rao, Aruna and Rieky Stuart (1997) 'Rethinking organisations: a feminist perspective', in Caroline Sweetman (ed.) *Gender in Development Organisations*, Oxford: Oxfam.

Ravazi, Shahra and Carol Miller (1995) *Gender Mainstreaming: A Study of the Efforts by the UNDP, the World Bank and the ILO to Institutionalize Gender Issues*, Geneva: UNRISD.

Staudt, Kathleen (ed.) (1990) *Women, International Development and Politics: The Bureaucratic Mire*, Philadelphia: Temple University Press.

Thomas-Slayter, Barbara, Rachel Polestico **et al.** (1995) *A Manual for Socio-economic and Gender Analysis: Responding to the Development Challenge*, Worcester MA: ECOGEN Publication, Clark University and Virginia Polytechnic Institute and State University.

Wallace, Tina (1998) 'Institutionalising gender in UK NGOs', *Development in Practice* 8(2):159–72.

Young, Kate (1993) *Planning Development with Women: Making a World of Difference*, Basingstoke: Macmillan.

# Sustainable investments: women's contributions to natural resource management projects in Africa[1]

## Barbara Thomas-Slayter and Genese Sodikoff

## The problem

The growing linkages between poverty, resource decline, and ecological degradation constitute a formidable challenge to development policy and practice. In many African countries, the natural resource base on which significant populations depend for their livelihood is deteriorating markedly. Gender is one of the key variables defining access to and control over natural resources. Women—as well as men—use and manage resources and have different roles, responsibilities, opportunities, and constraints in doing so, both within the household and in the community. Gender is a determining factor in the division of labour, rights, and responsibilities, and, therefore, affects sustainability of livelihoods and the equitability of development (see, for example, Berry 1989; Braidotti et al. 1994; Collins 1991; Gianotten et al. 1994; Mehra 1993; Rocheleau et al. 1996).

Can prospects for improving livelihood security and building sustainable environments in Africa be increased if women have greater influence over decisions about how resources are managed? For development scholars and practitioners who are convinced of the importance of gender considerations and women's contributions in donor-driven environmental planning in Africa, an affirmative answer is self-evident. But the question was recently posed by the Office of Technical Resources in the Africa Bureau of USAID, which suggests doubt on the part of the donors and inadequate reports on the part of implementers. If bilateral and multilateral agencies lack substantive, comparative data that demonstrate measurable social and environmental improvements from women-focused natural resource management projects, then such a lack could jeopardise future donor support for such work.

First published in *Development in Practice* 11(1) in 2001

From our perspective, the development 'project' approach is often narrowly and inappropriately conceived. We hope that new forms of international assistance will eventually help to avert failed plans and tragedies linked to or aggravated by development. Indeed, the project approach to development, as illuminated by Uvin (1998) in his analysis of Rwanda, can lead to a myopia which may foster negative forces of exclusion, oppression, and structural violence. We do believe, however, that the international community has a moral obligation to share its wealth and technical knowledge with poor nations. Our intention is that the views and suggestions presented here contribute to a shift in prevalent institutional approaches to development by emphasising process rather than aggregate results, the integration of social and environmental indicators, and a commitment to assessing accomplishments, as well as failures, with the stakeholders themselves. We hope that this paper will contribute to ongoing efforts to rethink the strategic use of projects as an approach to development.

Anecdotal evidence from Africa and other regions in the South attests to the advantages of giving women greater managerial control over donor-driven natural resource management projects which have traditionally vested authority in men. However, anecdotal evidence alone does not do justice to the knowledge and labours of African women involved in such efforts. It is clear that few development agencies perform systematic evaluations with gender-disaggregated data, despite nearly two decades of development literature describing the pitfalls of failing to do so. We were motivated to find case studies that contain qualitative and quantitative information on project process and effect, the kind of 'hard evidence' that we believe is necessary to institutionalise donor support firmly for African women's contributions to creating sustainable environments and economies. After an extensive literature search, we selected five case studies from an array of donor-sponsored natural resource management projects across sub-Saharan Africa.[2] Our paper seeks to assess:

- the effects of women's involvement in project-related resource management decisions;
- those conditions which foster their involvement; and
- indicators of impact, process, and sustainability which denote changes in equity and effectiveness in natural resource management projects.

We elucidate data that irrefutably show 'success' in local and foreign organisational terms, and we emphasise the common denominators that form the basis of their positive outcomes. Finally, to remedy the gap in the institutional records and to ensure equitable and beneficial natural resource management projects, we offer a methodology that allows stakeholders to evaluate the project process with attention to social, economic, and ecological effects.

## Analytical approach

This paper analyses the findings of five case studies culled from an extensive literature search across Africa. The cases selected are from The Gambia, Kenya, Malawi, Nigeria, and Rwanda, and are based on extensive documentation and fieldwork. Each case offers specific insights for understanding the complexities, issues, outcomes, and explanatory variables in regard to the roles of women in decisions related to resource management projects. They highlight in very different ways the primary data, analysis, and synthesis needed to build indicators which assess effective and gender-inclusive resource management. Informed by our broad literature search and extensive experience in Eastern and Southern Africa, we find that the case studies are characterised by recurrent themes, despite the fact that they differ in scale and magnitude. From them, we identify five enabling conditions, develop indicators, and suggest several hypotheses for future exploration.

Experience leads us to affirm Kabeer's conceptualisation of poverty as both *state* and *process*. Defining poverty as a situation in which resources are insufficient to meet basic needs, the *state* of poverty focuses on shortfalls in needs satisfaction, while the *process* of poverty is concerned with the causes and mechanisms of the generation and transmission of poverty (Kabeer 1991:243). Resources are distributed in a society through a complex system of entitlements which are in turn shaped by the social relations and practices governing possession, distribution, and use in that society. Impoverishment occurs because of a deterioration in the value of the two main parameters— endowments and exchange entitlements—which constitute the basis of household or individual claims to the social product (Sen 1990; Kabeer 1992). Like Kabeer and many others, we are concerned about the social relations established around resource tenure, access and control, and emphasise what has perhaps become common knowledge that 'in general women's rights to property and natural resources in many regions are much more restricted than men's' (Lastarria-Cornhiel 1994:3; Rocheleau et al. 1996).

When we discuss the enabling conditions of successful natural resource management projects, we are addressing both an enabling state (such as a secure livelihood) and a desired condition, an outcome linked to a process. Certain enabling conditions are thus both fundamental starting points of equitable social relations and viability, as well as continuing features of 'sustainable' development. For example, the involvement of stakeholders in decision making can be perceived as both an enabling condition and also, if successfully maintained or enhanced, as an outcome. Here our perspective reflects, in a positive sense, Kabeer's conceptualisation of poverty as both state and process.

Analysis in this study relies on an ecological approach which emphasises the interaction of the environment and human beings in a diversity of complex land-use systems. An ecological approach allows us to see land-use and technology change as a dynamic, interactive process rather than one of incremental and unilinear movement. We are interested in both household and community levels of activity and the ways these relate to broad policy analysis and implementation. In addition, local organisation and grassroots movements are critical to progressive social change (however that may be locally defined) and more equitable and effective management of resources.

## Summaries of cases selected

The five cases offer insights into the conditions that enable women's effective management of resources and benefit the community at large. Kenya's Chanderema Women's Group in Vihiga District exemplifies competent group organisation for management of high, milk-yielding dairy cattle, soil erosion control, and fodder cultivation activities. Further, the collaboration of the group with Farming Systems of Kenya, Africa 2000, and the government of Kenya, demonstrates the value of local to global partnerships.

The Women in Agriculture Development Project in Malawi (WIADP) highlights the importance of women's production in smallholder agriculture. It also shows how two very important institutional changes have led to policy changes that have benefited both agriculture and women: collecting gender-disaggregated data and introducing gender concerns at different levels of government.

A study of Nigeria and the adoption of soybean technology among men and women farmers documents the rate and effectiveness with which women and men make land-use decisions regarding the adoption of a new technology. This research testifies to the value of gender-disaggregated statistics to disclose data and clarify misinformation and misinterpretations concerning men's and women's respective roles in agriculture.

The fourth case, Rwanda's aquaculture sector, explores wetland land-use systems where women are the key workers. Data were collected in 1992 and 1993 before the genocide of 1994. Aquaculture is based on recycling and refurbishing land with organic manure and using local plant and crop waste for fish production. The case illustrates the importance of local cooperatives in the community which collaborate with Rwandan and international researchers and extension workers. More importantly, the case also illustrates a fundamental critique of the development community, as revealed by Uvin (1998) in his examination of Rwanda and events leading up to the genocide. The project evaluations—exploring aquaculture, community, and gender roles—judged the effort a success. Yet the project was functioning within a broad context of ethnic politics, human rights abuses, and violence; analysts ignored the relationship between the project itself and the big picture of state policy and social structure. By ignoring the context, the development community contributed to the destructive processes underway.

The Gambia case relates the complexity of gender politics with regard to competing crop production systems. Into the thicket of gendered competition over the low-lying land and groundwater sources come the development/donor agencies, promoting their own conflicting agendas. The donors encourage, on the one hand, women's commercial vegetable gardens to enhance food production and incomes, and, on the other hand, men's orchards to stabilise land resources. Tree planting on garden beds became a mechanism for land-holders to alienate surplus female labour and subsidies that were embodied in concrete-lined wells and permanent wire fences. At the same time, shade effects from tree planting threaten to undermine the productivity of gardeners, who play a key role in providing for the subsistence needs of their families. Gender is clearly a critical aspect of the political ecology of The Gambia and is little understood by the donor community, something which has jeopardised productivity, sustainability, and community welfare.

In total, these cases are complementary in that they emphasise different sectors, highlight diverse enabling conditions, and provide data across a variety of activities. Moreover, they offer evidence to support the claim that opportunities for environmental sustainability and economic productivity are increased when women are vested with authority to make land-use management decisions. All cases also reveal some of the ambiguities and complexities of the development process. Two in particular, Rwanda and The Gambia, reflect the short-sightedness and conflicting objectives of the donor community, as well as the myriad ways in which development efforts can become entangled in domestic policies and social issues.

## Deriving enabling conditions from the cases

There are common themes emerging in these case studies which we have called 'enabling conditions', signifying attributes favourable to fostering sustainable economic activity and equitable social relations. Findings from the case studies permit us to cluster enabling conditions in five categories:

- gender-disaggregated data;
- extension and training;
- local participation and organisation;
- livelihood security;
- local to global linkages and partnerships.

We discuss each of these enabling conditions in turn, drawing on evidence from at least two cases for each.

### Gender-disaggregated data

The case has been made persuasively for nearly 15 years (see Overholt et al. 1985) that knowledge of gender-based activities, access and control over resources, involvement in decision making, and responsibility for productive activities is essential in order to formulate effective projects and programmes. We can readily demonstrate the relevance of gender-disaggregated data to establishing programmes and policies to improve livelihoods, increase food security, and lead to an enriched and sustainable natural environment.

The Malawi case illustrates this point emphatically. WIADP conducted research on gender roles in the diverse farming systems in Malawi, disaggregated by gender a number of data sets, and presented these data to policy makers. According to Spring (1995), WIADP made a major national breakthrough in statistical data gathering by studying two of Malawi's largest surveys—the National Survey of Agriculture

(NSSA) and the Agro-Economic Surveys (AES)—and determining a way to distinguish the sex of the household head in both of them.

WIADP subsequently convinced analysts at the National Statistical Office (NSO) to disaggregate its data. As a result, the NSO had its first publication containing the percentages of female-headed households by area and development project for the entire country. To the amazement of all, female-headed households constituted nearly 30 per cent of all rural households, with a range from 15 to 45 per cent. These data became the rationale to assist women in several programmes and to shift policy towards women farmers (Spring 1995:6)

Subsequently the WIADP approach for disaggregating data became a model for most data sets in the country. WIADP used the data on extension to show gender differences in the delivery of extension services. Only with accurate gender-disaggregated data were the members of the WIADP project able to develop convincing arguments and interventions for policy and programme changes. The data collected on women farmers, and specifically on female-headed households, were sufficient to 'allow' women access to some portion of development resources. Analysis of the data sets confirmed that women not only contributed a large percentage of the labour to Malawi's smallholder agriculture but also made agricultural decisions in many rural households. The data also showed the variable nature of the division of labour by gender in terms of crop, task, location, and family composition. These data were invaluable in making the case for policy change to policy makers (Spring 1995:18).

The data collected by WIADP thus provided the foundation for launching gender-specific training such as on-farm maize and soybean trials, new technologies, and credit programmes among smallholders in two resource-poor, drought-prone areas. The programmes greatly improved the productivity and levels of food self-sufficiency within the participating households.

The Nigeria case also points to the importance of obtaining gender-disaggregated data. As in many other African countries, women in Nigeria take increasing responsibility for family farms, while men migrate to cities and sometimes abroad to seek employment. Kehinde explores the differences in the degree of soybean technology adoption between men and women farmers. The population for the study included all resource-poor farmers involved in soybean production in Oyo State, with a sample of 200 stratified according to gender and age taken from three different ecological zones. Twenty-two per cent of those selected for the sample were women. Using analysis of variance to test the effect of gender on soybean technology adoption, Kehinde found that the only statistically significant differences between men and women pertained to the acreage of soybeans planted and the unit price per measure of soybeans. Men had a higher total acreage planted (yet a slightly lower proportion of land planted to soybeans compared with women), and women received higher unit prices from soybeans than men. The study demonstrated beyond a doubt that women farmers are just as capable as men in adapting to new crops and innovations. Logically, the next step is to link this study (and others of its type) to policy change. If the trend of male out-migration continues, it will be increasingly important for Nigerian policy makers to address research and extension to women farmers to ensure the food supply for the country.

Thus, we have in these two cases hard evidence of women's key roles in managing land, and in making agricultural and resource-use decisions. The Nigeria case provides data which now need to be integrated into policies and programmes. The Malawi case demonstrates the potential when data analysis is effectively linked to policy and programme design through political and administrative processes.

## Extension and training

Effectiveness of extension services and training emerges from all the cases as central to their success. For the Kenya project with the Chanderema Women's Group, training constituted an integral part of project management. The local NGO, Farming Systems Kenya Ltd (FSK), in charge of administering the project, organised preliminary sessions to teach proper upkeep of exotic Jersey cows, and how to establish napier grass plots for fodder and construct zero grazing units. Moreover, FSK organised ongoing field days—two per month—on calf-rearing and cow maintenance as well as fodder management and use. In addition, an extension agent visited farms of group members every two months. Thus, at the local level, there was a close integration of group members, NGO programme staff, and extension agents involved in the Chanderema project. FSK specifies that the programme seeks to (1) train farmers in crop and livestock production techniques; (2) train farmers in record keeping and credit management; (3) provide in-kind credit for seed, fertiliser, and heifers; and (4) advise farmers on market conditions and provide some marketing and supply services. The training was largely carried out by the NGO (Njoroge 1995).

Working at a higher scale within the Malawian government, the WIADP worked with the Ministry of Agriculture in refocusing and reorganising its extension services. First, they encouraged a client-centred approach, drawing on the data on women farmers to facilitate a reorientation in this regard. This meant targeting agricultural services to women as well as men. It meant that gender awareness became integrated into the agricultural service and delivery system. Second, WIADP engaged in retraining female extension agents in certain agricultural topics, as opposed to home economics, which had been their traditional emphasis.

Third, WIADP was able to generate a climate which permitted male extension staff to work with women clients and managed to legitimise this approach at the policy level. Fourth, they gained assurance that seats would be set aside for women in agricultural training classes, and they secured these seats through national policy directives. Fifth, they fostered interdisciplinary work within the Ministry of Agriculture, encouraging both social and agricultural scientists to work together in an interdisciplinary fashion.

## Local participation and organisation

All five cases reflect high levels of local participation and organisation. What does this mean? Passive participation is one-way communication of information from a sponsoring agency to members of the community. This kind of participation is easily manipulated by local leaders to build patronage, and it tends to promote dependence rather than self-reliance. Reactive participation is usually controlled by the external development agent. There may be donations of labour, money, or other resources, but the initiative lies with the outside party and there are rarely ongoing forms of community organisation. Over time the activity dissipates. Active or full participation arises within a community. Community members themselves are the agents of change, though they may act in concert with outside sources of funds, technical expertise, or other resources. The advantages of this form of partici-pation are that leadership and initiative are based within local communities and that grassroots organisations often arise through general community mobilisation.

These cases all demonstrate the utility of well-organised groups in effective resource management. The Rwanda case is illustrative. Fish ponds in Rwanda are developed in the publicly owned *marais* lands or wetlands. Government law institutionalised the traditional rules of collective use of wetlands (Balakrishnan et al. 1993:14). Rwandan women and men share responsibilities in the aquaculture production system. A primary advantage of organising in farmer groups is the access to land for production. Farmers cultivate the *marais* land as a production group, and this collective production allows access to the rich farmland for a large number of farmers (Hishamunda and Moehl 1989).

In the integrated aquaculture system, the pond bunds are used for garden crops, which are cultivated by women. Most women state that they have taken up fish culture to provide for family food needs, since fish from ponds are regarded as a ready and relatively cheap source of protein. In addition, some women's groups have benefited financially by selling the fish and saving the cash returns, which have been used later to purchase inputs for agricultural production.

Yet the project analyses were not sensitive to issues of ethnicity, poverty, and collective behaviour, nor were there assessments of the interplay of social structures and project outcomes. Since this project, like others, was considered in isolation from its surroundings, the development community was inadvertently contributing to the build-up of frustrations and animosities leading to genocide (Carnegie Commission 1997; Uvin 1998).

Local women's market garden groups have been spectacularly successful on the North Bank of the Gambia River, the region investigated by Schroeder. Over the past two decades, this area has developed into one of the most intensive vegetable-producing enclaves in the country. The pool of women gardeners grew from 30, selected to take part in a pilot onion project in the mid-1970s, to more than 400, registered during an expansion project in 1984, to 540 in 1991 (Schroeder 1995). At least a dozen separate projects have been funded by international NGOs and voluntary agencies, bringing the total invested in this Mandinka-speaking community to at least US$40,000 between 1978 and 1995. The funds have been used for fences, wells, seed, fertiliser, and other inputs for the gardens which send truckloads of fresh produce to market outlets up and down the border between The Gambia and Senegal.

Women's groups supervise day-to-day operations of the gardens, including maintenance of perimeters, seasonal land clearing, and administering fines to those who do not cooperate. In general, fences are managed by the group, but women work their own land allocation individually or as a family group. Water management and marketing are collective operations. Schroeder's observations of 1991 sales suggest that aggregate annual returns to the 540 growers in the village he studied were in the order of US$80,000, clearly an important addition to household income. It was group organisation that facilitated the strategies and inputs that made the market gardening so successful.

In both of the above cases, the groups were engaged in productive activities leading to greater food availability, increased income, and improved management of the resource base. Groups may focus on productive activities and specific resource-management problems. They may also build capacities and collective strength, enabling them to take a more active part in political processes determining access to and allocation of resources. The Gambia case demonstrates the complexities of gendered politics, development objectives, and resource/land-tenure issues. The women's groups and their gardens on the North Bank of the Gambia River clearly became part of a larger set of questions embedded in local political economy and ecology.

## Levels of livelihood security

The programmes or projects described in these five cases have contributed substantially to improving levels of livelihood security. Recall that we identify the relevance of livelihood security as both enabling condition and outcome, in the manner in which Kabeer has defined the state of poverty as shortfalls in needs satisfaction, and the process of poverty as the causes and mechanisms which generate and transmit it. In both Malawi and The Gambia, the initial benefits to livelihood security from credit and extension programmes focused on women (Malawi) and group-managed vegetable gardens (The Gambia) led to the rapid growth of the programmes. Women could assess the benefits to livelihood security and became engaged, in increasing numbers, in the programmes.

The Malawi programme (WIADP) has had the most far-reaching consequences for smallholder farming households. This success is related largely to the fact that WIADP mainstreamed women into farm clubs and enabled them to participate in a seasonal credit programme. Seasonal credit, as dispensed in Malawi, provides inputs (seeds, fertilisers, and chemicals) in crop-specific packages through farm clubs. Individual farmers can choose the particular packages they want, and the club as a whole is responsible for seeing that the loans are repaid (Spring 1995:29). Defaults by members might result in the entire club being disbanded and denied future loans. The Ministry of Agriculture's policy specifies that both women and men must be members of farm clubs in order to receive agricultural credit.

Clubs are organised by farmers themselves, and it has been difficult for women to become club members. (For an in-depth discussion of this issue, see Spring 1995.) In fact, male extensionists were not supposed to register women into farm clubs. With WIADP working on behalf of women farmers, smallholder women overcame obstacles to club membership. Of all farm-club members obtaining credit in 1990–1991, 35 per cent were women and 65 per cent were men. Within another three years, the numbers of women in clubs who were receiving credit had jumped to 40 per cent.

In The Gambia, the 20-year development of market gardens along the North Bank of the Gambia River reveals that women are engaged in successful vegetable production for sale. As Schroeder (1993) emphasises, the economic and ecological pressures of the 1970s and early 1980s, including declining rice production, poor terms of trade for groundnuts, and drought, meant that families were having difficulty meeting household needs. Women began to intensify efforts to reclaim marginal land for gardening purposes; and, as seen above, the area under cultivation grew from five hectares in the mid-1970s to more than 30 hectares, with an increase to 540 growers in the village and returns measuring approximately US$80,000 (Schroeder 1995:7). This contribution to livelihood security is well understood by both the men and the women in the village, who are now engaged in a controversy over how that land should be used and how labour should be allocated among rice, vegetable, and tree crops. The controversy arose when an agroforestry project was funded by USAID in tandem with the women's garden project. The agroforestry project provided a vehicle for men to expropriate the land that women were using to cultivate vegetables, thereby undermining women's efforts. There is no doubt that women have been effective managers of the natural-resource base. The issue, however, is gender-based control over the land and who gets to benefit from its cultivation. Livelihood security—even generous livelihoods—is at the heart of this issue.

## Local to global linkages and partnerships

One way to strengthen equitable and effective resource management is to develop linkages among actors and groups at different scales through coalitions, alliance building, and networking. Such linkages and partnerships constitute a bridge between external opportunities and local initiatives. They have a number of advantages. We identify two.

First, they draw on the experience, knowledge, and skills of local, diverse groups, endeavouring to translate that experience in ways that can inform the decisions of development policy makers. WIADP in Malawi illustrates this advantage. WIADP carried out surveys and trials selectively within all three regions of the country, experimenting at the micro-level with new approaches to data gathering and providing extension services. When a new approach proved useful and suitable, WIADP then moved to influence the policy level through working with (1) women's units, national machineries, and professional women; (2) planning units responsible for writing national policy, five year plans, and country strategies; and (3) donors who could influence policy through funding. 'It was', says Spring (1995:14), 'departmental, then ministerial, and finally national policy that legitimated gender concerns in development endeavors'. But it was groundwork at the local level, linking evidence from farming households and communities to policy makers, which permitted these changes.

Second, planned linkages and partnerships can overcome a variety of problems reflecting suspicion, even contestation, that have plagued the development efforts of NGOs in Africa (Thomas-Slayter 1992:136). Kenya's Chanderema project illustrates the ways in which national or indigenous NGOs, an international NGO, the government, and the local community can build an effective partnership to meet a set of development objectives. To begin with, there is a locally organised group which identified its own concerns and needs. Second, the UNDP's Africa 2000 Network is an international donor agency specifically designed to provide small-scale assistance to local groups endeavouring to improve livelihoods in the context of building a sustainable environment. Africa 2000's Kenya office is managed by Kenyans who are knowledgeable about environmental and resource issues, and dedicated to addressing development problems at the local level.

Third, the Kenyan NGO, FSK, was established in 1981 as an independent affiliate of the African Inland Church in Nakuru District. Its overall goal is to increase the productivity and profitability of Kenyan agriculture and to enhance food security. Its specific objective is to strengthen the capabilities of smallholder farmers and their incomes through programmes of training and credit. FSK conducted a baseline study for the Chanderema project, carried out training in livestock management as well as business management and fodder production, and provided various follow-up support services.

Fourth, the Ministry of Agriculture, Livestock Development and Marketing was involved in the partnership by providing veterinary and artificial insemination services. While there were problems with these services, there was clear recognition of the division of responsibilities and the design of the partnership.

All participating entities recognised the need for collaboration and for each individual organisation to carry out its obligations if the project was to succeed. This recognition seemed to be at the heart of establishing supportive partnerships. This partnership included the community (the Chanderema group), the public sector (government), international donors (the UN's Africa 2000), local NGOs (FSK), and individual farming households. The process of building partnerships among local groups and external agencies links micro activities and macro structures, as well as transcending individual agendas, turf struggles, and entrenched roles. The dialogue enables groups to identify effective approaches to local development and resource management, and broadens their capacity for flexible, innovative action.

## Building indicators

After examining the five enabling conditions specified above—effective extension and training, local participation and organisation, gender-based data, livelihood security, and local to global linkages—we can identify indicators associated with each which clarify effectiveness and equity in resource management. Indicators communicate information about progress towards particular goals, provide clues about matters of larger significance, or make perceptible a trend or phenomenon that is not immediately detectable (Hammond et al. 1995:1). While indicators often quantify information as well as simplifying information about complex phenomena, those emerging in our analysis do not quantify data across the cases under consideration. Rather, they elicit from these cases the central elements of gender-inclusive project effectiveness leading to improved livelihoods and sustainable environments. Individually, each case provides quantitative data revealing problems and successes. The indicators are based on a qualitative, not quantitative, aggregation of the findings.

Indicators can be used for many purposes, such as providing a framework for collecting and reporting information, providing guidance to various organisations on needs, priorities, and policy effectiveness, and facilitating local community efforts to undertake and strengthen development plans. The choice of indicators depends on the purpose for which they are required and on the audience. For an audience focused on development practice and research, we have chosen to be explicit about the ways in which we are developing the indicators, and to suggest tools which are useful for primary data collection, as well as processes for analysing the data. Figure 1 presents our conceptualisation of the information needed for building indicators.

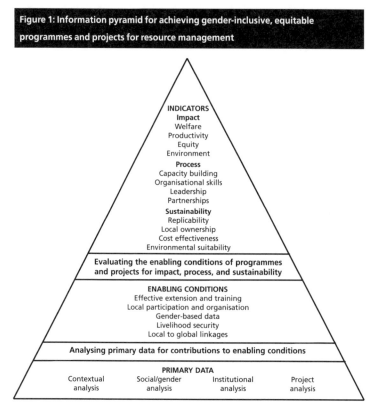

**Figure 1: Information pyramid for achieving gender-inclusive, equitable programmes and projects for resource management**

INDICATORS
**Impact**
Welfare
Productivity
Equity
Environment
**Process**
Capacity building
Organisational skills
Leadership
Partnerships
**Sustainability**
Replicability
Local ownership
Cost effectiveness
Environmental suitability

**Evaluating the enabling conditions of programmes and projects for impact, process, and sustainability**

ENABLING CONDITIONS
Effective extension and training
Local participation and organisation
Gender-based data
Livelihood security
Local to global linkages

**Analysing primary data for contributions to enabling conditions**

PRIMARY DATA
Contextual analysis | Social/gender analysis | Institutional analysis | Project analysis

(Source: adapted from Hammond et al., *Environmental Indicators: A Systematic Approach to Measuring and Reporting on Environmental Policy Performance in the Context of Sustainable Development*, p. 1)

Three categories of indicators determine whether progress is being made towards the objectives of improved livelihoods and sustainable environments: impact indicators; process indicators; and sustainability indicators. For each category, we suggest four sub-topics. These indicators, of course, require baseline data to determine the nature and rate of progress towards the objectives. We discuss each in turn.

## Impact indicators

Impacts have both quantitative and qualitative dimensions:

- *Productivity* can be measured in terms of increased output per given unit of land, inputs, labour, or period of time. Improved productivity may also be a matter of decreased labour time for the same output, and it can be determined by measuring income.

- *Welfare* has many dimensions. It should be possible to select those most relevant to the type of project, e.g. health, educational opportunity, nutrition, improved housing, better sanitation.

- *Equity* as a measure will suggest how broadly based are the improvements in welfare and productivity. It requires consideration of social groups and suggests that the contextual analysis (as part of the primary data-gathering exercises) is an important component of building indicators.

- *Environment* requires measures of the ways in which a project is affecting soil fertility, water quality and retention, erosion, natural vegetation, and biodiversity.

## Process indicators

There are a great many 'process' issues which might be measured in connection with projects, all leading to increased capacities and self-reliance. We identify four:

- *Capacity building* on the part of individuals or a local group in a community. What new skills have been acquired; what local knowledge has been identified and used; what institutions have been strengthened?

- *Organisational skills* suggest the development of group capabilities in identifying problems, prioritising solutions, implementing programme, dealing with conflict, consensus building, negotiation, and problem solving.

- *Leadership* is an essential element in strengthening local communities. The emergence of local leadership committed to these goals and able to mobilise and organise local groups is an important part of this process.

- *Partnerships* can strengthen development efforts through linking the various stakeholders in a common effort. Partnerships which build relationships between local communities and external agents, regional, national, and even international, can help bring a project to fruition and can serve as an indicator that the project is not likely to wither in isolation and neglect.

## Sustainability indicators

These are essential for determining not only the viability of the project at the moment the evaluation is being prepared, but also its longevity and influence. We identify four:

- *Replicability* suggests that others can readily undertake a similar project. If there is spontaneous replication, so much the better. The project is spreading on the basis of its own merits without an outside organiser or initiator.

- *Local ownership* is an important indicator of the project's lifetime. If local people find it useful, want it to continue, and are prepared to assume responsibility for assuring its continuation, local ownership has been achieved and so has a new level of local empowerment.

- *Cost-effectiveness* is an essential part of sustainability, although it may be difficult to separate it from the impact indicators. If the project is not cost-effective—in the broadest sense of the term, including all levels of effort required of local people to sustain it—then it is unlikely to be supported by local residents. Three types of cost-effectiveness, each designed to meet the needs of different kinds of projects, include: (1) measures of costs in comparison with community resources; (2) the ratio of net benefits to costs; and (3) the ratio of per-unit costs.

- *Environmental suitability* is an essential element of sustainability. If the project or programme has, on balance, a negative impact on the environment, it may bring short-term benefits (such as some types of mining) but is not sustainable in the long term. Many projects have both positive and negative effects on the environment, and these must be weighed in each situation.

Table 1 clarifies how the indicators connect to the enabling conditions, revealing the latter's relevance to meeting environmental and economic objectives in the five cases.

| Table 1: Indicators, enabling conditions, and illustrative changes in the five cases | | | |
|---|---|---|---|
| **Enabling conditions** | **Impact** | **Process** | **Sustainability** |
| Extension and training | *Environment* Improved, intensive farming on farm-land resulting from new information (Nigeria) | *Partnerships* Household and community adoption of aquaculture over time (Rwanda) | *Local ownership* Group organisation of AI services (Kenya) |
| Local participation and organisation | *Productivity* Increased productivity /sales through communal efforts (The Gambia) | *Capacity building* Organised farmer production groups (Rwanda) | *Cost-effectiveness* Spontaneous repli-cation of communal vegetable gardens (The Gambia) |
| Gender-disaggregated data | *Equity* Extension services targeted to women-headed households (Malawi) | *Leadership* Household income earnings by men and women (The Gambia) | *Local ownership* (i.e. national instead of donor ownership) Integration of data into national plan-ning process (Malawi) |
| Livelihood security | *Welfare* Improved nutrition/ sales from aqua-culture (Rwanda) | *Organisational skills* Farmers keep records showing increased milk yield from high breed cows (Kenya) | *Environmental suitability* Group members rehabilitate soil with compost (Rwanda) |
| Partnerships and linkages | *Productivity* New technologies and higher yields resulting from inter-national and national research linkages (Nigeria) | *Capacity building* Long-term collabo-ration of extension services, farmer organisations, and researchers (Malawi) | *Replicability* New groups under-taking partnerships/ projects (Kenya) |

# Using the indicators to monitor the Chanderema dairy project

To demonstrate how a research project or organisation can monitor its progress and adapt to a changing situation, based on our discussion of relevant indicators and enabling conditions, we have structured the experience of the Chanderema Women's Group dairy project in a way which highlights our points. The primary objective of the Chanderema Women's Group involved generating income for the group. The group and FSK decided to launch a dairy project for the purpose of selling milk, and since the milk output of the exotic Jersey breed is superior to that of the indigenous breed, project personnel and participants opted to introduce Jerseys into the community.

Treating this project with the benefit of hindsight allows us to demonstrate how data-gathering tools can best be employed. Hypothetically, then, primary data are collected to inform project development. Various tools are used to gather data which permit the community to see the opportunities and constraints facing the proposed dairy project idea. Some of the constraints include, first, that the indigenous cattle are kept for dowry purposes. However, the indigenous breed consumes a large amount of fodder and competes with the Jersey cows, thereby jeopardising the health and milk-producing capacity of the new cattle. Second, the land and the cash crops are controlled by men, and one-quarter of household farmland is devoted to cash crops instead of staple crops; therefore a limited amount of land is available to women to plant fodder cultivars for the cows. Third, success of the project depends on a reliable artificial insemination service, but the government service is inefficient and cannot be relied upon. On the plus side, the government encourages the raising of exogenous cattle, notwithstanding the problem of its inadequate support services. If well organised, the Chanderema group may be able to mobilise to get government extension services to assist their enterprise.

Based on analysis of these primary data, the strategic details of the women's group's objective—to generate income for members' households—can be reformulated by the women's group and FSK. Strategies must negotiate the cultural, political, and institutional constraints confronted by the participants, as well as tapping into the opportunities. Perhaps cultural traditions, such as the passing on of indigenous cattle for dowries, can adapt to a changing situation, and men might choose to accept exogenous, milk-producing cattle instead. In this way, households could increase their Jersey herds and enjoy greater milk yields. Working on strategies may generate new objectives, therefore, which reach beyond pragmatic issues such as earning income. The new objectives may include lobbying to change the government policy that obliges households to keep cash crops on land, when they would rather replace cash crops with subsistence and fodder crops. They may also include training community members in artificial insemination techniques, so that they may at least get the necessary materials (if not the personnel) from the government to carry out artificial insemination services.

Once the objectives are reformulated, the participants and development agency can look ahead to a regular monitoring of the activity. This necessitates selecting well-defined indicators which pay attention to impact, process, and sustainability. When, for example, group members receive the new cows, does the higher milk production result in a noticeable increase in income, or is all money sinking back into veterinary or insemination services (impact)? What is the increase in income (impact)? If members succeed in reducing the number of indigenous cattle owned by their households, is fodder adequate for the new breeds (impact)? How did members accomplish the reduction of indigenous cattle, i.e. did they consult with the whole household (process)? Will men continue to accept the new arrangement (sustainability)? Does the increase in milk improve the nutritional level of the household (impact, sustainability)? Are more residents interested in joining the Chanderema group after seeing its success (sustainability)? Are group members motivated to address the relevant government agency concerning the problem of inadequate insemination services (process)? Regular evaluations should incorporate issues that span the range of indicators. It is largely due to the lack of regular, thorough evaluation that documented evidence concerning successful women-controlled resource management activities is scarce.

After the evaluation is complete, it is time to assess the current context. Have social changes in the community occurred as a result of the activity? Interviews and other tools can be administered, and the data can be re-analysed. Depending on whether the situation has changed, with objectives met or prevented, the participants can reformulate objectives and strategies once again, always with an eye to monitoring and evaluating indicators of impact, process, and sustainability. This cycle can continue until the donor or facilitating agency eventually pulls out of the project and the group is able to manage or redirect the activity independently, the true sign of sustainability. Table 2 reveals the usefulness of the indicators for a specific project.

## Concluding observations

The analysis of these five cases clarifies ways in which gender shapes the opportunities and constraints that African men and women face in securing viable livelihoods and strong community institutions

| Table 2: Using the indicators to monitor the Chanderema dairy project | | |
|---|---|---|
| **Impact** | **Process** | **Sustainability** |
| *Productivity* The change in levels of milk sales and income since the introduction of the Chanderema women's project | *Capacity building* Effectiveness of group members working together to solve problems | *Replicability* Other groups interested in undertaking similar projects |
| *Welfare* Improvement in nutrition with the increase in milk production among Chanderema Group members' households | *Organisational skills* New skills introduced to the Chanderema Women's Group | *Local ownership* Actions taken by group when a cow dies or a critical element in a project malfunctions |
| *Equity* Opportunities generated by the Chanderema Group which are equitably distributed among group members | *Leadership* Emergent leaders from group who have mobilising capabilities and commitment to project | *Cost-effectiveness* The ratio of per unit benefits to costs, including units of land and labour |
| *Environment* The use of land for fodder competing with other land users' claims | *Partnerships* Partner organisations working effectively towards mutually understood and agreed upon objectives | *Environmental suitability* Long-term prospect of land supporting dairy projects, accounting for smallholder farming, fodder management, and zero-based grazing |

across cultural, political, economic, and ecological settings. It further identifies both the conditions under which women can more effectively manage land and other resources and the ways in which women are crucial contributors to community livelihoods and adept resource managers. The case analysis suggests that if policy, programmes, and projects are to foster sustainable, effective, and equitable management of resources, they must address the concerns of men and women and the ways in which they, individually and collectively, relate to the State, the economy, and the resource base.

Researchers can help this process by sensitive awareness of the issues and careful contextual, social, institutional, and project analysis. Development professionals can assist by a sustained effort to build gender-inclusive programmes and to attend to capacity-building processes. Donor agencies must recognise the impacts their changing agendas may have on the larger context in which struggles over land, resources, and livelihoods occur. In fact, the development aid system itself can become part of the ongoing struggles within any community and can potentially bring harm or benefit.

These case studies have provided ample evidence to support the assertion that prospects for achieving livelihood security and sustainable environments in Africa will be improved if women have a more central role in resource-management decisions. These five cases highlight enabling conditions which facilitate effective involvement of both men and women in natural-resource management, including:

- pertinent *gender-disaggregated data* routinely collected for baseline, monitoring, and evaluation purposes;
- effective and gender-aware *extension and training*, to ensure that new technologies and new procedures are fully integrated into natural-resource management project efforts;
- local *participation and organisation*, central to capacity building at the local level, which, in turn, helps to strengthen projects and leads to their sustainability;
- positive impact on *livelihood security*, which can occur in a variety of ways, from dune-stabilisation or water-control measures, to access to new seedlings, new credit opportunities, or new technologies;
- *linkages and partnerships* across issues of infrastructure, research, policy, training, and institution building, which can build project success.

A variety of indicators can help to measure progress in terms of impact, process, and sustainability. They are useful both for researchers seeking careful analysis and presentation of their findings on matters of environmental and economic change and for development professionals who can build gender-inclusive programmes, thereby increasing women's involvement—and both equity and effectiveness —in resource management.

## Notes

1  This paper is based on data gathered in 1995 and 1996 through Clark University's Ecology, Community Organisation and Gender (ECOGEN) project. It resulted in a report by Barbara Thomas-Slayter, Genese Sodikoff and Eileen Reynolds entitled *Gender, Equity, and Effective Resource Management in Africa* (1996), which was funded through the Office of Technical Resources in the Africa Bureau of USAID. In-depth case materials were provided for this report by Dr Revathi Balakrishnan (Rwanda), Dr Lucy Kehinde (Nigeria), Dr Richard Schroeder (The Gambia), Dr Anita Spring (Malawi), and Ms Betty Wamalwa-Muragori (Kenya), who carried out the fieldwork in their respective sites. The works of these researchers are included in the references.

2　The projects were gleaned from a literature search from bilateral and multilateral development institutions that had implemented natural resource projects with a focus on gender issues. More than 50 cases from over 20 countries were reviewed. They included projects in a variety of natural resource management sectors including reforestation, improved agricultural technologies, land use, environmentally friendly technologies (e.g. solar or biogas energy or improved cooking stoves), extension and training, sustainable harvesting of plant products, water supply development, and soil erosion control. While the materials reviewed were largely in English, projects were reviewed from a range of non-anglophone countries, including Sudan, Madagascar, Senegal, Cameroon, Burkina Faso, Mali, Mauritania, Niger, and Cape Verde. Of the case studies, only five met the criteria of containing substantive data which demonstrated success.

# References

Balakrishnan, R., K. L. Veverica and P. Nyirahabimana (1993) *Rwanda Women in Aquaculture: Context, Contributions and Constraints*, Corvallis: Oregon State University, Office of Women in International Development.

Berry, S. (ed.) (1989) 'Access, control and use of resources in African agriculture', *Africa* 59(1):41–55.

Braidotti, R., E. Charkiewicz, S. Hausler and S. Wieringa (1994) *Women, the Environment and Sustainable Development*, London: Zed Books.

Carnegie Commission (1997) *Preventing Deadly Conflict*, Final Report of the Carnegie Commission on Preventing Deadly Conflict, New York: Carnegie Corporation.

Collins, J. L. (1991) 'Women and the environment: social reproduction and sustainable development', in R. S. Gallin and A. Ferguson (eds.) *The Women and International Development Annual*, Volume 2, Boulder, CO: Westview Press.

Gianotten, V., V. Groverman, E. van Walsum and L. Zuidberg (1994) *Assessing the Gender Impact of Development Projects*, The Hague: Royal Tropical Institute.

Hammond, A., A. Adriaanse, E. Rodenburg, D. Bryant and R. Woodward (1995) *Environmental Indicators: A Systematic Approach to Measuring and Reporting on Environmental Policy Performance in the Context of Sustainable Development*, Washington, DC: World Resources Institute.

Hishamunda, N. and J. F. Moehl Jr (1989) *Rwanda National Fish Culture Project*, International Center for Aquaculture Research and Development Series, No. 34, Alabama: Alabama Agricultural Experiment Station, Auburn University.

Kabeer, N. (1991) 'Gender dimensions of rural poverty: analysis from Bangladesh', *Journal of Peasant Studies* (18)21:241–61.

Kabeer, N. (1992) 'Evaluating cost–benefit analysis as a tool for gender planning', *Development and Change* 23(2):115–39.

Kehinde, L. (1995) 'Farmers' information-seeking behavior, and impact of information source on soybean technology adoption in Nigeria', unpublished dissertation, Urbana: University of Illinois.

Lastarria-Cornhiel, S. (1994) 'Policy guidelines for incorporating gender in natural resource tenure', unpublished draft.

Mehra, R. (1993) *Gender in Community Development and Resource Management:*

*An Overview*, Washington, DC: ICRW.

Njoroge, C. (1995) 'Evaluation Report of Chanderema/Gavudia Heifer/AI Project (Phase II)', Project implemented by Farming Systems Kenya and funded by Africa 2000 Network, Nairobi.

Overholt, C., M. Anderson, K. Cloud and J. Austin (eds.) (1985) *Gender Roles in Development Projects: A Case Book*, West Hartford, CO: Kumarian Press.

Rocheleau, D., B. Thomas-Slayter and E. Wangari (1996) *Feminist Political Ecology: Global Issues and Local Experiences*, London: Routledge.

Schroeder, R. (1993) 'Shady practice: gender and the political ecology of resource stabilisation in Gambian gardens/orchards', *Economic Geography* 69(4):349–65.

Schroeder, R. (1995) 'Contradictions along the commodity road to environmental stabilisation: foresting Gambian gardens', *Antipode* 27(4): 325–42.

Sen, A. (1990) 'Gender and cooperative conflicts', in I. Tinker (ed.) *Persistent Inequalities*, Oxford: OUP.

Spring, A. (1995) *The Women in Agricultural Development Project in Malawi: A Case Study*, unpublished case study, Gainesville: University of Florida.

Thomas-Slayter, B. (1992) 'Politics, class and gender in African resource management: the case of rural Kenya', *Economic Development and Cultural Change* 40(4):809–28.

Thomas-Slayter, B. and D. Rocheleau (1994) 'Research frontiers at the nexus of gender, environment, and development: linking household, community, and ecosystem', in *The Women and International Development Annual*, Boulder, CO: Westview Press.

Uvin, P. (1998) *Aiding Violence: The Development Enterprise in Rwanda*, West Hartford, CO: Kumarian Press.

Wamalwa-Muragori, B. (1995) Project reports from Chanderema Dairy Project, Nairobi: Africa 2000 Network, UNDP 1992–1995.

# Critical Incidents in emergency relief work

## Maureen Raymond-McKay and Malcolm MacLachlan

## Introduction

Emergency relief work is now routinely undertaken by many local and international NGOs, national governments, and UN agencies. In the economically less developed countries of the 'Third World', such work is often set in motion by wealthier Northern countries, which send specialist personnel to assist with the disaster response. Where human life is at risk, nurses and doctors are commonly among those who are dispatched. Such *technical assistance* (as it is referred to) understandably emphasises the importance of professional and technical qualifications. However, it is hard to imagine what could prepare one for the altogether overwhelming experience of, for instance, being a Charge Nurse in a well-resourced rural Scandinavian hospital on a Monday, and then by Wednesday being responsible for the provision of scant basic health services to thousands of malnourished, possibly traumatised, and certainly distressed, people in a dust-bowl of a refugee camp, miles from any form of back-up or respite.

Resource-poor environments, such as desolate refugee camps, seem to cry out for *technical assistance*—food, medicine, shelter, machinery, sanitation, and so on, and the expertise to provide them. However, those who provide such assistance are often seen simply as the conduits of international aid. The development literature, in general, has been relatively silent about the people who deliver international aid, even though there is considerable evidence to suggest that *individuals*, rather than simply the materials with which they are associated, determine the success of an aid project (Cassen 1994; Kealey 1990; Carr et al. 1998).

Parallel with this emphasis on material, rather than human, resources, is a focus on *outcome* rather than *process* (MacLachlan 1996). Again, this is entirely understandable, as international aid aims to return distressed, impoverished, and/or unhealthy people to a state of well-being. However, the danger is that by looking towards that goal we look past the processes necessary to achieve it. By focusing on the 'hardware' of technical assistance in relief and/or development work, we do not recognise the importance of '*people* skills' in facilitating interventions. A quarter of a century ago Schnapper (1973) stated that 'The history of international development is strewn with the wreckage of many development projects. One of the major conclusions that emerges from this history is the lack, not of technical skills, but of interpersonal and intercultural adaptation skills' (quoted in Kealey 1990:2). This conclusion is as apt today as it was then: O'Dwyer states that one of the main reasons why aid projects fail is ' ... poor design, including the failure to take full account of the human and social environment' (1994:436).

It is well known that working in another culture can be a stressful experience (MacLachlan 1997). Furnham (1990) describes seven factors which are related to the degree of stress experienced by expatriates: distance from home, how similar the new country of residence is to home, how similar the new job is to the previous one, the quantity and quality of social support in the new environment, how secure the person's job is at home, and to what extent individuals have moved on a voluntary basis. Clearly the context of one's placement, in personal, social, and geographical terms, is very important for coping with cross-cultural transitions. In a study of more than 1,000 Swedish business expatriates, men (rather than women), the better educated, those who socialised more with host nationals, those who had a special interest in the host country, and those whose spouse was more satisfied with their move, found that adjustment was easier. Again, both the way in which individuals interacted with their new environment, and their social and personal relationships, were key factors in their adjustment. Perhaps surprisingly, previous overseas experience was not associated with better adjustment, a finding that has been confirmed for international aid workers in developing countries (Gow 1991; Kealey 1989).

While working cross-culturally may present personnel with significant challenges, such challenges are surely augmented by the materially impoverished contexts that characterise many developing countries, which are major recipients of international aid. Bennett (1986) suggests that disconfirmed expectations, role ambiguity, social isolation, confrontation with one's own prejudices, and general anxiety may be experienced. Also, the lack of material resources and professional support to which they are accustomed can undermine the confidence of health professionals.

When individuals are dispatched to emergency relief operations, the speed of response may be crucial, leaving these people inadequately prepared psychologically, socially, domestically, and simply in terms of the pragmatics of arranging for leave from their regular job and organising their departure. Given that the environment into which emergency relief workers are deployed is often so very different from that in which they received their training or currently practise, it is important to identify the sorts of skill which are instrumental in attempting to achieve their goals.

To identify such skills it is necessary first to know what goals individuals are working to achieve. While such goals may seem obvious, in emergency relief work there are often many competing needs which can call for fieldworkers' attention. This is an important issue, as clarity of objectives and of work roles has been shown to correlate with job satisfaction, emotional reactions, tension, personal adjustment, job commitment, and *job performance* (Jackson and Schuler 1985; Ilgen and Hollenbeck 1991; Netermeyer et al. 1990).

While there has been voluminous academic discussion and theorising on what technical assistance *should* be about, and what sorts of skill *should* be taught, insufficient attention has been given to fieldworkers' experiences of what actually happens *in situ*. In the present study we used the Critical Incident Technique (CIT) to investigate emergency relief workers' goals and the skills that they themselves found most useful in trying to achieve them.

## Method

### Subjects

The participants were 15 nurses (all women), with a mean age of 39 years (range 29–50 years), all of whom had been engaged in emergency relief work within the past three months to five years. This study was undertaken with the co-operation of Comhlamh (an umbrella organisation for returned development workers in Ireland), which forwarded a letter to the addresses (stored on its database) of a randomised quota sample of 100 people living in or around Dublin, who had returned from international aid assignments within the time period specified. This sample received a letter inviting them to take part in a project 'looking at the experiences of Irish development workers during their period of work overseas'. The letter indicated that informal interviews would take approximately one hour and be held in Trinity College, Dublin. The letter emphasised that '[i]t will *not* be an evaluation of you or your organisation. ... The long-term aim of the project is to improve training programmes for international aid workers. It is therefore important for us to learn about your personal and first hand experiences in the field.' Invitees were asked to complete a form indicating their willingness to participate in the project, and return it in a stamped addressed envelope. They were also given a number to telephone in case they wanted any more information about the research project before committing to it. Participants were offered no payment or any other form of inducement to take part in the research.

Replies were received from half of the sample, although many of these were on behalf of the person we had written to, informing us that they were not presently in the country. Twenty-two people agreed to participate in the study and were interviewed within two months of receiving the invitation. Seven of these people were engaged in long-term development assignments, and their data constitute part of another project. The present study reports on the interview data derived from 15 nurses who had been engaged in emergency relief assignments.

## Critical Incident Technique (CIT)

Since the CIT is a methodology which is not widely used in research on health or international development, we briefly describe its origins, rationale, and procedure.

Flanagan (1954) developed the CIT and described it as ' ... a set of procedures for collecting direct observations of human behaviour in such a way as to facilitate their potential usefulness in solving practical problems and developing broad psychological principles. The Critical Incident Technique outlines procedures for collecting observed incidents having special significance and meeting systematically defined criteria' (p. 327).

The CIT is a technique for collecting incidents which the respondent feels have been critical to his or her experience of the job. The incidents are recorded, and discussion of these incidents helps to elucidate a composite picture of job behaviour. The particular form of eliciting Critical Incidents was the same as that used by MacLachlan and McAuliffe (1993) and Kanyangale and MacLachlan (1995).

After a brief introduction, participants were told that 'in this interview we are going to ask you to identify some incidents which have occurred during your emergency relief assignment. These incidents should be "critical incidents". They should be events which have made a strong impact on you. A Critical Incident has a beginning and an end, and its outcome is relatively important to the objectives of your assignment.'

## Statements of objectives

'The first stage of identifying Critical Incidents is to define what the objects of your work are, as you understand them. We do not want to know how other people have described what the aims of your work were, we want to know your opinions based on your experience of the work. You are the "expert" on the job *you* were doing. You are therefore in the best position to define its objectives, as you have experienced them.' The interviewees were asked to try and name four to six objectives 'which are specific, not general or ambiguous'.

## Recording of Critical Incidents

Following the identification of objectives, which were read out by each interviewee, they were then asked to try and relate one incident which had had a positive impact on them and one which they regarded as negative. They were given Incident Sheets, which were vertically divided into two columns. One column was headed 'Incident Details' and the other 'Abilities/Characteristics'. The interviewees were asked to write brief notes, under the 'Incident Detail' column, on each of the two sheets.

# Probing of Critical Incidents

Once the incidents had been recorded, the interviewer then concentrated on each one in turn. The first part of the interview involved probing the interviewee for more information about the incident: 'What led up to the incident?', 'Why did the incident occur?', 'Who was involved?', 'What were you thinking/feeling?', 'How did you attempt to deal with it ... ?', and 'If the incident occurred again, how would you deal with it?' The function of these probes was to make the incident as vivid as possible, and in doing so heighten the interviewee's recall of the learning experience.

## Specifying job-related attributes

Once a full description of the incident had been obtained, interviewees were asked the following question: 'Taking this incident as an example of the sort of work your job requires, what would you say are the main abilities or characteristics that somebody should have, in order to perform well in the job?' The interviewer then noted the attributes that were described by the interviewee, and continued the discussion to probe further and clarify some of the ideas put forward by the interviewee.

Once the discussion of a particular incident seemed to be drawing to a close, the interviewer read through the list of attributes which had been identified as relevant to dealing with the job-related Critical Incident described. This process was completed for each Critical Incident; the whole procedure took between two and three hours for each participant.

# Results

## Identification of work objectives

Table 1 presents a thematic content analysis of the work objectives identified by the 15 participants. Only those themes mentioned by two or more individuals are included. In total, 61 different work objectives were mentioned, with 15 of these being mentioned by only one person. On average, participants identified four work objectives each. By far the most frequently mentioned theme (by 12 participants) was the provision of basic medical and/or food aid. The second most frequently mentioned objective (by seven participants), was the desire to fulfil a personal ambition to help 'Third World' or developing countries, and thirdly, to train indigenous workers to provide the service that the expatriate was currently providing (mentioned by six participants). However, it is noteworthy that fewer than half of the sample mentioned the second and third most common objectives, reflecting the variety of objectives held by the participants during their emergency relief work. In some instances this may have been due to the very specific nature of the project (e.g. 'to assess needs of prisoners of war', 'to encourage those with TB to remain in the area for the full term of the TB programme', 'to trace families of unaccompanied children'; each mentioned by one person), or due to specific motivations (e.g. 'to enhance managerial skills as the co-ordinator of a programme', 'to educate myself regarding the political situation of the country', 'to set a good example to indigenous workers'; each mentioned by one person). It is clear from Table 1 that in our sample the 15 nurses were not focused on the same few objectives, but sought to achieve a diverse range of objectives.

| Table 1: Objective of the work of emergency aid assignees | |
| --- | --- |
| Statement of objectives | Frequency |
| Provide adults/children with basic medical/food aid | 12 |
| Fulfil personal ambition to help 'Third World'/developing countries | 7 |
| Train indigenous workers to enable them to run/staff the project | 6 |
| Improve and help conditions in the 'Third World'/developing countries | 5 |
| Use experience and skills to assist where most needed | 4 |
| Accept and integrate into the host nation's culture | 3 |
| Increase own knowledge of 'Third World'/developing countries | 3 |
| Undertake a new challenge | 2 |
| Keep good written records to ensure continuity of care | 2 |
| Encourage local people to foster orphaned refugee children | 2 |

## Identification of job-related skills

To illustrate how the job-related skills were identified, and something of the character of the incidents described, we present summaries of four Critical Incidents (two positive and two negative): Each of these relates the experiences of nurses working in refugee camps. The first incident cited here was rated as *negative* by the interviewee. She was engaged in assessing the feeding and basic medical requirements of refugees, and prioritising for assistance to those most in need, according to the standards set by the aid agency. Approximately 3,000 people per week would pass through the feeding centre. A six-month-old infant had been identified as being in urgent need of nutritional assistance and to this end was provided with a gastro-nasal feeding tube. The mother subsequently removed the feeding tube and the infant died. It emerged that the mother had decided that available resources would best be given to her other children who had in her opinion a more realistic chance of surviving. The interviewee was shocked and distressed at first, but eventually came to terms, as best she could, with what turned out to be a not infrequent occurrence.

The principal skills identified here were the ability to respect the dignity, customs, and traditions of others (specifically the tendency of the mothers to reject the weakest child in order to maximise the survival chances of the sturdier children); to recognise the limits of the job—especially in regard to handing out advice which has little relevance in a war-torn situation (evidenced by the mother's response to aid workers' intervention to save the child). The remaining skills identified were related to how best to cope on a personal level with a survival ethos which is generally uncalled for in a stable Western environment. These include being able to express one's emotions; good interpersonal relationships with colleagues; being able to nourish oneself after a day's work without feeling guilty.

The second Critical Incident describes the experience of a nurse who managed a feeding centre for refugees. This incident was also rated as a *negative* one. On taking up the post, she realised that it was more appropriate to a nutritionist than a nurse. She felt swamped and unable to cope. She decided to find as many books as possible on the subject. She sought advice from medical colleagues and the organisation's field director. She established a rapport with local employees whom she found to be a valuable source of information. After about three weeks, she felt competent to set out to achieve her objectives.

The job skills identified from this incident were being able to identify the requirements of the job (from the recognition that the job was more appropriate to a nutritionist); making full use of available resources (by asking for help and advice from colleagues and getting hold of the appropriate textbooks); and openness to learning from local workers (by entering into the team spirit).

The third Critical Incident, which was rated as *positive*, concerns the relationship between personnel within a refugee agency. A satellite telephone dish was stolen from outside the residence of the donor organisation. An investigation was carried out by the local (indigenous) assistant co-ordinator of the project, who attributed blame to the 'opposing' tribe. The organisation's co-ordinator directed that the wages of the indigenous workers (belonging to the 'opposing' tribe) would be cut by 25 per cent to pay for the cost of the new dish. The interviewee felt very strongly that this was an unjust course of action; but she found that other expatriates who agreed with her were disinclined to challenge this unilateral decision of the group leader. The indigenous workers organised a protest, and the decision to cut the wages was rescinded. Instead, a reward was offered for the return of the dish. The dish was returned a week later and, it seems, had not been stolen by the accused tribe. A considerable amount of damage was done to the relationship between the indigenous and expatriate workers by the way in which the matter was handled.

The characteristics identified from this incident included the employment of fair practices in dealing with co-workers (because of the failure to do so in this case); assertiveness (because of the reluctance of some expatriate workers to challenge their manager); showing sensitivity to the feelings of others (because of failure to do so); and the ability to resolve conflict (following the protest by indigenous workers).

The fourth Critical Incident, also rated as *positive,* concerned the selection and training of an indigenous worker to assess who, of his own people, were most in need of being admitted to a refugee-feeding programme. The interviewee selected a young man who she considered to have the necessary ability to undertake the job. The young man had great difficulty at first in turning away his own people who did not meet the required criteria for acceptance to the feeding centre. However, after a week's training she (the interviewee) felt confident that the trainee would be capable of carrying out the job with only intermittent supervision and she was happy to hand it over to him.

The characteristics identified from this example were ability to assess suitable workers (the trainee turned out to be an able worker, despite his initial misgivings); willingness to hand over the job to indigenous workers (which is what subsequently happened); ability to pass on skills; having trust and belief in indigenous co-workers (in allowing the trainee to work unsupervised).

Table 2 summarises the job-related skills identified through analysis of the 34 Critical Incidents reported by participants. This table presents only those skills mentioned by two or more individuals. In total, 139 job-related skills were derived; these were collapsed into 54 distinct skills. Thirty-one of these skills, or characteristics, are described in Table 2, the basis for their inclusion being that they were derived from two or more Critical Incidents. As an aid to further analysis, we have presented these under five broad themes, although some items could easily be classified under more than one of these themes. The number of times a particular skill was mentioned is given, along with the number of times it arose in a positive or negative Critical Incident. Sub-totals for each of the five themes are also presented.

## Coping skills

A sense of humour, ability to relax and detach when off duty, and knowing one's own limitations were identified as coping skills. These skills were mentioned twice as often in the context of negative Critical Incidents as in the context of positive ones, suggesting that it was often the lack of these skills that produced negative outcomes for the participants. Other coping skills, each mentioned by only one person, included accepting failure, knowing how to express emotions appropriately, and knowing how to deal with homesickness.

## Table 2: Job-related skills identified from Critical Incident analysis

| | Positive incident | Negative incident | Total |
|---|---|---|---|
| **Coping skills** | | | |
| Sense of humour | 3 | 4 | 7 |
| Ability to detach and relax off duty | 1 | 4 | 5 |
| Knowing one's own limitations | 1 | 2 | 3 |
| Sub-totals | 5 | 10 | 15 |
| **Relationship skills** | | | |
| Sensitivity to values of other cultures | 5 | 2 | 7 |
| Patience (adapt to local pace) | 4 | 3 | 7 |
| Being able to ask advice from colleagues | 3 | 2 | 5 |
| Openness to learning from local people | 3 | 1 | 4 |
| Willingness to hand over to local workers | 3 | 1 | 4 |
| Sensitivity to feelings of indigenous population | 1 | 1 | 2 |
| Sub-totals | 19 | 10 | 29 |
| **Communication skills** | | | |
| Diplomacy/tact | 3 | 4 | 7 |
| Good social skills | 4 | 2 | 6 |
| Negotiating skills | 1 | 3 | 4 |
| Good relations with expatriate colleagues | 0 | 3 | 3 |
| Ability to establish rapport | 1 | 1 | 2 |
| Use of touch with seriously ill people | 1 | 1 | 2 |
| Sub-totals | 10 | 14 | 24 |
| **Analytical skills** | | | |
| Good interviewing skills for recruiting locals | 3 | 0 | 3 |
| Ability to achieve closure | 0 | 3 | 3 |
| Ability to predict project sustainability | 1 | 2 | 3 |
| Use of democratic practices with all workers | 2 | 1 | 3 |
| Not being impulsive | 2 | 1 | 3 |
| Good programme evaluation skills | 1 | 1 | 2 |
| Regular evaluation of programme | 2 | 0 | 2 |
| Motivating locals to accept responsibility | 1 | 1 | 2 |
| Sub-totals | 12 | 9 | 21 |
| **Internal motivations** | | | |
| Assertiveness | 2 | 2 | 4 |
| Adaptability | 1 | 3 | 4 |
| Flexibility | 4 | 0 | 4 |
| Initiative | 2 | 0 | 2 |
| Decisiveness | 2 | 0 | 2 |
| Tolerance | 0 | 2 | 2 |
| Resourcefulness | 2 | 0 | 2 |
| Stubbornness | 1 | 1 | 2 |
| Sub-totals | 14 | 8 | 22 |
| **Grand totals** | 60 | 51 | 111 |

### Relationship skills

Relationship skills were the most frequently mentioned sort of skill, being mentioned almost twice as frequently in the context of positive incidents as in negative incidents. Sensitivity to the values of other cultures and a willingness to adapt to the (slower) pace of life were each noted by seven participants. Some of the relationship skills mentioned by only one individual included entering into a team spirit with local workers, and having a genuine interest in the people whom one is helping.

### Communication skills

Being diplomatic/tactful, having good social skills, and being willing to negotiate were the most frequently cited communication skills. The importance of establishing good relationships with expatriate colleagues was also noted in three different negative Critical Incidents. Communication skills, including non-verbal communication such as touching; using simple straightforward language, and having the ability to probe, were each mentioned by one person.

### Analytical skills

No particular analytical skills dominated this category; all the skills derived through analysing Critical Incidents were found for either one, two, or three individuals. The pragmatics of selecting local colleagues to work with showed interviewing skills to be important, and such skills were cited in three positive incidents. On the other hand, the ability (or inability) to bring matters to a satisfactory conclusion and achieve a sense of closure was cited in three negative incidents. Skills cited in only one instance included responding to the needs of the local community rather than those dictated by the fieldworker's role, the ability to pass on skills, and recognising one's mistakes and apologising when necessary.

### Self skills

While all of the above skills relate in some way to how the relief worker treats herself, the skills grouped under the theme of 'Self skills' especially emphasise this ability. Assertiveness, adaptability, and flexibility were the most frequently cited skills. We use the term 'adaptability' to refer to the ability to move on to another area of work when required to do so, rather than seeing oneself as having competence in only a specific narrow area. By 'flexibility' we mean flexibility in matters such as the interpretation of rules. Less frequently mentioned skills included perseverance, autonomy, and maintaining optimism (each mentioned by only one person).

## Discussion

### Work objectives

The degree to which people share work objectives can be taken to reflect their 'cohesion of purpose'. Clearly, however, we would not expect people responding to different emergency situations in different parts of the world, and under different local living conditions, to specify the same objectives. Indeed, although 12 of our 15 participants reported the provision of basic medical or food aid as one of their objectives, more than 60 different work objectives were derived through the CIT, with a quarter of these being given by only one person. In the evaluation of any project it is, therefore, important to realise that not everybody is motivated to achieve the same objectives, and that an individual's objectives may differ from those of the sending agency, or of the recipient community.

The objectives reported in Table 1 reflect three broad themes: *helping* (e.g. 'To improve and help conditions in the Third World'), *benefiting* (e.g. 'To undertake a new challenge') and *being task-focused* (e.g. 'To keep good written records to ensure continuity of care'), with many objectives reflecting more than one of these themes (e.g. 'To fulfil personal ambition to help the Third World'). The 'helping' or altruistic motives reported by Irish workers in this study coincide with previous surveys in Ireland which have noted strong support for helping developing countries (ACDC 1990). While aid motivated by personal, humanitarian, or charitable concerns may have its value, it should also be informed by awareness of the larger structural causes of poverty, and in Ireland this has not necessarily been the case (ibid.). While it is certainly desirable for aid workers to be motivated by altruism, this is never going to be sufficient, and more emphasis should be placed on educating them on the social, economic, and political context in which relief and development operations occur.

The second theme of 'benefiting', or personal fulfilment, is an aspect of international development and/or relief work which is becoming increasingly recognised. In their study of Irish development workers, O'Dwyer and Woodhouse (1996) note that development workers, in common with volunteers in general, have self-interested motivations such as career development and the opportunity to acquire new knowledge and skills. It is entirely reasonable that such 'pay-offs' be explicitly acknowledged, and indeed promoted, for the purposes of recruitment.

Being 'task-focused', the third theme to emerge from the objectives reported, reflects objectives which are rather specific to the context of intervention. However, it may also reflect a concern with the achievement of specific goals—a focus on outcomes, rather than on a more abstract 'reason for being there'—and perhaps a concern for *how* progress is made.

## Skills

We grouped the themes concerning job-related skills under five headings: 'Coping', 'Relationships', 'Communication skills', 'Analytical skills', and 'Internal motivations'. Perhaps the most striking aspect of the skills that emerged from the analysis of Critical Incidents is that they are, by and large, concerned with *how things get done*, rather than with *what* is done. That is to say, they reflect a concern with *process skills* rather than with *technical skills*. Only the category 'Analytical skills' (which had less than one fifth of the skills elicited) explicitly incorporates a concern with outcomes (by, for instance, having an 'ability to achieve closure' or 'ability to predict project sustainability'). However, even when a lack of technical skills is seen as a problem, for instance in the second Critical Incident described, where a nurse felt that the skills of a nutritionist would be more appropriate, the ability to do something about this was derived from openness to learning from indigenous workers, making full use of available resources, and the ability to recognise the requirements of the job.

The four specific skills that achieved the highest endorsement (by seven different people) were sense of humour, sensitivity to the values of other cultures, patience, and diplomacy/tact. If these are indeed among the most important skills for aid workers to possess, few professional training or pre-departure courses can claim to provide a grounding in them. The first three categories of skill are essentially concerned with how individuals operate in their work environment, be it in relation to others (relationship and communication skills) or in relation to themselves (coping skills). While such skills may be related to personality characteristics, the fifth category of Internal Motivations is more explicitly concerned with this. Although Kealey (1994) suggests that most donors appreciate the value of adaptability, communication skills, motivation, flexibility, cross-cultural sensitivity, initiative, realism, and patience, MacLachlan and Carr (1998) argue that there is often no systematic way of assessing such requirements, or of measuring how effective such skills are in the field. Recruitment policy, we argue, should be empirically, not theoretically, driven (MacLachlan and Carr 1998).

Given recognition of the importance of relationship and communication skills, it is surprising that language skills do not feature in Table 2. As long ago as 1961, the US Peace Corps introduced a requirement for each volunteer to be proficient in the local language of their assigned country or area, and this is generally looked upon as a landmark decision. The nature of the assignments investigated here, i.e. emergency relief work, probably militates against the practicalities of language training. Even so, we would have expected the lack of language skills to be a feature of some Critical Incidents, but this was not so. If language skills were not seen as critical to job performance as assessed through the Critical Incident methodology, then it is important to know why. Further research with emergency relief workers should probe this important area of communication between expatriate aid workers and the people they were assigned to work with.

In 1966, Byrnes described 'role shock' as an occupational hazard of technical assistants working abroad. It refers to the stresses and frustrations concomitant with discrepancies between expected, ideal, and experienced roles. Role conflict and role ambiguity have received considerable attention from occupational psychologists, and its psychosocial and health costs are well documented (see, for example, Winnubust 1984). Analysing the work practices of Irish development workers, O'Dwyer (1994) has noted 'considerable differences' between the perceptions of development workers and those of their 'supervisors' of the roles that development workers should be filling. It seems very likely that the same will apply to emergency relief work, where expectations may be relatively naïve, especially for 'first timers'.

Among the 'ways of working' identified by our methodology were patience, tact, openness to learning, being able to ask for advice, willingness to negotiate, adaptability, flexibility, initiative, tolerance, and resourcefulness. These all reflect a 'fluid' approach to working, as opposed to relying solely on more crystallised technical skills. Such 'fluid' skills are likely to promote tolerance of ambiguity. Given the confused, hectic, and unstructured nature of much relief work, tolerance in both social and work relationships may be very important for an individual's work performance and well-being.

## Limitations

It is important to recognise certain limitations to the present study. First, the participants were self-selected, and their willingness to take part in the research may reflect biases in terms of cultural values, personal experiences, self-perception, recall of events, age, sex (all females) and so on. While the aim of qualitative research is to develop a richer and deeper understanding of particular human experiences, it is difficult to assess the legitimacy of generalisation. However, while there were only 15 subjects in the present sample, this is a relatively large number, compared with other applications of the CIT (e.g. MacLachlan and McAuliffe 1993). It would clearly be desirable to evaluate the construct validity of the CIT by using other methods of job-skills analysis and comparing the outcome with that derived from the CIT. It would also be important for future research to investigate whether there are gender differences in the skills identified through the CIT.

Notwithstanding these limitations, the present research represents the first attempt to assess job skills in emergency relief work; and it has furnished behaviours and attitudes which have proved critical to the achievement of the objectives towards which people worked. As such, these job-related skills reflect valuable empirical data which could be incorporated into preparatory training courses for emergency relief work. While Critical Incidents have provided the 'data' for the present research, these same incidents could be used as the content of experiential learning, where participants on training courses could work through, and perhaps role play, the protagonists in various Critical Incidents, subsequently providing their own analyses and interpretations of the skills required for particular types of work in particular situations. Such a perspective could also profitably be used at the recruitment stage, where applicants could be asked to role play and subsequently analyse Critical Incidents in order to identify the applicants who are sensitive to the importance of the sorts of skill described above. Thus, Critical Incident analysis can provide a mechanism for returned aid workers effectively to feed back their own experiences into the training of those who may be sent to replace them on the same or similar assignments. Such a cycle of learning from experience, especially contextualised experience, may be one way in which fluid process skills can be identified, specified in terms of clear behaviours and attitudes, and enacted.

# References

ACDC (1990) 'Aid to Third World Countries: Attitudes of a National Sample of Irish People', Dublin: Advisory Council on Development Cooperation.

Bennett, M. J. (1986) 'A developmental approach to training for intercultural sensitivity', *International Journal of Intercultural Relations* 10:179–96.

Byrnes, F. (1966) 'Role shock: an occupational hazard of American technical assignments abroad', *Annals of the American Academy of Political and Social Science* 368:95–108.

Carr, S. C., E. McAuliffe and M. MacLachlan (1998) *Psychology of Aid*, London: Routledge.

Cassen, R. (1994) *Does Aid Work?*, Oxford: Oxford University Press.

Furnham, A. (1990) 'Expatriate stress: the problems of living abroad', in S. Fisher and C. L. Cooper (eds.) *On the Move: The Psychology of Change and Transition*, Chichester: Wiley.

Flanagan, J. C. (1954) 'The critical incident technique', *Psychological Bulletin* 51:327–58.

Gow, D. D. (1991) 'Collaboration in development consulting: stooges, hired guns or musketeers?', *Human Organisation* 50:1–15.

Ilgen, D. and J. Hollenbeck (1991) 'The structure of work: job design and roles', in M. Dunnett and L. Hough (eds.) *Handbook of Industrial and Organisational Psychology*, California: Consulting Psychologists Press.

Jackson, S. E. and S. R. Schuler (1985) *Organisational Behaviour and Human Decision Processes*, New York: Academic Press.

Kanyangale, M. and M. MacLachlan (1995) 'Critical incidents for refugee counsellors: an investigation of indigenous human resources', *Counselling Psychology Quarterly* 8:89–101.

Kealey, D. J. (1989) 'A study of cross-cultural effectiveness: theoretical issues, practical implications', *International Journal of Intercultural Relations* 13:387–428.

Kealey, D. J. (1990) *Cross-cultural Effectiveness: A Study of Canadian Technical Advisors Overseas*, Quebec: CIDA.

MacLachlan, M. (1996) 'From sustainable change to incremental improvement: the psychology of community rehabilitation', in Carr and Schumaker (eds.) *Psychology and the Developing World*, Westport: Praeger.

MacLachlan, M. (1997) *Culture and Health*, Chichester: Wiley.

MacLachlan, M. and E. McAuliffe (1993) 'Critical incidents for psychology students in a refugee camp', *Counselling Psychology Quarterly* 6(1):3–11.

Netermeyer, R. G., M. W. Johnston and S. Burton (1990) 'Analysis of role conflict and role ambiguity in a structural equations framework', *Journal of Applied Psychology* 70(1): 145–57.

O'Dwyer, T. (1994) 'An Identification of the Training Needs of Irish Development Workers in the Context of Appropriate Criteria for Development', PhD thesis, University of Bradford.

O'Dwyer, T. and T. Woodhouse (1996) 'The motivations of Irish Third World development workers', *Irish Journal of Psychology* 17(1):23–34.

Winnubst, J. (1984) 'Stress in organisations', in J. Drenth, et.al. (eds.) *Handbook of Work and Organisational Psychology*, Volume 1, London: Wiley.

# Tools for project development within a public action framework

## David Wield

### Introduction[1]

The growing professionalisation of development management has grown out of, and involved, acceptance of new public management approaches. These include goal-setting — increasingly quantitative — with outcomes overtly described and evidently achievable, in the name of efficiency and financial and/or managerial accountability. In terms of project design and implementation, this suggests the use of technical tools such as Logical Framework Approach (LFA). LFA tools were originally developed and used as design tools for 'blueprint' approaches, and as such they have been highly constraining, quantitative, and boundaried. More recently, as many development agencies, particularly NGOs and aid agencies, have addressed the pressure to 'professionalise', they have adopted such tools. However, these agencies have at best exhibited an ambivalent attitude to their use and their applicability to the complex and uncertain realities of development practice.

The paper looks at ways of thinking about the LFA in various types of application. There have been many well-publicised attempts to use the LFA in process-based ways.[2] However, with the countervailing pressures for project management to become more managerialist, these interesting efforts can be threatened. We consider the process-based use of the LFA and argue that this should not be lost in the drive for professionalisation, and that such application is useful to practitioners in complex, value-driven, and qualitative contexts. We also consider the limitations of the LFA from a public action perspective, where public means a wide range of institutions — not only government institutions but aid agencies, NGOs, community groups, collectives, and political movements.

# Development management and tools

Development management is a process that includes the social definition of needs and it is embedded in public action. Development management is more than policy implementation in a rigid sense. Rather, it involves activities that steer and facilitate intervention towards the identification and meeting of human need. This style of management 'differs from the simple idea of getting the work done by the best means available' (Thomas 1996: 101). It means steering effort outside the particular organisation for which one works. Since there are never enough means available, it involves balancing resources, often from many sources, all with different needs and priorities. Agencies, institutions, groups, and individuals may never completely agree on what has to be done. Ideas such as influence, steer, facilitate, and sustainability point to the overriding importance of process and continuity. And development management involves learning lessons and feeding them back into practice.

Thus, among development agencies, there is fundamental doubt and considerable cynicism about whether LFA tools can possibly be relevant to process-based management, given that they appear to promote the very project-based styles, with a tendency to technocracy and non-participation, that many agencies believe weaken the overall effectiveness of development interventions.

# Development projects and development processes

Development management takes place in a variety of development contexts and institutions, always involving a range of agencies and individuals (i.e. a diversity of stakeholders). There is a tension between the need to focus and clarify development interventions in manageable ways, often artificially simplified, and an understanding of the limitations set by such a narrow focus on boundaried projects, interventions, and activities. Interventions take place in a complex, highly populated landscape of human activity.

One starting point for such initiatives in development is the project. At a simple level, this allows a complex series of processes to be broken down into an organised set of tasks which follow a decision to implement a project. There are great variations in what constitutes 'a project', including:

- the installation of a single new piece of equipment;
- the introduction of a single new job category;

- an agency expanding its activities to another location;
- the development of a whole new sector of activity.

Because of this diversity of scales it is important to develop approaches that, in effect, step back from a project and see it in its full context as part of a longer and broader process. The importance of this is illustrated by a comment made by one practitioner/academic:

> Moving from ideas to action (at whatever level) is one of the trickiest issues [in development]. It requires identifying what actually needs to be done once one has the bright idea, who will do it, and how they will be accountable. Failure to spell this out can be intentional or unintended. For example, government departments often come up with grand plans without concretely working out the institutional base, the impact on incentives, and the power relations that will result. Donor agencies and governments alike, especially recently, talk to stakeholders at great length but the who's and how's are unspecified and vague. NGOs also waste a lot of time and effort in this way. Result — all the lovely discussion and plans for participation come to naught.

### Policy and action: projects and environments

How then, in a process-based way, can we situate the intervention (project or whatever) within the 'highly populated landscape'? Considering the relationship between policy and action, and between projects and the wider activities of operations and institutions (i.e. its environment), another practitioner said:

> There is a tension between the need to focus projects and interventions and the need to appreciate the complexity of the environment of the new activity. It is obvious that at any one moment the focus may be entirely at project level with no sense of its context. Conversely, those responsible for implementation, may feel they have little control over decisions outside their project.

The following quotations further illustrate the tension:

> For example, in a very unstable environment the managers will probably need to adjust project design more often, and there will be a different planning and management approach than in a more stable environment. Account has to be taken of the breadth of impact of a particular project — and the full range of factors that may affect its course — and of the long term character of change. There are major differences between, and concern

*with, development processes more broadly — which are likely, at the very least, to involve several projects over a significant period of time, and most likely a complex interaction between different individual projects.*
(NGO employee)

*Most practitioners/project managers are focused on, or perhaps even blinkered by, the project level. Many are so busy managing 'their' project that the wider picture is lost. It is also perhaps a reflection on the fact that most project managers feel little responsibility for, or influence over, events outside their project. In reality, there is often a lack of influence.*
(Aid agency employee)

*Projects: Are they discrete, technical initiatives to achieve defined objectives, or should they be viewed as socio-political processes in which competing and collaborating actors seek to achieve stated and unstated objectives?*
(Academic)

## Policy as blueprint or as process

This tension is always there, a reflection of the conflicting images of what projects are.[3] The tension can be described, perhaps simplistically, as that between blueprint and process. The term blueprint comes from engineering images of detailed drawings showing exact product specifications, suggesting 'that projects need to be systematically and carefully planned in advance, and implemented according to the defined plan' (Cusworth and Franks 1993: 8) — perfect imagery for both state-led and scientific management approaches, but not for the idea of multi-agent, complex, process-based approaches. The process approach, on the other hand, 'allows for flexibility in project design: although wider objectives must be defined from the outset, project inputs and outputs ... are not set in stone .. and lessons are learnt from past experience' (ODA 1995: 104). It seems clear that the polarised either/or approach to blueprint versus process is not the way ahead. Rather, it may be 'a question of which form of blueprint or process, in which circumstances, and even of what means may be used to integrate blueprint and process approaches' (Hulme 1995: 230).

So, account must be taken of the breadth of impact of a project, of the relationship between projects and ongoing activities, and of the development processes of which it is part. Projects take place in a sea of linked activities that involve multiple agencies, 'an aggregate of organisations which are responsible for a definable area of institutional life' (Anheier 1990), where 'the objectives of individual organisations involved in a project do not necessarily add up to, and coincide with, those of the project or the target group', and where issues are 'complex, ill-structured, interdependent and multi-sectoral'.

In practice, many managers and practitioners prefer working with relatively tight routines and blueprints, but they also recognise that these, in fact, exist within processes.

## Influencing environments

Such a recognition implies that a simple boundary between the project and its environment is not that helpful. Smith et al. (1981) developed a framework that recognised the environment as more complex than 'all the elements outside a project, or outside an organisation, that cannot be controlled'.[4] They use a three-level model of the environment. In the centre is the *controlled* environment, then what they call the *influenceable* environment — those activities and institutions which can be influenced by the project or organisation but not directly controlled. Outside this is the *appreciated* environment, which includes activities and institutions that 'can neither be controlled nor influenced by its management', even though their actions affect project or organisation performance.

Such an approach overlaps with that of Vickers' appreciative system (1965; 1970). This is a process whose products condition the process itself, 'but the system is not operationally closed ... the appreciative system is always open to new inputs' (Checkland 1994: 83–84). Research in the evolutionary theory of technological change strongly suggests that during periods of rapid innovation, the boundaries between businesses (or firms) and their environments are in constant flux (Amendola and Bruno 1990).

## Projects and ongoing public action

There is, then, a tension between the need to focus projects and actions and the need to appreciate the complex environments in which interventions take place. Many development practitioners think of their work as project-based and development as a series of projects and programmes — a vast interlocking series of them. In many parts of the world, projects are an increasing element of development activity. Not only has there been a major decrease in state activity, but much of that activity has been turned into projects — a process of projectisation. In many countries and sectors, there has been a major decline in routine, ongoing activity and a corresponding increase in support for NGO activity (sub-contracted with short time-frames). Aid agency funding, much of it on a project or programme basis, is increasingly important. Many large loans and grants have thus been projectised. But, despite the recurrent debates on the disadvantages of projects as instruments of development intervention, no effective alternatives have emerged, and projects are likely to remain a basic means for translating policies into action programmes (Cernea 1991).

Nevertheless, many development practitioners work in organisations that facilitate and coordinate many different actions simultaneously, rather than having prime responsibility for one project. For example, at a local level, someone in charge of primary health may be responsible for pulling together many projects (that in turn link to many different agencies) into some sort of coherent whole. Their work includes balancing the need for overall coherence against the need to keep up the enthusiasm of project workers. Or rather, the need to combine coherence of action with punctuated intervention. One serious problem in many locations is that the work of project intervention is separated from that of building or preserving coherence — that is, different people do the different tasks, with one type of work (the project work with donor funds) valued more highly than the routine, ongoing activities which try to continue in the face of diminishing budgets. Such balancing involves serious tensions between many different organisations, all with different cultures, resources, and agendas.

## Understanding the LFA in a public action perspective

We have argued so far that development issues are generally complex and messy. They usually involve problems that are strongly interconnected, and multiple agencies. They cannot easily be reduced into neat individual problems that can be resolved within one organisation — they require those involved to go outside their organisation, to where they may have little leverage to implement change. Untangling the different casual processes is not possible solely by following a set of routines.

If tools are used as process-tools, the extent to which they can assist in steering and forging coherence of action in situations with multiple actors and many interests can be assessed. So it is with the LFA.

Framework planning is a tool used to improve clarity and focus in the planning of interventions. The tool, which has many different forms, was established as a structure to assist project planning, but has grown into an approach that can aid the process of consensus-building in project design and management. The LFA has become ubiquitous in the development business, defying those who prophesied its demise as simplistic and just another form of technocratic management by objectives. The basic idea of the tool is to provide a structure to allow those involved in projects to specify the different components of activities, and carefully and causally relate the means to the ends. The framework aims to aid logical thinking about the ways in which a project or other intervention may be structured and organised. It also allows the different groups associated with the intervention to participate in discussions and decisions about it and its underlying assumptions, and to continue involvement as the project develops and changes. Coleman argues that the approach 'is an "aid to thinking" rather than a set of procedures' (1987: 259). Framework planning can be used in a mechanistic manner. There are anecdotes of framework plans being developed in hotel bedrooms by visiting consultants after a day or two's discussion with those most affected by the intervention, or even just with those in favour of it. One practitioner said: 'Consultants are not given much time but expected to come up with a project document and log-frame (framework plan) as part of their terms of reference. This means that a log-frame is sometimes constructed by the consultant alone, which is not intended. If handled badly it can set back an intervention severely'.

There is no shortage of analyses of the LFA in terms of its efficacy as a blueprint and/or process tool. The ambivalence and cynicism mentioned earlier has been encapsulated in a range of good publications.[5] We will not rehearse these arguments here. Rather, the question we consider is how the change from state-led to multiple-actor involvement in development can be reflected in, and inform, micro-level project design (see Table 1).

State-led development implies that a single actor is able to implement or at least to control implementation. The 'public action' perspective assumes, on the other hand, plurality of financing, and multiple actors with plurality of interest. With state action it is easy to imagine that there is a *public interest*, which the state's role is to reflect and act on. This implies a concept of planning with a single actor doing things. The implications for project design and planning are that techniques are required for identifying, prioritising, and evaluating such action. The big problem for development and project planning was how to plan development more effectively so that the state could better achieve those tasks that were its responsibility. The development planning and project appraisal literature from the 1950s onwards shows a gradual improvement in these techniques. The 1970s and 1980s brought a massive growth in programming tools and social and qualitative techniques, so that:

*...there is now a much wider range of techniques and procedures available for policy analysis. Models can more easily be designed to match the constraints and policy objectives of individual countries, rather than using a standard framework. Also, the shift towards simulating market outcomes means that policy analysis has shifted away from the setting of targets to the comparison of instruments and programmes* (Chowdhury and Kirkpatrick 1994: 4).

This categorisation of public interest is simplified of course, but if we consider it from the perspective of the new policy agenda (NPA) it becomes much more complex. The public interest is contested by different interests and different stakeholders. The idea that there can be coherence of planning cannot be assumed. Who should act in the so-called public interest? NGOs? Donors? Local government? The state? If they all act independently in the same sector, how does it all add up? Under these conditions, the old concept of project appraisal is insufficient. Techniques can be used for assessing individual projects, but, overall, how does it pull together? In the 'old', blueprint approach to planning, an unchallenged single actor can plan by allocating resources it controls. Now, with concepts like 'planning as steering' and 'influencing behaviours to get agreed outcomes', a new approach to project design is needed. What would be its characteristics? Intervention as a process means consensus-building and giving priority to coherence so that 'things add up'. The implication is that tools and techniques are needed to seek such consensus and coherence, and that tools are also needed to illustrate and display the results of one actor going it alone in a multiple-actor situation. The right hand column of Table 1 is an attempt to express this situation.

## The LFA as process-tool?

So, the LFA can be a blueprint tool restricted to matrix box-filling, but evidence from a range of cases we have analysed suggests that, as one part of a range of tools, it can assist practitioners faced with managing complexity but also having to state goals for which they are accountable.

However, a straightforward strengths and weaknesses analysis of the LFA does not really capture the complex practice of the approach. Rather, it is the ways the LFA are used which are important. Ironically, as Gasper has well described, it is the ZOPP (objectives-oriented project planning system) method which, while using the LFA in a process-based way, has also stuck to the most top–down, managerial style of

**Table 1** State-led and multiple-actor development policy, and implications for planning and projects

|  | 'Old', state-led approach | 'New', public action approach |
|---|---|---|
| **Type of actor** | State-led single actor | Public action by multiple actors with plurality of interests |
| **Public interest** | Yes, the state knows what public interest is, and acts on it | Public interest is not immediately obvious. Definition of 'public' interest' contested. Different interests, different stakeholders |
| **Planning** | Planning with one actor. Techniques needed to identify, prioritise, evaluate actions | Coherence cannot be assumed. Who should act? NGOs? Donors? State? If they all act, how does it add up? |
| **Problem** | How to do it better? | How best to steer and influence behaviours of various actors? |
| **Tools** | Project appraisal, cost benefit analysis, etc | Techniques to build coherence. Tools for seeking consensus for coherence of action. Tools to illustrate and display the results of one actor 'going it alone', e.g. participation analysis, stakeholder analysis, framework planning as process. And so on. |

implementation (Gaspar 1996: 15). Although it has the rhetoric of participation, it ends up being one of the most imposed tools in development policy and practice. Similarly, some of the most interesting uses of the LFA have been as part of a raft of tools used as and when needed. However, some agencies have tried to turn the raft of tools into a prescriptive list of 'must dos'. And all the time the LFA has become increasingly used by agencies worldwide.

In our teaching (with, so far, around 250 practitioners), we emphasise that the LFA and other tools are approaches that have evolved and will continue to evolve, perhaps into something quite different; and that the tool is not a 'precious thing' — it can be treated roughly and used in whatever ways assist with the process of clarifying and focusing. It is not a 'pure' method. We use a range of well-known tools, and also emphasise the importance of power and contradiction at various levels — macro, meso, and micro. Table 1 is an expression of how we have conceptualised the relationship between tools and 'new' approaches within a public action perspective.

## Reflections

To date in our use of the LFA for teaching purposes, at least three issues have arisen which illustrate its limitations as a stand-alone tool.

### Form over substance

In the aid business, form often substitutes for substance. In the case of the LFA, the victory of form over substance can be 'the filling in of the matrix', or it can be the tyranny of the manipulated 'participation'. One practitioner had this to say about one particular participatory tool, Participatory Rural Appraisal: 'PRA leads to genuine participation and ownership. One of the problems ...is that agency staff or consultants are not properly trained, and in fact start creating short cuts in the methodology. Hence the "quick and dirty" type of PRA work that is now very common.'

But if public action is contested, as we have argued, and if 'public interest' is plural, there must be an analytical framework to handle it. So, in that case, there are some key aspects of LFA which are essential.

These are the tools that give an analytical handle on *public interest as contested terrain* — in situations of multiple interest, tools are needed that help to identify the 'stakes' and 'interests' in particular activities and interventions. But more, tools are needed to ensure that 'you get somewhere' — that a platform for action emerges. So, for example, tools are needed that show stakeholders the results of pursuing self-interest, and that subordinating some interests can improve the overall solution for most stakeholders.

To argue for the identification of interests is not to argue for an ideal or perfect consensus where none exists. Indeed, the identification of interests is needed to develop an understanding of a blocking or controlling interest — which could well include the donor — that would need to be confronted. In the framework plan matrix, the column of measurable output may be a donor's controlling device, for example, which means, 'I will only fund this project if it has these predetermined outcomes'.

The LFA can also be used to bring out disagreements and so used in a process to investigate the possibilities for collective action. It is only by identifying such interests that coherent action can be forged, and that is what makes it so difficult. The search for coherent action will almost always involve institutional change. And transformation is not only an organisational question, but also a political issue. A cynical response to that might be 'Who said it was going to be easy?' Analytical tools are certainly required to improve the conceptualisation and practice of making connections between, and sense of, complex personal interactions.

### Assumptions

The second issue for reflection is that of assumptions, the vital importance of which is always emphasised in the LFA. The success of an intervention depends on being clear what is likely to constrain it. However, there is another side to the need for serious analysis of the assumptions that may adversely affect an intervention. Assumptions can also be seen as things you have to work on and change.

A slavish adherence to the LFA would focus on making the most of the constraints rather than on changing them. LFA experts would argue that that is precisely why there need to be iterations of the LFA in a process-based way, but there are numerous examples where the emphasis on assumptions has cemented a constraint rather than trying to change it.

Breaking boundaries and constraints is, of course, quite normal in the steering of development activities. It is also an important aspect of strategic management. Michael Porter (1990) for example, a classic author in this field, has analysed these issues both at a business (firm) level and national level. He argues against the idea of comparative advantage — that nations always produce what they can produce most productively with, for example, some producing low-value products like cotton while others produce computer software. He argues instead that comparative advantage — and thus competitive advantage — can be reshaped by national and firm-level action.

Although Porter is writing in the context of business or national competitiveness, the same argument can be made for other types of organisation. One way of building advantage is to work on the constraints and continually improve. This key notion in innovation theory is as relevant in development projects and programmes as it is in firms. Those who study 'the behaviour of the firm' are constantly looking to understand why some 'adapt' to their environments more favourably than others. Similarly, some organisations and programmes appear to be able to engage in 'adaptive behaviour'. A narrow focus on framework planning can deflect from the need to work on the assumptions and constraints associated with an intervention. Adaptive action can widen the scope of an intervention and increase its effectiveness.

## Conclusion

In working on this practitioner-based material, a metaphor kept springing up — one that has been well used in management and development circles to signify both survival and evolution. Ironically, a metaphor that is much used in social constructions of Africa — that of the dance — emerged also at the Harvard Business School in the 1980s with Moss Kanter's *When Giants Learn to Dance* (1989), a study of corporate attempts to transform organisations and institutions. In writing on Africa, it is used as a metaphor for survival, as, for example, in Stephanie Urdang's book on women's survival strategies in Mozambique, *And Still They Dance* (1989). The different uses of the metaphor — dance as flexibility and dance as survival — come together quite nicely when we think of how to improve learning from interventions, and how to use tools without being dominated by them. In multi-actor environments the ability to steer in complex yet practised movements and at the same time to continue to dance — to be 'active' and evolve new, creative forms of movement — lie at the heart of notions of public action.

## Notes

1  This paper results from reflections on approaches to teaching these tools within a public action perspective, and has benefited from the large quantity of practitioner insights and feedback, some of which is cited throughout. Thanks particularly to Marc Wuyts for insights and discussions, both on our joint attempts to teach and at the same time critique cost–benefit analysis in the 1970s, and on the relationship between the LFA and the moves from state to public action. Thanks also to David Daniels, Des Gasper, Mark Goldring, Caroline Harper, David Hulme, Penny Lawrence, Carolyn Miller, Berit Olsson, Gita Sen, Graham Thom, Adrian and Timlin for their contributions, some of which are inside 'quotes', and especially to my colleagues Dorcas

Robinson and Simon Bell who assisted with the production of teaching materials for The Open University's Global Programme in Development Management.

2 See for example, INTRAC/South Research (1994) and Gasper (1997).

3 Hulme (1995) provides a useful analytical framework in which to examine such tensions.

4 I am grateful to David Hulme for this insight on Smith et al.

5 See, for example, Coleman 1987; Gasper 1997; INTRAC/South Research 1994; Biggs and Smith 1998.

# References

Amendola, M. and S. Bruno (1990) 'The behaviour of the innovative firm: relations to the environment', *Research Policy* 19: 419–433.

Anheier, H. K. (1990) 'Private voluntary organisations and the Third World: the case of Africa', in H. K. Anheier and W. Siebel (eds.) *The Third Sector: Comparative Studies of Non-Profit Organisations*, New York: de Gruyter.

Biggs, S. and G. Smith (1998) 'Beyond methodologies: coalition building for participatory technology development', *World Development* 26: 239–48.

Cernea, M. (1991) 'Using knowledge from social science in development projects', World Bank Discussion Paper No. 114, Washington DC: The World Bank.

Checkland, P. (1994) 'Systems theory and management thinking', *American Behavioral Scientist* 38: 75–91.

Chowdhury, A. and C. Kirkpatrick (1994) *Development Policy and Planning: An Introduction to Models and Techniques*, London: Routledge.

Coleman, G. (1987) 'Logical framework approach to the monitoring and evaluation of agricultural and rural development projects', *Project Appraisal* 2: 251–59.

Cusworth, J. W. and T. R. Franks (1993) *Managing Projects in Developing Countries*, Harlow: Longman.

Gasper, D. (1997) 'Logical Framework: a Critical Assessment, Managerial Theory, Pluralistic Practice', ISS Working Paper.

Hulme, D. (1995) 'Projects, politics and professionals: alternative approaches for project identification and project planning', *Agricultural Systems* 47: 211–33.

INTRAC/South Research (1994) *A Tool for Project Management and People-driven Development* (2 Vols), Oxford: INTRAC and Leuven: South Research.

Kanter, R. M. (1989) *When Giants Learn to Dance: Mastering the Challenge of Strategy, Management and Careers in the 1990s*, New York: Simon and Schuster.

ODA (1995) *A Guide to Social Analysis for Projects in Developing Countries*, London: HMSO.

Porter, M. E. (1990) *The Competitive Advantage of Nations*, London: Macmillan.

Smith, W. E., F. J. Lethem and B. A. Thoolen (1981) 'The design of organisations for rural development projects: a progress report', World Bank Staff Papers No. 375, Washington DC: The World Bank.

Thomas, A. (1996) 'What is development management?' *Journal of International Development* 8(1): 95–110.

Urdang, S. (1989) *And Still They Dance: Women, War and the Struggle for Change in Mozambique*, London: Earthscan.

Vickers, G. (1965) *The Art of Judgement*, London: Chapman and Hall.

Vickers, G. (1970) *Freedom in a Rocking Boat: Changing Values in an Unstable Society*, London: Penguin.

# Ethnicity and participatory development methods in Botswana: some participants are to be seen and not heard

## Tlamelo Mompati and Gerard Prinsen

As participatory methods are increasingly preferred in the effort to develop communities, and as development initiatives increasingly take place at the grassroots, practitioners are discovering that ethnicity and ethnic identity are among the most important factors influencing the opportunities for change at village level in most African countries. This paper discusses the understanding and practice of participatory development methods in Botswana. In particular, it examines the role that ethnicity plays in determining the involvement of the various ethnic communities in development planning, and in community decision-making processes more generally.

After delineating the concept of ethnicity, the article describes the traditional consultation process in Botswana, with the *kgosi* (chief) as the key player in the process. It will be shown how this process systematically excluded ethnic-minority groups. The implications of ethnicity for present-day village consultation in rural Botswana will then be analysed. In the concluding section, the authors identify five problem areas for participatory development methods and indicate how such methods could possibly address these problems.

To illustrate ethnic prejudice and exclusion, the article uses experiences from a Participatory Rural Appraisal (PRA) project that was commissioned by Botswana's Ministry of Finance and Development Planning in 1995–1996.[1] The general objective of this project was to assess the potential use of PRA in existing development-planning practices. Teams of extension workers in four districts were trained in PRA and subsequently applied it in selected villages. Having produced village-development plans through these exercises, which took about two weeks per village, the project also assessed their implementation after several months (Prinsen et al. 1996).

# Defining ethnicity

'Ethnicity' is an anthropological term that came into conventional usage in the 1960s to refer to aspects of relationships between groups which consider themselves, and are regarded by others, as culturally distinctive. It is concerned with the sense of belonging or affiliation to a cultural-linguistic group and the uniqueness of such a group. The term denotes a social identity which is both collective and individual, externalised in social interactions, internalised in personal self-awareness, and publicly expressed (Jenkins 1999). A necessary accompaniment of 'ethnicity' is some consciousness of kind among members of an 'ethnic group', which can be defined as a subsection or subsystem more or less distinct from the rest of the population, and is based on membership defined by a sense of common historical origin, shared culture, language, value orientation, shared social norms, and sometimes religion (Schermerhorn 1996; Banks 1996). According to Tonkin *et al.* (1996: 22), the terms 'ethnic' and 'ethnicity' 'seem to have rediscovered, even without intention, the "us" and "them". ... In their common employment, the terms have a strong and familiar bias towards "difference" and "otherness".' Therefore, 'ethnicity' is concerned with identity and distinctiveness of an 'ethnic group' (Banks 1996) and is something that inheres in every group that is self-identifying (Tonkin et al. 1996).

However, the term 'ethnicity' has undergone a gradual shift as an analytical framework from a term that merely denotes 'ethnic affiliation' to a concept increasingly characterised by negative interactions and competition between ethnic groups (see Nnoli 1995; Clements and Spinks 1994; Braathen et al. 2000). Thus, it manifests itself in phenomena such as cultural stereotyping and socio-economic and political discrimination. Stereotyping does not allow people to be judged and treated as individuals in their own right. Instead, 'the other person is labeled as having certain characteristics, weaknesses, laziness, lack of honesty and so on, and these labels obscure all the other thinking about the person' (Clements and Spinks 1994:14). These labels result in prejudice, which encompasses negative assumptions and pre-judgements about other groups, who are believed to be inferior. As such, prejudice is rooted in power—the power of being a member of a primary group and feeling more important than people in 'secondary' groups. Ultimately, the feeling of exclusiveness as a group, and the negative images held about other groups, lead to discrimination, which Clements and Spinks (1994) see as 'prejudice in action'.

# Participatory development

Participatory development methods are born out of the recognition of the uniqueness of an individual as an entity who is capable of making unique contributions to decision making. Currently, participatory methods are very much in vogue in development thinking. The entire spectrum of development agencies, from grassroots organisations to the World Bank, seems to have embraced the concept of participation in development planning and implementation (Chambers 1994a, b, c; World Bank 1994). The major actor who is expected to participate is the 'community', an entity that is hardly ever described beyond 'all those living in a certain geographic area'. However, although various authors have pointed out that a community is rarely a homogeneous entity (Butcher et al. 1993; Clark 1973; Plant 1974), very little research has been done to determine the precise nature and workings of the heterogeneous rural African village.

PRA is a method that seeks to maximise the equal involvement of all adult members of a community in planning their collective development. It is purported to overcome cultural, political, and economic barriers to meaningful participation in development planning. However, the literature on this popular consultation method focuses almost exclusively on the stakes held by different material interest groups (rich versus poor, pastoralists versus settled farmers) or by men versus women (Mosse 1994). It deals far less with the cultural dichotomy of superior versus subordinate ethnic groups.[2] This is probably a result of two factors. First, most writers on participatory methods in Africa are of European or North American origin. Even though they may have extensive experience in a particular African country, they are less likely to comprehend the subtle details of ethnic identities in most of these countries. Indeed, the average child in a sub-Saharan African country, having been socialised to ethnic divides from birth, can probably multiply several times over the list of ethnic identities that a European or North American is able to identify.

Second, the minority of sub-Saharan Africans who write on participatory methods may be hesitant to address the matter of ethnicity, because the concept effectively undermines the foundations of their already rather weak 'nation-states' (Davidson 1992). Indeed, recent history in sub-Saharan Africa shows horrifying experiences of what happens when ethnic identity prevails over national identity.

Notwithstanding the above, the issue of ethnicity cannot be ignored when community participation is becoming a cornerstone for development planning. This is not only because most communities are composed of different ethnic groups, but because if participatory development efforts prioritise the most marginalised areas for intervention, as they often do, then it is likely that it is precisely these areas that are also characterised by strong ethnic divisions.

From the above, it is clear that ethnicity is antagonistic to the basic concepts underlying participatory methods. Ethnicity has exclusiveness, prejudice, and discrimination as core characteristics. Participatory methods, on the other hand, have taken as their cornerstone liberal concepts such as 'one person one vote' and 'the freedom of one should not be to the detriment of another'.

## Socio-political realities of ethnicity in Botswana

By custom, the major ethnic groups in Botswana, called *Tswana*, were organised in villages according to distinct sub-groups, such as *Bakwena, Bangwaketse, Bakgatla*, and *Batlokwa*. However, villages were not necessarily formed of ethnically homogeneous groups of people. They were further divided into specific sub-ethnic groups (*merafe* and *meratshwana*) that were associated with particular wards, according to kinship or common ancestry. In this context, *merafe* refers to people belonging to one of the *Tswana* groups that constitutes the regional majority, and *meratshwana* refers to all other ethnic groups. A ward was made up of a number of family groups or households, most of whom would be related to the ward head, while others would be family groups from other ethnic groups placed under the head's care (Ngcongco 1989).

The arrangement of wards within a village was such that the highly regarded wards were located close to the *Kgosing* ward (the main ward, where the *kgosi* lived), and the wards that were poorly regarded on ethnic grounds were situated on the outskirts. Thus, the subordinate ethnic groups were physically relegated from the social, cultural, and political life of the village. The importance attached by villagers to this physical separation extends, at least in some cases, to the deceased. For example, one of the plenary sessions dealing with the village map in Artesia became hotly debated, as one of the villagers complained to the audience that his late aunt, related to the *kgosi*, was buried too close to the graveyard for subordinate ethnic groups. What was contested was whether the two graveyards were or were not too close to each other, not whether there should be two separate graveyards (Botswana Orientation Centre 1996a).

The inhabitants of the subordinate wards were marginalised in many respects. For instance, Datta and Murray (1989:59) note that *Batawana* and *Bayei* tended to have a master–serf relationship, with *Bayei* seemingly ' ... accepting their lower status in that they would refer to themselves as *Makuba* (useless people), the *Batawana* term for *Bayei*'. Similarly, *Bakgalagadi* in the *Bangwaketse* and *Bakwena* areas show acceptance of their lower status by referring to the dominant groups as *Bakhgweni*, which connotes 'master'.

This pattern, in which the negative 'image of the other' of the dominant group is incorporated as the 'image of the self' by the subordinate group, completes a cycle of repression to which resistance can develop only with difficulty. If a subordinate group wished to oppose the *status quo*, it would have to start with the most difficult part of change: reversing its self-perception; that is, thinking of the world upside down (Freire 1972). The situation described above was observed during the PRA project.

The PRA process involved the selection and training of ten people in each village to assist in the proceedings and to lead project implementation when the PRA team was gone. As villagers were 'free' to elect their trainees, almost invariably members of the dominant ethnic group were elected. Even subordinate ethnic groups generally tended to vote for a candidate of the dominant group. The well-entrenched belief among the ethnic-minority groups was 'We cannot speak so eloquently and do not understand things.' In the case of Kedia, the authors learned that once, owing to external pressure, a member of the subordinate ethnic group of *Basarwa* was appointed supervisor of a construction programme in which most labourers also belonged to the subordinate ethnic group. Soon the labourers requested the *kgosi* to appoint somebody from his own ethnic group, claiming that their supervisor was often absent, could not manage the work, and drank too much. In short, they did not want one of their own group as supervisor (Botswana Orientation Centre 1996b).

As an almost inevitable consequence of these ethnically related imbalances of power, subordinate ethnic groups were systematically impoverished by being denied the right to own cattle and access to land and water. Consequently, their livelihoods were usually relegated to economically and ecologically marginal areas, and some groups, such as the *Basarwa*, were even forced to become hereditary serfs, called *balata, balala,* or *batlhanka* (Datta and Murray 1989). This relationship relegated *Basarwa* to the level of personal and private property.

Systematic impoverishment is a major source of concern for the ethnic-minority communities in Botswana. The introduction of the Tribal Grazing Land Policy (TGLP) in 1975 is a case in point. This policy commercialised huge areas of land that were formerly communally owned around the Kalahari desert, resulting in the annexation of land from the indigenous people of the area, particularly *Bakgalagadi* and *Basarwa*, and its re-allocation to the more economically powerful members of the majority ethnic groups from all over Botswana. Large numbers of the indigenous people of the area were forced to work for the new master-landowners (Mogalakwe 1986). In Kedia, for example, the PRA exercise stimulated a discussion about opportunities to develop a rather marginal area of 33,000 ha which was 40 km away from the village but nevertheless belonged to it. The introduction of livestock, wildlife management, and commercial production of veldproducts were suggested options. While the dominant ethnic group considered the ideas with enthusiasm, the suggestions were a source of major discomfort to members of the ethnic minorities. They used the land for hunting and for gathering veldproducts, and were afraid of losing access to it if it was commercialised (Botswana Orientation Centre 1996b).

Stratification of communities according to ethnicity is not only visible in the physical set-up of villages and the social, economic, and political relations among ethnic groups, but is also enshrined and protected in Sections 77 and 78 of the Constitution of Botswana (1965). These Sections of the supreme law of the country legitimise the superiority of the eight so-called major tribes, all belonging to the *Tswana* (*Bakgatla, Bakwena, Balete, Barolong, Bangwato, Bangwaketse, Batlokwa,* and *Batawana*). All other ethnic groups in the country are usually referred to as 'minor', 'subordinate', or 'subject' groups.

Although the Constitution explicitly mentions eight major tribes, the issue of ethnicity is downplayed under the motto 'We are all *Batswana*'. Thus, there is no official government record with data related to ethnicity. For example, population censuses do not contain reference to ethnicity. Therefore, it is difficult to determine how many people belong to a particular ethnic group or know the proportion of the *Tswana* to other ethnic groups in Botswana's 1.5 million population. Consequently, Hitchcock (1992) resorts to extrapolating such figures from the 1946 census dating from the time of the colonial Bechuanaland Protectorate Government, which describes 70 per cent of the population as belonging to the eight *Tswana* sub-groups and the remaining 30 per cent to minority groups, most of which have their own languages (*Bakgalagadi, Balala, Basarwa, Batswapong, Bayei, Herero, Kalanga, Mbukushu, Nama, Pedi, Subiya, Teti*).

## Consultation in traditional society

The understanding and practice of 'consultation' is not much different in Botswana from that in the West. Consultation is a process through which decision makers and planners solicit the views of the people for whom decisions are being made. An important feature of consultation is that the consulting party does not necessarily have to use the views of those consulted.

Botswana had, and still has, an extensive consultation system to inform decisions. Traditionally, the key player in this process was the *kgosi* (chief). The *kgosi* headed the governance system and was the custodian of the custom, culture, and welfare of his people. He ruled over his subjects through ward heads, who were appointed by him. The ward heads connected their own people to the *kgosi* and vice versa (Ngcongco 1989). However, they were more accountable to the *kgosi* than to their subjects. Although the strong convention of consultation played an important role in checking against the risk of absolutism on the part of the chief, nothing compelled him to consult his advisers. Consequently, while the *kgosi* would from time to time meet with his subjects to 'consult', this consultation meant predominantly the imparting of information or issuing of instructions.

The *kgosi* promulgated new laws at the *kgotla*. The *kgotla* is a traditional meeting place found in all *Tswana* communities, which the *kgosi* used 'to advise or admonish his followers as well as to impart information to them' (Ngcongco 1989:44). The persuasive skills and power of the *kgosi* in this regard were critical. So too was the role of the *malope a kgosi* (commoners who do things in order to be loved by the chief or to receive favours from him), who helped to detect and discourage any dissenting views.

The following example from the PRA project illustrates the importance of the continuing role of the *malope a kgosi*. Ethnic conflict was rife in Artesia, and the *kgosi* and the ethnic minorities upheld several conflicts. In order to circumvent the effects of power imbalance, the PRA project team organised separate sessions in the ward of the ethnic minority. This proved to enhance their participation greatly on the first day. However, on the second day the villagers observed that one of the village elders (*lelope*) noted down names of villagers who spoke out against the established order. Once villagers became aware of this, most of them withdrew from the meeting. In the evening, the conflict expanded, when all the villagers who were elected to be trainees threatened to quit. They informed the project team that the elder was summoned to the *kgosi* every evening to report on 'who said what'. They did not want to get into trouble with the *kgosi*. The problem was solved after extensive talks with all parties involved (Botswana Orientation Centre 1996a).

In practice, there was very little room for debate once the *kgosi* had issued his orders; 'the *kgotla* after all is not a participatory but a consultative institution' (Molutsi 1989:115). Participation in this context denotes people actively taking part in the decision-making process, whereas consultation entails being informed about decisions to be or already taken. In short, the word of the *kgosi* was highly respected and was almost always final. Hence the *Setswana* saying '*Lefoko la kgosi le agelwa mosako*', meaning 'The word of the *kgosi* is to be supported and respected by all'. In this respect, the *kgosi* was regarded almost as an omnipotent being. As will be explained shortly, consultation in modern Botswana differs a little from the way in which it was conceptualised traditionally.

## Ethnic exclusionism in the community forum

Theoretically, all adult members of the community have unrestricted right of speech at the *kgotla*. This principle is reflected in the *Tswana* proverb '*Mmua lebe o abo a bua la gagwe*', meaning 'Everybody is free to speak out, and even to make mistakes'. However, practice in traditional communities was very different, as subordinate groups were denied participation. The perpetuators took comfort in this practice by blaming the victim. For example, in the case of the discrimination practised by *Bangwaketse* against *Bakgalagadi*, the usual explanation given was that by nature *Bakgalagadi* are timid and bashful, and find it difficult to stand up and speak at gatherings (Ngcongco 1989).

The agenda of the *kgotla* meeting was the responsibility of the *kgosi*, and only on rare occasions could ordinary members of the *merafe* (not the *meratshwana*) add to the *kgosi*'s agenda through their ward heads. Participation, in the sense of 'having a say' in this kind of decision-making process, was restricted. Only a few people could participate, and these included the chief's uncles and brothers (who were also the chief's advisers) and members of the dominant ethnic groups. In an ethnically heterogeneous community, these restrictions were rigidly enforced. For instance, in *Bakwena* and *Bangwaketse* areas, *Bakgalagadi* were not, as a rule, expected to speak at the *kgotla*, even though they were free to attend like any other *Motswana*. 'As children in the home, they were to be seen and not to be heard. ... *Bakgalagadi* were children and their overlords were the ones who could and did speak for them' (Ngcongco 1989:46).

Even the physical arrangement of the *kgotla* indicated its undemocratic nature. The *kgosi* sat in front, surrounded by his advisers—mostly his male relatives and a few handpicked village elders. Immediately behind the chief's advisers sat the *merafe*, and behind them the *meratshwana*. This pattern was also observed in all villages where PRA plenary sessions took place at the *kgotla*. The male members of subordinate ethnic groups hardly spoke, and then usually only when directly addressed. Women and youngsters of ethnic minorities almost never spoke. They were seen but not heard. When one of the PRA team members naïvely suggested once that the *kgosi* should also solicit the views of people from the ethnic-minority wards, the *kgosi* looked at them and replied: 'Ah, these people never come to the *kgotla*, I cannot see them' (Botswana Orientation Centre 1996a:3).

In this regard, the *kgotla* provides a forum for the dominant ethnic groups to exercise power and authority. It is natural, therefore, that the groups in power will feel threatened when members of the subordinate groups attempt to speak in this forum, as this is viewed as undermining their power-base. This point is illustrated in an interview conducted by Ngcongco (1989:46) with a *Mongwaketse* elder who related an incident that demonstrated the undemocratic nature of the *kgotla*. 'A member of the *Bakgalagadi* who attempted to speak at a particular *kgotla* meeting was rudely pulled down by *Bangwaketse*, who said: "*Nna hatshe o tla re tlholela.*" This literally meant: "Sit down, you will bring us bad luck."'

The following example shows how a *kgosi* used a police officer to enforce this practice of ethnic exclusionism during the PRA pilot project. In Kedia the authors observed a participatory planning meeting in which one particular woman from a subordinate ethnic group spoke out loudly against discriminatory practices of the dominant group. It was evident that she was helped in breaking gender and ethnic rules by a serious intake of alcohol, but quite a number of other participants were also rather inebriated. The *kgosi* quickly pointed at a policeman, who took the woman by the arm, lifted her off the ground, and brought her to the shade of a tree about 50 metres from the meeting place. Thereafter, the meeting continued as if nothing had happened.

Participatory methods aim to change such practices by involving people directly in the decision-making processes that affect their lives and livelihoods.

## Consultation in present-day Botswana

In the opening lines of a paper presented to a conference on Democracy in Botswana, Mpho (1989:133) observed that 'Democracy appears to exist in Botswana because the majority of the people belonging to the so-called "minority" tribes have remained peaceful and patient about their oppression.' However, this situation is changing. One reason for this change is the deepening socio-economic inequality in the country. Botswana receives ever-increasing revenues from diamond mining, and the country has risen from being a very low-income country in the 1960s (with a per capita income of US$22 at independence in 1966) to a middle-income country in 1995 (per capita income of US$3,082). Nevertheless, this wealth is very unevenly distributed, with the richest 20 per cent of the population receiving 61 per cent of the total national income, while the poorest 40 per cent, many of whom belong to subordinate ethnic groups, receive only 9 per cent (MFDP 1997:3). At the same time, however, the economic boom led to an extensive and well-developed infrastructure, which increased mobility and educational levels. This development empowered ethnic minorities to challenge the *status quo*. Increasingly, ethnic groups at the lower end of the ladder now organise themselves and voice protests, even though this is still incomprehensible to members of the dominant ethnic groups.[3]

Against this background of, on the one hand, a rather rigid, ethnically stratified social order and, on the other, an increasingly mobile society in which traditional values are being eroded and in which subordinate ethnic groups question the *status quo*, the government has built a long-standing practice of 'consulting' villagers on development. Since independence in 1966, the government has formulated five-year development plans to inform and guide its path of development. Preceding the making of a new development plan, district-level extension teams visit all villages and hold meetings, in which the villagers put forward the needs and wishes that they would like to see incorporated in the upcoming development plan (Byram *et al.* 1995). This consultation process takes place along lines similar to those used by the chiefs. Every village has elected members of a Village Development Committee (VDC), which is a body charged with leading development programmes at village level. In ethnically heterogeneous communities, members of the VDC usually belong almost exclusively to the dominant ethnic group, and the *kgosi* is an *ex officio* member. VDCs are similar, therefore, to the traditional union of the *kgosi* and his advisers. The *kgosi* and ward heads manage the community's internal relations, while they gather in the VDC to deal with its relations with government. The exercise in which government officers descend on villagers to 'consult' on development plans always takes place at the *kgotla*. The VDC does the groundwork by informing and consulting villagers beforehand, and as such the actual consultation exercise at the *kgotla* bears resemblance to a ritual—pleasing to those who feel comfortable with the customary social order, but unappreciated by others.

This consultation process is now facing problems and increasing criticism from various sides. The number of villagers attending the *kgotla* is steadily declining. The chiefs complain nationwide that people no longer heed their calls to come to the *kgotla*. This may have two explanations. First, villagers from subordinate groups no longer wish to partake in a ritual in which they have no right to stand up and speak (while the chiefs no longer have the authority to enforce attendance). Second, villagers may feel that their input into government's planning is not taken seriously, because they hardly get any feedback, nor do they see their input really influencing policies and practices. This problem arose during the PRA project, as described below.

A recurrent complaint of every chief involved in the PRA project was that 'villagers no longer come to *kgotla* when I call them'. Indeed, a low and/or declining attendance of villagers at the *kgotla* was a continuous worry for the PRA team (Botswana Orientation Centre 1996a, b, c, d). The matter of low attendance at the *kgotla* has various causes, one of which is the diminishing authority of the chiefs without the void being filled by others. On the other hand, the pilot project revealed extensive proof that villagers do not feel treated respectfully in the established consultation procedures. Group-interviewed respondents in eight of the nine villages researched almost unanimously concluded that they are 'treated like children' in consultations (Prinsen et al. 1996:28).

Another criticism of the consultation process comes from government officers. With an increasing frequency and openness, the government expresses its disappointment with the disappearing 'self-help spirit', one of the nation's leading principles (MFDP 1994:7). It is concluded that *Batswana* have become increasingly dependent upon government to provide them with infrastructure and the commodities and amenities of life, without making any contribution themselves. Government sees proof of this in the ever-recurring 'shopping lists' that villages produce after the consultations.

The last criticism comes from planners and analysts. In their view, as government has invested heavily in infrastructure over the past two decades, development now needs to shift focus. First, ' ... the initiative must be seized by those in the private sector', because too few viable economic enterprises have emerged from the citizenry (MFDP 1991:28). Second, the time has come to look at the quality of service provision or the 'poor productivity' of civil servants (MFDP 1994:9). Both these areas need a forum for dialogue between citizens and the state that is qualitatively well beyond the present practice.

## Conclusions: problems and opportunities

In view of the problems with the long-practised approach to consultation, the Ministry of Finance and Development Planning piloted Participatory Rural Appraisal (PRA) over 13 months in 1995–1996 in four of the country's ten districts. Besides trying to address the inherent inadequacies of consultation as practised in Botswana, the Ministry also felt, in line with international trends, that 'there is significant evidence that participation can in many circumstances improve the quality, effectiveness and sustainability of projects' (World Bank 1994: i).

In the light of the above discussion, it will be clear that the issue of ethnicity was politically far too sensitive to be addressed explicitly in the PRA project. However, the practical experiences acquired during the project clearly revealed the tensions between various ethnic groups and the traditional consultation structures, on the one hand, and the Western liberal values underlying participatory methods, on the other. These tensions create obstacles for meaningful and effective participatory planning exercises. Sometimes during the project, PRA offered opportunities to surmount or circumvent these obstacles. However, there were also instances where it could not offer workable solutions. A preliminary inventory of the obstacles results in five categories of problems related to ethnicity; these are listed below, with some of the opportunities that PRA offers to address them.

### Physical segregation

Subordinate ethnic groups may be invisible at first glance: their houses, their livelihoods, and even their cemeteries may be separated (subtly or otherwise) from those of the dominant groups. Not only can this apparent invisibility lead to their being overlooked altogether, but when participatory methods deal with the physical planning of a village, ignorance of minorities' physical segregation may further damage their interests. Even assisting in developing their marginal income resources may require scrutiny, as subordinate ethnic groups may lose their access to these resources to dominant groups, once such resources become more attractive.

To overcome these pitfalls, some PRA techniques (transects, random household interviews, farm sketches) take the facilitators (i.e. extension workers, planners, and other professionals) away from its central meeting places. Provided that these outsiders observe well and ask open questions (assuming that their guides feel free to talk in such informal settings), the outcomes of these enquiries may be raised in plenary PRA reporting to the village at large.

### Political exclusion

Participatory methods usually require the establishment of a community-based committee to serve as a counterpart or complementary body to external development agents. These committees play a central role in implementing and following up development activities. Generally, the fact that the community has elected the committees satisfies the participatory requirement by external development agents of having empowered the community to be the local partner. However, it may well be that subordinate groups are effectively excluded from these committees. Subsequently, the local partner may use its 'empowerment' to further marginalise subordinate groups under the guise of democratic elections.

Temporary and outsider-initiated interventions can rarely change power balances directly. Participatory programmes are no exception. It can only be hoped that subordinate groups gradually develop a claim-making power through small-group work, careful facilitation, and confidence-building activities. However, this may well require a continued role for the outsiders in monitoring and carefully following up the activities at grassroots level. This continued involvement in events at village level will be legitimised only as long as the outsiders' contribution to development is appreciated or at least tolerated by the ethnically dominant groups.

### Prejudice and feelings of inferiority

Even when problems of political and administrative exclusion are overcome through participatory methods, and subordinate ethnic groups take a seat in the community organisations that join hands with development agents, the ethnic minority's contribution may be limited. Their self-esteem and perception of their skills and capacities may be so low that they are prevented from making a significant contribution. Simultaneously, dominant groups will continuously reproduce negative attitudes towards the subordinate groups in these organisations.

Participatory methods are often based on working in small groups. A repressive atmosphere is less likely to be felt and enforced in such groups, especially if their work takes place outside the symbolic courts of power. If properly facilitated, these small groups offer a learning opportunity for subordinate groups to practise negotiating skills and build self-confidence. It should be noted, however, that often the outsiders (especially government officers) also belong to the dominant ethnic groups. Consequently, they may also display prejudices in their interaction with ethnic minorities. It is, therefore, very important for outsiders to be self-critical.

## *Reprisals*

Even if outsiders succeed in involving subordinate ethnic groups in local development processes, there may be reprisals against these groups for defying the *status quo*. It is unlikely that the local powers will take such 'corrective' measures while the outsiders are around. But the danger of reprisals is real as soon as the outsiders have left. It is also unlikely that upon their return to the village the outsiders will be made aware of these reprisals. Subordinate ethnic groups are very conscious of the risk of reprisals and will normally withdraw before they expose themselves to such risks.

One of the central objectives of participatory methods is to give people control over procedures, plans, and events. This is especially important when working with subordinate groups. The more these groups feel in control, the less likely they will be to venture into areas where they can expect reprisals. Participatory methods do not offer opportunities to address the problem of reprisals by dominant ethnic groups but, if carefully and properly applied, they can prevent the problem arising.

## *Risk avoidance*

Participatory methods are based on the assumption that people are able and willing to voice their interests and that they mean what they say. However, in ethnically divided communities, subordinated ethnic groups may be unwilling to voice their views on their medium- and long-term interests, when this could immediately destabilise or endanger their limited certainties and self-image, however feeble these may seem to outsiders. Development projects usually aim to change, i.e. improve, an existing situation. However, for many ethnic minorities living on the brink of survival, avoiding risk and maintaining the status quo are paramount priorities. This attitude is largely the culmination of all the problems elaborated above, and it will not begin to change until the weight of these problems decreases.

The inventory presented above has explicitly been called 'preliminary' because an understanding of the implications of ethnicity for participatory development methods is only beginning to emerge, along with their increased use. This inventory is preliminary also because it is based on experiences in the particular context of Botswana. As explained, the strengthening and expanding state apparatus in Botswana has created tensions between the traditional and ethnically oriented socio-political order and the modern liberal Western order. In this process, traditional systems seem to lose power to the new order, thus potentially creating room for subordinate ethnic groups to exert themselves politically. However, it is unclear whether this space exists, and whether participatory methods can broaden it in those African countries where the state apparatus is crumbling. Nevertheless, at this stage, it is already clear that participatory methods are likely to remain scratches on the surface of the ethnically coloured African rural reality, unless its practitioners are able and willing to address ethnicity and ethnic identity openly.

## Glossary

Batswana: A term officially used to indicate a citizen of Botswana (singular: motswana). However, in an ethnic context it may also refer to members of the dominant eight Tswana sub-groups, sharing at least the same language, even though they may differ in some cultural practices.

Kgosi: Chief.

Kgotla: A traditional meeting place, especially for the major ethnic Tswana groups.

Merafe: A term that refers to villagers belonging to the dominant ethnic group in a particular village.

Meratshwana: A term that refers to all villagers who do not belong to the dominant ethnic group in a particular village.

| Tswana: | The majority ethnic group in Botswana, composed of eight sub-groups which have only slightly different cultural practices and share the same language. |
| Setswana: | An official language in Botswana (mainly spoken by members of the dominant eight *Tswana* sub-groups). |

## Notes

1   A precise description of what PRA entails is not necessary here. In brief, it is a popular participatory planning technique in which outsiders (i.e. government officers, employees of NGOs and/or donor agency representatives) co-operate with local people in undertaking a number of steps based on special techniques for gathering and analysing information. The various steps assess the features and resources of the community, identify problems and opportunities, and then prioritise actions to address the problems. For further details see Chambers (1983, 1994) and the monthly publications of the International Institute of Environment and Development.

2   The major exception in this respect are publications about particular ethnic groups—usually minorities referred to as the 'indigenous people'—whose history, culture, and lifestyle differ strongly from other ethnic groups in a country and have attracted favourable attention from the international community (e.g. Pygmies in Cameroon or Bushmen (*San, Basarwa*) in Botswana and Namibia). Hitchcock's (1986) inventory suggests that in four decades more than 150 academics or

professionals, from at least five universities, dedicated studies to the *Basarwa*, a minority of about 40,000 people in Botswana.

3   An Assistant Minister is quoted in a newspaper as having said to a *Basarwa* delegation: 'You think these outsiders [donor agencies] will always help you. Well, one of these days they will be gone and then there will only be us, and we own you and we will own you till the end of time' (Good 1996:59).

## References

Banks, M. (1996) *Ethnicity: Anthropological Constructions*, London: Routledge.

Botswana Orientation Centre (1996a) *Artesia, Village Development Plan*, Gaborone: BOC.

Botswana Orientation Centre (1996b) *Kedia, Village Development Plan*, Gaborone: BOC.

Botswana Orientation Centre (1996c) *Lentsweletau, Development Planning through PRA*, Gaborone: BOC.

Botswana Orientation Centre (1996d) *East Hanahai, Village Development Plan*, Gaborone: BOC.

Braathen, E., M. Boas, and G. Saether (2000) 'Ethnicity kills? Socials for power, resources and identities in the neo-patrimonial state' in E. Braathen et al. (eds) *Ethnicity Kills? The Politics of War, Peace and Ethnicity in Sub-Saharan Africa*, Houndmills: Macmillan.

Butcher, H., A. Glen, P. Henderson and J. Smith (1993) *Community and Public Policy*, London: Pluto Press.

Byram, M., A. Molokomme and R. Kidd (1995) 'Local consultation process', in Ministry of Local Government, Lands and Housing, *District and Urban Planning—The Way Forward: Report of the Proceedings and Evaluation of* the 1995 Planners Seminar, Gaborone: Government Printer.

Chambers, R. (1983) *Rural Development: Putting the Last First*, London: Longman.

Chambers, R. (1994a) 'The origins and practice of participatory rural appraisal', *World Development* 22 (7): 953–69.

Chambers, R. (1994b) 'Participatory rural appraisal (PRA): analysis of experience', *World Development* 22 (9): 1253–68.

Chambers, R. (1994c) 'Participatory rural appraisal (PRA): challenges, potentials and paradigm', *World Development* 22 (10): 1437–54.

Clark, B. D. (1973) 'The concept of community: a reexamination', *Sociological Review* 21 (3): 32–8.

Clements, P. and T. Spinks (1994) *The Equal Opportunities Guide: How to Deal with Everyday Issues of Unfairness*, London: Kogan Page.

Datta, K. and A. Murray (1989) 'The rights of minorities and subject people in Botswana: a historical evolution', in J. Holm and P. Molutsi (eds.).

Davidson, B. (1992) *Black Man's Burden: Africa and the Curse of the Nation-state*, New York: Times Books.

Freire, P. (1972) *Pedagogy of the Oppressed*, Harmondsworth: Penguin.

Good, K. (1996) 'Towards popular participation in Botswana', *Journal of Modern African Studies* 34: 53–77.

Hitchcock, R. K. (1986) 'Ethnographic research and socioeconomic development among Kalahari San: some tables', in M. A. Biesele, R. J. Gordon and R. B. Lee (eds.) *The Past and Future of !Kung Ethnography: Critical Reflections and Symbolic Perspectives, Essays in Honour of Lorna Marshall*, Hamburg: Buske.

Hitchcock, R. K. (1992) 'The rural population living outside of recognised villages', in D. Nteta and J. Hermans, *Sustainable Rural Development*, Gaborone: Botswana Society.

Holm, J. and P. Molutsi (eds.) (1988) *Democracy in Botswana*, Gaborone: Macmillan.

International Institute for Environment and Development (1994) *Notes on Participatory Learning and Action (PLA Notes)*, London: IIED.

Jenkins, R. (1999) 'Ethnicity etcetera: social anthropological points of view' in M. Burmer and J. Solomos (eds) *Ethnicity and Racial Studies Today*, London: Routledge.

Ministry of Finance and Development Planning (MFDP) (1991) *National Development Plan 7*, Gaborone: Government Printer.

Ministry of Finance and Development Planning (MFDP) (1994) *Mid-term Review of National Development Plan 7*, Gaborone: Government Printer.

Ministry of Finance and Development Planning (MFDP) (1997) *National Population Policy*, Gaborone: Government Printer.

Mogalakwe, M. (1986) *Inside Ghanzi Farms: A Look at the Conditions of Basarwa Farm Workers*, Gaborone: Applied Research Unit.

Molutsi, P. P. (1989) 'The ruling class and democracy in Botswana', in J. Holm and P. Molutsi (eds.).

Mosse, D. (1994) 'Authority, gender and knowledge: theoretical reflection on the practice of participatory rural appraisal', *Development and Change* 25 (3): 497–525.

Mpho, M. K. (1989) 'Representation of cultural minorities in policy making', in J. Holm and P. Molutsi (eds.).

Ngcongco, L. D. (1989) 'Tswana political tradition: how democratic?', in Holm and Molutsi (eds.).

Nnoli, Okwundiba (1995) *Ethnicity and Development in Nigeria*, Aldershot: Avebury.

Plant, R. (1974) *Community and Ideology: An Essay in Applied Social Philosophy*, London: Routledge and Kegan Paul.

Prinsen, G., T. Maruatona, N. Mbaiwa, F. Youngman, N. Bar-on, T. Maundeni, T. Modie and T. Mompati (1996) *PRA: Contract and Commitment for Village Development, Report on the Ministry of Finance and Development Planning's Participatory Rural Appraisal Pilot Project*, Gaborone: Government Printer.

Republic of Botswana (1965) *Constitution of Botswana*, Gaborone: Government Printer.

Schermerhorn, R. (1996) 'Ethnicity and minority groups' in J. Hutchison and A. D. Smith (eds) *Ethnicity*, New York: Oxford University Press.

Tonkin, E., M. Mcdonald, and C. Mcdonald (1996) 'History and ethnicity' in J. Hutchison and A. D. Smith (eds) *Ethnicity*, New York: Oxford University Press.

World Bank (1994) *The World Bank and Participation*, Washington, DC: World Bank.

# Logical Framework Approach and PRA: mutually exclusive or complementary tools for project planning?

## Jens B. Aune

### Introduction

The overall purpose of project planning is to improve project performance. However, there is no general consensus with regard to how to undertake this. One planning system used by many donor agencies is the Logical Framework Approach (LFA) or 'logframe'. An alternative system is Participatory Rural Appraisal (PRA), which has further evolved into Participatory Learning and Action (PLA). LFA and PRA systems are considered by Chambers, the father of PRA/PLA methods, to be mutually exclusive (Chambers 1996, 1997). This paper questions that view and proposes a method for how it is possible to combine the two methods.

There are several pitfalls in project planning. One is the position that the plan should be fulfilled at any cost. However, circumstances (external factors) might change during project implementation, thus necessitating adjustments to the original plans (Hersoug 1996). If these factors develop negatively during the project period, the project may have to be terminated or redesigned in order to circumvent them. External factors may also develop favourably, thereby opening up new possibilities. If planning and implementation are viewed too rigidly, these opportunities will be foregone. The third pitfall is not to have any plan or to have a plan with few or no implications for project implementation. This causes frustration among project staff and beneficiaries because it is not known where the project is heading. Project planning is, therefore, a question of finding a suitable balance between stability and flexibility (Hersoug 1996). As a general rule, the more you know about the external factors which can influence a project, the more you can plan in detail. More realistic goals may also be established during project implementation. This is also in line with the current thinking that project implementation should be a learning process.

Planning, implementation, monitoring, and evaluation are parts of a continuous project cycle. It is of special importance that the lessons learned during project implementation feed back into the ongoing planning process.

## Planning according to LFA

LFA is a method that is used widely for planning development projects. The reasons for introducing logframe systems have been (NORAD 1995; Vanoppen 1994; Steigerwald 1994):

- to assist projects in establishing clear and realistic objectives;
- to promote logical thinking and check the internal logic;
- to provide a basis for monitoring and evaluation and make planners think in evaluatory terms;
- to make planners state the assumptions that they are making;
- to encourage people to consider what their expectations are;
- to focus attention;
- to summarise key information in one document;
- to improve communication between donor and recipient.

LFA proposes a seven-step procedure in the planning of a development project (NORAD 1995):

1 *Participatory analyses*—identify the groups affected by the project. The main groups are analysed with regard to main problems, interests, potentials, and linkages. A decision is taken on whose interests and what problems are to be given priority.

2 *Problem analyses*—identify a focal problem and establish cause/ effect relationships through the use of a 'problem tree'.

3 *Objective analyses*—transformation of the 'problem tree' into an 'objective tree'.

4 *Alternative analyses*—assess different options for the project. This assessment can be based on technical, financial, economic, institutional, social, and environmental feasibility.

5 *Identify the main project elements*—goal (long-term overall objective), purpose (operational objective), outputs (results that are guaranteed by the project), activities, and inputs.

6 *Assumptions*—describe conditions that must exist if the project is to succeed but which are outside the control of the project.

7   *Identify indicators*—the performance standard to be reached in order to achieve the goal, purpose, and outputs.

These steps are normally undertaken in an LFA workshop. The elements from steps 5 to 7 are also combined in the project planning matrix.

In LFA, the development process is seen as a causal link of events. The outputs are produced if the activities take place and the assumptions in relation to output are fulfilled; the purpose is attained if the outputs have been produced and the assumptions in relation to purpose achieved. Finally, the goal is achieved if the purpose is attained and the goal-related assumptions are fulfilled. By adopting such a procedure, the project is forced to think through its internal logic and reflect on the factors that influence its performance.

## Planning according to PRA

Development projects often show some success during the project period, but the outcomes are frequently not sustained (Pretty 1995). One important shortcoming has often been that the local beneficiaries do not develop a true sense of ownership of the project and therefore take little or no responsibility for sustaining the infrastructure or organisation that have been developed by it. Irrigation dams, soil conservation structures, credit groups, and even women's groups are often considered as belonging to the project alone. A critical point in development planning is, therefore, to identify local priorities and encourage stakeholders' responsibility. A tool which has been developed to ensure stakeholder participation in planning, monitoring, and evaluation is the PRA method. Empowerment of the local people is an important principle in PRA, which seeks to give local people a key role in all aspects of development projects in which they are to be involved. PRA also emphasises the building of local problem-solving capacity and acknowledges that different groups in a society have different needs.

The origins of PRA lie in participatory action, agro-ecological analyses, participatory observation, applied anthropology, farming systems research, and Rapid Rural Appraisal (Chambers 1997). It is an assembly of different methods such as wealth-ranking, ranking matrices, seasonal profiles, mapping, transect walks, etc. The approach emphasises the active participation of the local population in the collection and analyses of data, use of visual techniques, group discussions, and information sharing.

Participatory planning has been shown to increase uptake of services, decrease operational costs, increase transparency, and increase the mobilisation and capacity of local people to act for themselves (Pretty 1995). Participation can also be considered as a fundamental right (ibid.).

## Comparing the methods

Chambers (1997) considers PRA as completely opposed to LFA, while others think that LFA does not necessarily contradict the people-oriented approach of PRA (Mikkelsen 1995).

One clear difference is that the LFA method takes no stand with regard to who is present and by whom decisions are taken (NORAD 1995). On the other hand, an important principle of PRA is empowerment of weak and vulnerable groups (Chambers 1997). This principle is not, however, a guarantee for the active participation of local stakeholders. There are good and bad practitioners of both LFA and PRA methods. The success of either method in project planning depends very much on the skills and attitudes of the facilitators.

One of the criticisms of the LFA is that its difficult vocabulary excludes local people from participating (Chambers 1997). This gives more power to 'élite groups', as these know how to articulate their needs using the 'LFA language'. This language makes frequent use of the term 'target group', something which may convey the idea of passive recipients of aid and undermine the idea that the overall objective of development assistance is to enable people to act for themselves and determine their own destiny.

Another criticism is that in LFA the different challenges that people face are reduced to one core problem (Chambers 1997), while different groups within a community may well have different problems, making establishment of a core problem a struggle between different groups. Consensus is not always possible.

A major strength of LFA is its structured approach. It is easy to get an overview of the project, and the indicators that are identified can be used as a basis for monitoring and evaluation. This is perhaps one of the reasons why the method has become so popular among donor agencies. Planning according to PRA has no clear structure and it may, therefore, be difficult to get an overview of the project.

# Combining LFA and PRA

Each of the two methods has its weaknesses and strengths and it is therefore of interest to discuss how it is possible to use the two methods in a complementary way. One approach is to use LFA for giving the overall structure of the planning process and the checklist of factors to consider, while PRA is used in discussions and decision making at the grassroots level. Thus, unlike the conventional LFA approach, the key decisions are not taken in an LFA workshop, but by the local stakeholders. The project staff should facilitate, but the final decision making should be in the hands of the project beneficiaries.

PRA should be used to identify vulnerable groups (step 1 in the LFA), local problems and their causes (step 2), to discuss with local stakeholders the goals of the project and which activities should be given priority (steps 3–5), to identify the external factors which can influence the project (step 6), and to define the indicators (step 7). PRA tools to be used include, among others, wealth ranking and matrix scoring. Wealth ranking is used to identify different wealth groups in the villages, and the subsequent analyses of problems and alternatives are undertaken within the different wealth groups. This enables the weakest groups to express their needs and to decide on their priorities for the project. The outcome of such a process is often that differences emerge between the priorities of the different groups, and a decision will have to made with regard to whose interest will count the most in the decision-making process. There will always be a power struggle, regardless of which planning system is used. However, what this process seeks to ensure is that the weakest groups are able to express their needs. Identification of indicators should be a participatory process, and the selected indicators should reflect how local stakeholders measure progress.

LFA is used to organise the decisions from the PRA exercise into a project matrix (PM). The PM will provide an overview of the project, show what is to be expected from it, and which indicators are to be used to measure project performance. The structuring of the PM is a joint responsibility of project beneficiaries and project staff. LFA should only be used to assist in planning and should not be used rigidly. It is mainly a tool to assist the project in asking the right questions and in structuring the main elements of the project.

# Conclusions

It is proposed that LFA and PRA be used in a complementary way. The LFA method is used to structure the overall planning process while PRA is used to identify local problems and to foster decision making at the local level. The strength of LFA lies in structuring the main elements of the projects whereas PRA is an important tool in promoting participation and empowerment of local stakeholders.

# References

Chambers, Robert (1996) 'Participatory learning approaches and ZOPP', remarks at the GTZ workshop 'ZOPP Marries PRA?', Eschborn, Germany.

Chambers, Robert (1997) *Whose Reality Counts? Putting the First Last*, London: IT Publications.

Hersoug, B. (1996) 'Logical framework analyses in an illogical world', *Forum for Development Studies* 2:377–404.

Mikkelsen, B. (1995) *Methods for Development Work and Research: A Guide for Practitioners*, New Delhi: Sage.

NORAD (1995) *Guide to Planning and Evaluation NGO Projects, Number 2: Core Elements in Planning Development Assistance*, Oslo: NORAD.

Pretty, Jules (1995) *Regenerating Agriculture*, London: Earthscan.

Steigerwald, V. (1994) 'Recent development in GTZ's use of the ZOPP', in *Proceedings of INTRAC and South Research Workshop on LFA and OOIP*, Keuven, Belgium, 16–18 May 1994, Part 2 Annexes.

Vanoppen, J. (1994) 'The use of OOIP in Coopibo-supported programmes in Zimbabwe', *Proceedings of INTRAC and South Research Workshop on LFA and OOIP*, Keuven, Belgium, 16-18 May 1994, Part 2 Annexes.

# Critical reflections on rapid and participatory rural appraisal

## Robert Leurs

## Introduction

This paper starts by addressing the question of the purpose(s) of Rapid Rural Appraisal and Participatory Rural Appraisal (RRA/PRA). It outlines three broad contexts in which they are undertaken in practice. It then considers some of the challenges facing PRA. These include introducing and spreading PRA within communities; institutionalising PRA into development organisations and their projects or programmes; assuring and maintaining quality, both of the PRA process and its facilitation; and, finally, the lack of a methodological critique of PRA.

The paper was inspired by the author's belief that there has been a lack of critical writing in the PRA literature, although this is now starting to change. It is offered as a small contribution to this emerging literature (some of which is listed in the bibliography at the end of the paper).

## RRA/PRA for what?

RRA and PRA methods are being used in different ways by many different kinds of people for very different purposes, and the labels RRA/PRA are used rather indiscriminately to cover all of these.

### PRA as a research methodology

PRA is increasingly seen and used as an alternative or supplement to conventional surveys and other methods of social research (such as participant observation), by consultants and other development professionals, as well as academics. I would call most such work RRA (although it is often called PRA), whenever the selection of issues, questions, methods, and applications is determined by outsiders. In this context, RRA and PRA are located on a mainly methodological continuum.

## PRA for (project) appraisal

Many other PRAs appear to have been initiated by outsiders (NGOs, government organisations) as a way of encouraging communities to describe their situation, identify and prioritise their needs, formulate a plan of action, diagnose problems during implementation, or engage in participatory monitoring and evaluation), using PRA methods.

The agenda and objectives for this sort of PRA work are also usually set by outsiders, but the emphasis here is often on learning from communities, in order to make development work more appropriate and responsive (as opposed to the objective of getting an academic degree or providing information for donors, policy makers, or others involved in development work).

## PRA as part of a process of participatory development

PRA seems to be much less commonly used to initiate and/or sustain a process of participatory development.

The difference between PRA as process and PRA as appraisal has more to do with who sets the agenda and what the objectives are than with who uses the methods. The objective of PRA in this case appears to be to empower people and support a process of self-reliant development, on the terms set by the communities themselves.

# Challenges facing PRA

## Introducing and spreading PRA within communities

This is the main challenge for those using PRA as part of a process of participatory development. It involves identifying, training, and other-wise assisting some sort of local animator network, until no further support is felt to be necessary. PRA, understood primarily as a set of methods, will be only a small part of such a process, as well as of the repertoire of skills required to support it. On the other hand, the behavioural principles and attitudes underlying PRA will be crucial.

However, there is nothing new about these. Perhaps the contribution of PRA to participatory development therefore lies in the contribution that training in the methods and, more importantly, the practice of facilitating them in communities can make to developing the analytical, decision-making, and other capabilities (such as working together) that are necessary for self-help development.

The question then becomes one of how training and supporting local PRA facilitators can best be done, and how the lessons of experience can be shared where this has been attempted (for example, selection criteria for community PRA facilitators, details of their PRA training, incentives and support requirements, capabilities developed, changing relationships, etc.).

## Introducing PRA into development organisations and projects

An increasing number of development organisations worldwide are enthusiastically adopting a PRA approach for project appraisal, as defined above (which includes diagnosing problems of implementation as well as monitoring and evaluation).

However, many of these organisations (or projects) are now encountering obstacles related to the objective of making their work more responsive to community needs. These obstacles may be external or internal. External obstacles include an unfavourable policy environment. Internal obstacles are more obvious and numerous. They include the hierarchical culture of management; the lack of incentives for PRA work, or conflict with prior top-down planning and evaluation mechanisms; and rigid or inappropriate accountability requirements (and other agendas) of donors, central ministries, and politicians.

In short, PRA does not really fit into the conventional project framework. So-called process projects may be a contradiction in terms, certainly as projects are conventionally defined.

## Quality (and quality assurance) issues in PRA training

**Focus on methods, not principles, behaviour and attitudes:** There still appears to be a focus on methods in PRA training. This is understandable, as the methods are easy to understand and practise, although far more difficult to learn how to facilitate. On the other hand, while the primacy of attitudes, behaviour, and principles is often emphasised, it is less clear how these can be developed in training situations. There is also a danger of mechanical application (and standardised mixing or sequencing) of methods, if these aspects of PRA are neglected.

**Focus on content (what was learned), rather than process:** Most PRA training reports talk about what was learned and what methods were used. They do not contain much reflection on process (such as who participated, what they did, how they did it, etc.).

**Locating PRA methods within an analytical framework:** The selection of PRA methods by outsiders often appears not to be situated in a coherent analytical framework of development. This may also explain the lack of contextual analysis in many PRA reports. However, some attempts have been made to do so. For example, one model, developed by Sam Joseph at ActionAid, attempts to locate PRA within a framework for the analysis of livelihoods.

**Familiarisation, field-based training, and training of trainers:** There is a widespread view that there are at least three different types of PRA training, which have not been sufficiently distinguished to date, namely familiarisation workshops, field-based training, and training of PRA trainers.

Familiarisation workshops are short-term classroom-based events for people who will not be facilitating PRA in the field, but whose support might be required for a PRA approach.

Field-based training is a longer-term process, intended for PRA facilitators. A distinction between support agency and community PRA facilitators would also be useful.

Training of PRA trainers is another type of training of which more is required, given the common view that there are not enough 'good' PRA trainers available. The problem with this view is what does 'good' mean, and who decides (or should decide)?

Most of the current writing (and experience) appears to be about the second type of training, and more writing and sharing of experience about the first and third types is needed.

**Different levels of PRA training:** This is related to the previous point. PRA trainers and others seeking to promote PRA may need to identify and prioritise their audiences more strategically.

**One-off versus on-going PRA training:** Too much field-based PRA training seems to be a one-off affair, often in communities where there is no other on-going relationship with the training organisation concerned. There is now an increasing realisation that this is not sufficient, and that follow-up training or support of some kind is needed, even though PRA facilitators (community-based or agency-based) should, ideally, learn as they go along.

**Role of the PRA facilitator and skills required:** This will obviously depend on the context (research, project, or community) in which the PRA facilitator is working. Growing experience is showing that an understanding of the methods and (practice of) PRA principles is not enough. Facilitation and communication skills are crucial, and conflict-resolution skills may also be required.

What are (and should be) the roles of PRA facilitators, in different contexts and settings? Similarly, what are (and should be) the skills required, not just of PRA facilitators, but also of PRA trainers, and trainers of trainers? More thought and discussion about this would be useful. No doubt there will be many answers and even more further questions!

## Lack of a methodological critique of PRA

This is perhaps understandable, given the enthusiasm generated by the application of PRA methods, as well as their relative novelty and obvious practical 'hands on' usefulness. Nevertheless, questions are increasingly being asked about PRA methodology.

The initial debate was about the reliability and validity of the results of these methods, as compared with those generated by other approaches. In the few cases where comparisons have been made, the results of PRA have either been similar to those of conventional methods, or it has been the latter, not those of PRA, upon which some doubt has been cast.

Similarly, anthropologists in particular remain sceptical of the rapidity of PRAs, conceived as one-off exercises by outsiders, and the limitations thought to be associated with this, particularly the lack of initial understanding and familiarity with the environment, and thus the likely superficiality of any information or knowledge gained.

More recently, there has been some literature questioning the cultural appropriateness of the PRA approach or particular PRA methods. One author, for example, has focused on possible distortions related to the public nature of much PRA work, such as the gender bias which this may create in many cultures, as well as the inhibiting effects on the participation of some of those who are present.

The same author also highlights the unequal power relationships that exist, both between PRA facilitators and communities (with the consequent syndrome of 'I'll tell them what I think they want to hear') and within communities themselves.

It is also questionable whether all cultures necessarily learn and communicate best in a pictorial fashion. More fundamentally, how far can any means of communication transcend cultural and other differences (for instance, of experience)? Surely these differences affect our interpretation of what we hear or see in important ways, no matter how well we listen!

Yet, despite these and other recent methodological concerns (and principles such as critical awareness), the literature on PRA seems to be remarkably silent on questions of who did or did not participate, as well as on other process questions, such as why particular methods were used, and how these might have affected those involved.

What is also surprising, finally, given the emphasis on local perceptions, is the lack of information about local perceptions of the PRA approach and methods (other than from PRA training-course participants). Most of the PRA literature appears to have been written 'top–down', by outsiders, usually at a fairly high level.

## Conclusions

A number of conclusions suggest themselves on the basis of the views expressed above.

Firstly, those involved in promoting RRA/PRA should be clear about the context(s) and purpose(s) of its use. RRA/PRA can be used for development research, at various stages in the project cycle, and for community-led development. The nature and levels of PRA training, as well as of its facilitation, should reflect these different contexts and purposes.

Secondly, the two main operational challenges continuing to face PRA are how to introduce and spread PRA within and between communities, and how to introduce and spread RRA/PRA within government development organisations and programmes.

Thirdly, the main process-related challenges facing RRA/PRA are how to measure and maintain quality. Current concerns in this area include the continuing focus on methods rather than principles, and the focus on content (i.e. what was learned) rather than process.

A methodological critique of RRA/PRA (largely absent at present, with a few notable exceptions) is required to help resolve these 'quality assurance' challenges.

## Bibliography

Chambers, Robert (1994) 'Participatory rural appraisal (PRA): challenges, potentials and paradigm', *World Development* 22 (10).

'Draft Statement of Principles', IIED/IDS Workshop, May 1994, reproduced in *PLA Notes*, February 1995.

Kar, Kamal and Christoph Backhaus (1994) 'Old Wine in New Bottles?', unpublished paper. See also Christoph Backhaus and Rukman Wagachchi, 'Only playing with beans?', *PLA Notes*, October 1995.

Mosse, David (1993) *Authority, Gender and Knowledge: Theoretical Reflections on the Practice of Participatory Rural Appraisal*, ODI Network Paper No 44.

Pottier, Johan (1991) 'Representation and Accountability; Understanding Social Change through Rapid Appraisal', unpublished paper.

Pretty, Jules (1991) 'The Trustworthiness of Findings from Participatory Methods', unpublished paper.

Shah, Parmesh (1993) 'A Note prepared for the IIED/IDS workshop on "Alternatives to Questionnaire Surveys"'.

Thompson, John (1994) 'From participatory appraisal to participatory practice: Viewing training as part of a broader process of institutional development', *PLA Notes 19*, February 1994.

Wallace, Tina (1994) 'PRA: Some Issues Raised by Experience in the North', unpublished paper for the 1994 DSA conference.

# Participatory methodologies: double-edged swords[I]

## Eliud Ngunjiri

At a PAMFORK workshop attended by Robert Chambers — the guru of Participatory Rural Appraisal (PRA) and Rapid Rural Appraisal (RRA) — a range of development organisations came together to exchange ideas on how to improve the Participatory Methodologies (PMs) they currently use. PAMFORK (Participatory Methodologies Forum of Kenya), whose mission is to foster an environment where people realise their rights, are empowered to organise, articulate, and promote sustainable community development, argues that '[A]lthough a multiplicity of methodologies and approaches exist, practitioners lack an organised system that facilitates the process of sharing these experiences especially within Kenya.' Hence one of its objectives is to harmonise what is good in different methodologies.

Participatory methodologies are double-edged swords that can be used to destroy or to build the capacities of those upon whom they are used. Development is about people becoming or being helped to become conscious about themselves and their environment, after which plans and actions are expected to follow. The involvement of people in the process of helping themselves is a cornerstone of good development — and their awareness of this explains why development organisations have attached so much importance to PMs.

## Principles

The two approaches that I would like to share with development practitioners are guided by the following philosophies:

- The principle and power of positive thinking — for instance that it is better to think of and build on what a community is or can become, rather than to focus on what it is not or cannot be. Instead of looking for the dark side of people or things, we should look for their bright side. Positive thinking is most likely to lead to positive actions and outcomes.

- Partnership of mutual knowledge and/or understanding between the two actors, rather than assuming that only one of them knows, or needs to know about, the other. Thus a community or NGO partner group should know as much as possible about the development agency working with it, without feeling restricted by the relationship between them. Without this mutual knowledge, many things can go wrong. For example, without knowing what it can or cannot do, the local group may have expectations that are beyond the agency's ability or mandate. If these expectations are not met, the group may then find it easier to let the agency decide what is good for them.

- The principle of reciprocal giving and taking. It is, of course, better to give than to receive, for receiving alone erodes the dignity of the recipient. Nobody can derive pride from always being on the receiving end, but one can do so if one also gives in return.

- The principle of shared credit and not where one actor steals the other's credit.

For example, an organisation can help a community solve water problems by giving it ten bags of cement to protect the spring. The community directly or indirectly meets the rest of the cost. When all is done, the community is so grateful to the organisation that it says 'were it not for your support we would not have been able to solve the water problem'. The organisation not only agrees with this but also allows its name to be inscribed on the protected spring. What would be more in order would be to let the community know what its contribution has been, in order to enable it to realise how able it is or can be. Unless this is done, communities will continue to be disempowered and to depend on external support.

- Local resources need to be identified and mobilised to address people's felt needs, rather than adopting an approach where these are not drawn upon.

- Constructive participation and involvement of the community in the entire process of helping itself rather than destructive participation. I regard this as a basic human requirement without which people's capacity continues to be destroyed.

- External support coming to supplement rather than to replace or duplicate local initiatives or efforts. Thus, people should be helped to pursue self-reliance materially, intellectually, organisationally, and management-wise.

- External forms of support should complement each other rather than compete among themselves. Unless different support organisations recognise a common goal and a common playground (that is, the community with whom they are working) for their different development activities, they will continue to undo each other's work, duplicate efforts, step on each other's toes, confuse each other and the community, waste time and money, as well as scrambling for the community. When such things happen, organisations waste a lot of time, energy, and money trying to sort out their differences, more often than not at the expense of what they set out to do in the first place.

Unless PMs are used well and guided by these and other basic principles, many aspects of development will continue to go wrong. The above principles, if applied, will go a long way to building rather than destroying the capacity of the people with whom we work.

## The problem approach

Many development organisations have poverty alleviation as part of their mandate. To be most effective in this, they choose to work with the poorest of the poor .

As part of their introduction to their potential partners, these organisations inform them not only of their mandate (poverty alleviation) but also about the type of people they like working with (the poorest of the poor). When it comes to wanting to know more about the potential partner group or community and whether it qualifies to get into partnership with it, the organisation asks what their problems are. Many use PMs to enter into the communities as well as to identify their problems. Even before being asked what their problems are, the potential partner group or community feels obliged to say who they are and what their problems are, in the hope of proving themselves to be the poorest of the poor the organisation is seeking.

When an organisation starts its interaction with a community by asking people to say what problems they have, the community thinks it has been given a chance to show whether it numbers among the poorest of the poor and how it qualifies for support. As a result, people come up with as many problems as possible that can be categorised as real or genuine, discovered and feigned.

They give examples of how they have not been able to do one thing or another because of poverty and lack of external support. Some potential partners even ask development workers from the organisation to tell them what their problems are — and many of them make the mistake of doing exactly that.

## Negative discovery

Asking people to say what their problems are, using all sorts of participatory methodologies, is tantamount to asking them to say how useless, weak, empty, powerless, and worthless they are in order for them to qualify to be helped. Yet this, to many, is called community involvement or participation.

It would be correct to say the community has participated in its own destruction in that after listing their problems, real, discovered, and unreal, they discover how useless they are and feel worse off than before the exercise. They actually discover how poor they are and feel they seriously need external support. This is a negative discovery and however real or otherwise it may be, it can disempower or depress a community. Negative discovery works the same way three people can have a bad effect on you by separately telling you that you look ill. At the end of this you most likely end up feeling ill and wanting medical attention. It is as serious as that.

## Adding insult to injury

After proving that it is the poorest of the poor, the community, as expected, comes up with a lot of expectations that it hopes will be met with the support of the development organisation. The community sees the organisation as its God-sent redeemer, endowed with the right skills, knowledge, and ability to identify and solve its problems. The funny and disturbing thing here is that the development organisation does not seem very much worried by the whole misconception. Rather, as a way of encouraging community participation, it asks the community to prioritise its problems. At some stage the development organisation invokes its programme themes and the community is left asking (without saying it) 'Why ask us all these questions if you knew what your area of interest was?' The community, already trying to heal the wounds of negative discovery, sinks deeper into disappointment and frustration on realising that its apparent redeemer can only help in a mediocre way. The heart of this community gets broken after going through such destructive participation.

# The available resources approach

The suggested positive and empowering approach requires firstly that the organisation, in the course of introducing itself to a community or when doing a needs assessment, makes it known that it works with people with resources, plans, aspirations, and who are willing to do things for themselves.

There is nothing wrong with an organisation having a poverty focus, or having poverty alleviation as a mandate, or wanting to work with the poorest of the poor . What is wrong is forgetting or not knowing that:

- poverty is a highly complex syndrome or problem with many signs, symptoms, and causes and is perceived differently in different communities;

- its origins can be traced in both national and international circles;

- poverty is linked to denial and abuse of basic rights;

- poverty is about lack of control over resources including land, technology, skills, knowledge, capital, social connections, etc.;

- poverty can be aggravated by negative discovery or negative self-consciousness;

- even in an apparently poor community there are things that keep it going which can be built on in poverty alleviation;

- poverty and problems are commonplace and if your mission is to look for them you will always find them;

- poverty will always emerge if you make a community think you are looking for the poorest of the poor or wanting to know what people's problems are as your starting point.

Using PM tools, a development organisation should help a community to identify its resources, and come up with aspirations and plans that its members would be willing to implement themselves. A community should be helped to come together — get organised — firstly to identify its resources. This is important because:

- people become their own resource or realise they are already;

- participation is triggered;

- accountability among themselves and between them and others can develop;

- people start to form a structure that can stand on its own and relate with others; and so

- they acquire a louder voice and gain strength.

When it comes to listing their resources or wealth, people do a lot of thinking and identify resources that are real and tangible, they discover new ones, and their creativity and innovativeness in themselves bring forth new resources.

At the end of this exercise, more often than not, the community will heave a sigh of relief on discovering how wealthy, resourceful, and powerful it is or can be. This is nothing short of positive self-discovery. People feel wealthier and stronger than before and full of energy that they are eager to utilise.

Positive self-discovery (a resources-oriented development approach), community participation, and community organisation are powerful community capacity-building tools.

## Problem listing

After a community has genuinely proved to have resources, and is ready to do things for itself, the development organisation should ask whether it has any problems it would like to address, using its own resources as far as possible. Let the community know right from the beginning that much as the external organisation would like to help, it may not have all the resources required to solve the problems.

With this approach, it is likely that the community will come up with genuine problems and expectations that the development organisation can help it to address.

## Facilitation and problem-solving

Once resources and problems have been identified, the development organisation and the community will have before them some of the vital requirements to genuine ways forward and partnership. Both actors should play the vital role of finding solutions to the problems from the available resources. The development organisation's main role should be that of a facilitator. Challenging questions and creative input from both actors will emerge and many problems will be solved.

The remaining ones can be prioritised and plans made to resolve them, through the processes of brainstorming placed in order of priority. Once a solution is defined, what should follow is a listing of the required resources, separating out those that are available and those that are not. Ways to get hold of the latter should be established, and this is where the development organisation and others should come in handy. The next steps are those of community organisation and mobilisation plus drawing of action plans.

# Conclusion

As double-edged swords, PMs can be used to destroy or to build themselves and their environment, after which plans and actions are expected to follow. Whatever the source and the direction of these plans and actions, it follows that people (beneficiaries) should not be denied participation in the process of helping themselves. The involvement of people in the process of helping themselves is a cornerstone of good development. This has been realised by many development agencies, hence the importance they attach to PMs. Today, no NGO or development organisation worth its reputation feels it is doing, or is seen to be doing, a good job without using a PM of one kind or another. I have no quarrel with PMs as such, it just depends on how one uses them. My main concern is that, despite the increase in the number of NGOs, PMs, and after many years of poverty alleviation, poverty continues to be rife and communities continue to languish in it. There is no doubt, then, that something is wrong. It must either be that NGOs and/or PMs — the tools of their trade — are ineffective, or that NGOs use PMs wrongly. My view is the latter.

## Note

1   An earlier version of this article was presented by the author at a PAMFORK Participatory Methodologies Workshop held on 24-27 September 1996 at Resurrection Gardens, Karen-Nairobi, and was published in Baobab, Issue 22 (May 1997).

# The Participatory Change Process: a capacity building model from a US NGO

## Paul Castelloe and Thomas Watson

### Introduction

This paper describes the Participatory Change Process (PCP), a new practice model which promotes the formation and action of sustainable grassroots organisations in poor and marginalised communities. This model uses participatory learning and action methods to provide people with the capacities, self-confidence, and organisational structures needed to plan and implement development projects and influence policy formation. The Participatory Change Process was developed by the Center for Participatory Change, a US NGO which nurtures the development of grassroots organisations in western North Carolina.

At the core of the PCP are the concepts of participation and capacity building. Participation occurs when people use their life experiences as the foundation for community assessment, the analysis of community issues, and the planning and implementation of projects to address those issues (Chambers 1997). It refers to a process whereby community members control their community's development, shape the policies that affect it, and influence its direction of change (Nelson and Wright 1995). 'Capacity building' refers to the process of supporting groups as they develop the skills, knowledge, confidence, and organisational structures to act collectively over time to improve their community's well-being (Eade 1997).

The PCP signals a confluence of three practice approaches that have rarely been integrated: Participatory Rural Appraisal (PRA), popular education, and community organising. PRA consists of a collection of exercises which enable grassroots groups to participate in the planning and implementation of development projects (Chambers 1997). Popular education refers to the use of small-group dialogues to help people to learn to use reflections on their everyday experiences to critically analyse the social, political, and economic systems in which they live (Freire 1970). Community organising refers to the process of bringing community members together in order to build their capacities and accomplish tasks related to fundamental social change (Alinsky 1969). The PCP builds on the strengths of these three practice approaches (Castelloe and Watson 1999).

## Overview of the Participatory Change Process

There are five major activities that make up the PCP.

1   **Forming community-based groups**. The Process begins with the recruitment of 10–15 community members to form a community-based group. This recruitment is based upon two methods from community organising: (1) developing relationships with grassroots leaders (via door-to-door canvassing and visiting hubs of community life); and (2) developing relationships with professionals who work at the grassroots level (e.g. religious leaders, staff from governmental and non-governmental organisations). In order to ensure wide participation, community-based groups generally include as much racial, gender, and generational diversity as possible.

2   **The Triple-A Methodology**.[1] The Triple-A Methodology is a systematic sequence of participatory exercises which enables members of grassroots groups to plan development projects that meet their needs and address their priorities (Castelloe and Watson 1999). These exercises are implemented over a four-month period of weekly two-hour meetings.[2] We use the term 'Triple-A Methodology' because it emphasises *assessment*, *analysis*, and *action*. Phases of the methodology include: (1) *assessing* the issues faced by the community, and potential resources for addressing those issues; (2) *analysing* the social, cultural, political, and economic causes underlying those issues; and (3) planning *actions* to address the issues. As we facilitate the Triple-A Methodology, we also teach it; hence participating groups develop the capacities to implement the methodology on their own. Most of the exercises in the Triple-A Methodology were adapted from the literature on popular education or PRA. They include the following:

### Assessment

- Cardstorming on community issues: brainstorm issues via index cards on wall.
- Community living-room assessments: pairs of group members conduct informal assessments of community issues with 7 to 15 community members.

- Community asset mapping: group members list and map community assets.
- Prioritising a community issue to focus on, via pairwise ranking.

## Analysis

- Who decides, who benefits, who loses? – in relation to community issues or problems.
- Root-cause analysis: analyse the root causes of community issues or problems.
- Community assets analysis: analyse the degree to which local assets meet needs.

## Action

- Identifying and ranking solutions to the identified community issue – via matrix ranking.
- Analysing outcomes of potential solutions: analyse what is gained in each solution.
- Force-field analysis: analyse helping and hindering forces in implementing the project.
- Project implementation plan: specify activities to implement highest-priority solution.
- GANTT Chart: clarify the timeline and major phases of the project.

3 **Action and Capacity Building**. After completing the Triple-A Methodology, the grassroots group has a plan for community action to address a high-priority community issue. It also has a deep and critical analysis of the larger contexts in which that action will take place. At this point, the group faces a choice. It can choose to engage in the Action and Capacity Building process, where the Center for Participatory Change (CPC) provides two forms of support: support for implementing the plan for action developed in the Triple-A Methodology, and support for building their capacities to form as a non-profit organisation.[3] Alternatively, it can choose not to engage in the Action and Capacity Building process, in which case CPC still provides support for implementing the plan for action developed in the Triple-A Methodology.

The Action and Capacity Building process is a systematic sequence of participatory education and training sessions that has two foci: action and capacity building. 'Action' refers to supporting groups as they implement a development project (planned during the Triple-A Methodology). 'Capacity building' refers to building grassroots groups' organisational capacities, developing their board of directors (i.e. the organisations' governance), and supporting their formation as independent non-profit organisations (in accordance with US laws). The Action and Capacity Building process is implemented over a five-month period of weekly two-hour meetings. Specific action and capacity building activities include Action meetings (held every other week) for ongoing support and revision of project implementation; and Capacity Building meetings (held every other week), involving the following exercises: developing an Organisational Mission to describe the organisation's purpose; developing an Organisational Vision, which sets forth the expected future of the organisation; forming a Board of Directors: the group responsible for governing the organisation; understanding incorporation as a nonprofit organisation, according to US laws; writing Organisational By-laws (two meetings): the organisation's rule book; completing forms related to incorporation as a US non-profit organisation. For the directors, there is a three-day retreat, held to approve the work so far (half day); learn the basics of grassroots fundraising (one day); and learn about board development in general: participatory decision making, working as a group, shared leadership, and group process skills (one and a half days). The ultimate outcome of a group's engagement in the Action and Capacity Building process is the formation of a sustainable non-profit organisation that is responsive and accountable to community members, and which will work to implement development projects and shape policy formation at a local level.

4 **Ongoing organisational support**. The PCP also includes ongoing support for the grassroots organisations that complete the Action and Capacity Building process. This takes the form of ten hours of consultation per month for at least three months, with the option of an extension after three months. The support can focus on organisational capacity building and/or on continuing to plan and implement development projects; the nature of the support is determined by the grassroots organisation.

5 **Grassroots Federation and Community Roundtables.** The Grassroots Federation refers to semi-annual meetings of a federation of grassroots organisations which uses participatory methodologies

(based on the Triple-A Methodology) to address regional development issues. The purpose of the Grassroots Federation is to enable
grassroots groups to learn from each other; support each other; and
plan the work needed for poor and marginalised people to
participate in shaping the policies that affect them. The Federation
is crucial to the Participatory Change Process. The Triple-A
Methodology and the Action and Capacity Building process
emphasise using people's priorities as a basis for development at a
micro or project level. Such a focus may be excessively local and
parochial; it may neglect the broader contexts of community change
and result in a failure to become involved in wider political processes.
Further, a single community-based group is simply too small to
effect fundamental social change. As a network of organisations, the
Grassroots Federation represents a form of grassroots social action
that moves beyond the parochialism of single-issue or single-
community efforts by aiming to have a significant influence on
policy formation at a regional and state level.

Community Roundtables are semi-annual meetings of a
coalition of grassroots organisations (i.e. the Grassroots Federation),
religious organisations, governmental and non-governmental
organisations, businesses, and/or elected and appointed officials
across western North Carolina. The Community Roundtables are
held only after the Grassroots Federation is fully established – after
it has set its vision, defined its goals, and prioritised the issues that
it plans to address. Their purpose is to enable grassroots organisations to develop collaborations and alliances with sympathetic
professionals in various fields, thus building a broad-based coalition
that can influence policy at a regional and state level.

## Conclusion

Facilitating fundamental change in social, cultural, economic, and
political structures cannot occur in a short period of time. To bring
about sustainable change, we need to create a new way of working with
grassroots groups over the long haul. We need to help grassroots
groups to develop sustainable organisations for building the power to
implement development projects and influence policy formation.
This is the goal of the Participatory Change Process. This is designed
to empower grassroots groups to assess and analyse community issues,
design and implement projects to address those issues, and develop the

capacities needed to form as independent organisations (in order to continue addressing community issues). A more long-term goal is the development of a federation of grassroots organisations that aims to influence resource distribution and policy formation at a regional and state level. The Participatory Change Process is based on the priorities of community members (rather than outside 'experts'), and the projects that result from the model are initiated, planned, implemented, and evaluated by community members themselves. This model signals a new way of structuring development work so that communities can control their own development, and so that community groups can build the capacities to influence fundamental change at a regional and state level.

## Notes

1  The term 'Triple-A Methodology' is adapted from a process ('the Triple-A cycle for social mobilisation') developed by the Iringa Nutrition Project in Tanzania (see Krishna et al. 1997).

2  Holding weekly two-hour meetings is consistent with the culture of US community development. In other settings, the timeframe for implementing the Participatory Change Process might differ.

3  A 'non-profit organisation' is a US NGO that meets the tax-code requirements for tax-exempt status.

## References

Alinsky, Saul (1969) *Reveille for Radicals*, Chicago: University of Chicago Press.

Castelloe, Paul and Thomas Watson (1999) 'The Triple-A Methodology: integrating participatory development, popular education, and community organising', unpublished.

Chambers, Robert (1997) *Whose Reality Counts? Putting the First Last*, London: IT Publications.

Eade, Deborah (1997) *Capacity-building: An Approach to People-centred Development*, Oxford: Oxfam.

Freire, Paulo (1970) *Pedagogy of the Oppressed*, New York: Continuum.

Krishna, Anirudh with Urban Jonsson and Wibald Lorri (1997) 'The Iringa Nutrition Project: child survival and development in Tanzania' , in A. Krishna, N. Uphoff, and M. J. Esman (eds.) *Reasons for Hope: Instructive Experiences in Rural Development*, West Hartford, CT: Kumarian Press.

Nelson, Nici and Susan Wright (eds.) (1995) *Power and Participatory Development: Theory and Practice*, London: IT Publications.

# Two approaches to evaluating the outcomes of development projects

## Marion Meyer and Naresh Singh

Development strategies and theories have evolved over the past 50 years in response to lessons learned and changing circumstances. While there are many schools of thought on the issue, two main trends have emerged in practice. The first is where 'development' starts with the outsider providing some good or service (most likely a good) which a community may or may not need. This, known as the 'top–down approach', still occurs. But as people resented being treated as objects, and 'development' projects failed to achieve their goals, the emphasis moved towards the so-called 'people-centred' approach, or 'bottom–up' development. This concentrates on the needs of people, what *they* want and need. *They* define the goals of development and participate in development 'projects' from the beginning (Goulet, 1995).

The key is participation. However, the degree of participation varies. Some development projects involve an outsider coming in with an agenda and then harnessing the community's knowledge, people, and so on, in that research. Other projects involve an outsider offering services to a community, which sets the research agenda itself. Still others involve development taking place within a community without the help of outsiders. Certain underlying principles are common to all these types of participation.

What finally counts is whether the 'project' goal or outcome is achieved, by evaluating its performance. Reviewing the different principles and characteristics embodied in these two development philosophies, this article discusses evaluation in terms of two approaches: *the subjective and the objective*. We examine each, and discuss whether they are mutually exclusive or compatible, and indeed whether evaluating project outcomes is worthwhile.

While participatory development projects are highly fashionable, less attention has been paid to determining whether their stated outcomes[1] will be achieved. Traditional top–down projects have usually been evaluated with respect only to their outputs[2] and not to their outcomes. We hope to help to fill the gap in development thinking about how to evaluate so-called development projects effectively.

## Approaches to development projects

Most participatory development projects have similar characteristics and operate according to a general set of principles.[3] Firstly, these projects are supposed to be bottom–up, informed by the participants themselves. Secondly, participatory development claims to be holistic, taking into account a community's emotional, psychological, cultural, and spiritual needs as well as its physical needs (Goulet, 1995). Thus project outcomes are often intangible. For example, a project may set out to achieve empowerment, which is a state of being and not easily observable.

Furthermore, (the) development (project) is regarded as a process with no distinct end in sight. It takes place in a dynamic environment and responds and adjusts to changing situations. The major source of change in any community is probably not the development project. Hence, participatory development involves a long-term commitment of time and resources, and often involves a personal commitment to the people involved (Jiggins, 1995).

Evaluating an intangible process is difficult, for evaluation also then has to become a process. It must take place simultaneously and run parallel to development itself (Patton, 1982; Richards, 1985). The function of evaluation in this context is to inform, guide, and encourage the participants. Information is fed back, and appropriate adjustments are made, thus facilitating learning. Evaluation in a participatory context is subjective and based on culture. Understanding human behaviour and development from the participants' own frame of reference is considered important. Thus, social relations, power structures, and institutional factors are all taken into account (Salmen, 1987).

Non-participatory approaches are characterised by top–down activities and projects. These have a defined duration with a distinct end, and usually provide some tangible output (such as a dam). They involve a commitment of time and resources for a fixed period, regardless of whether the original goals are achieved. Such projects are linear, adhering to a plan drawn up prior to implementation. The fundamental assumption is that a causal relationship exists between the actions, the outputs, and the outcomes (Jiggins, 1995). The project is regarded as the major source of change. Most such projects are evaluated with regard to the achievement of the stated outputs as a function of allocated time and resources. The outcomes or goals are hoped for.

Table 1 compares participatory and non-participatory projects.

| Table 1: Comparison of participatory and non-participatory projects | | |
|---|---|---|
| | **Participatory** | **Non-participatory** |
| Locus of control | Bottom–up | Top–down |
| Duration | Indefinite | Defined period |
| Process | Cyclical, social learning process | Linear |
| Type of commitment | Long-term, often personal too | Length of the project |
| Hypothesis | The project is not the major source of change. It is only one part of a complex system. | A direct causal relationship exists between inputs and outcomes. |
| Outcomes | Intangible, as is the project itself | Tangible project and outcomes |
| (Table 1 summarises the experience of Goulet, 1995; Jiggins, 1995; Richards, 1985; and Salmen, 1987.) | | |

## Approaches to evaluation

There are many definitions of evaluation. According to Patton (1982: 15):

> *The practice of evaluation involves the systematic collection of information about the activities, characteristics, and outcomes of programs, personnel, and products for use by specific people to reduce uncertainties, improve effectiveness, and make decisions with regard to what those programs, personnel or products are doing and emphasizes (1) a systematic collection of information about (2) a broad range of topics (3) for use by specific people (4) for a variety of purposes.*

This definition is useful, since it is comprehensive, flexible, and broad, while others tend to be more specific. It is good to be flexible enough to understand which definitions of evaluation are appropriate and meaningful in a particular context.

It is also helpful to realise that many types of evaluation exist along with many methods. Here, two main approaches are examined. Generally these are referred to merely as *evaluation* and *participatory evaluation*; here we call them *objective* and *subjective evaluation* respectively, in order to avoid confusion. The former refers to any evaluation which follows the standard paradigm of seeking quantitative facts in an objective, technocratic manner. Emphasis is placed on measurability; and reviewing timeliness, efficiency, and value for money is standard. Analysis is generally objective and scientific, reducing reality to its smallest possible components. Conclusions are then drawn from these findings. If such an evaluation does look at social phenomena, the facts or causes are sought, with little regard for the subjective states of the individuals.

A distinction needs to be made between participatory evaluation and the evaluation of participation. Subjective evaluation refers to the former. Evaluating participation, on the other hand, could be done using either the objective or the subjective approach. Subjective evaluation is concerned less with measuring efficiency or value for money, and more with measuring the effectiveness of an action, or not measuring anything at all. It concentrates on the qualitative aspects of development, assessing what is taking place, and making recommendations accordingly (Jiggins, 1995). Models are not used to explain reality, because it is felt that reality is too complex to simplify in this way. In trying to simplify it, some important insight or observation could be lost. Thus, goal-free evaluation is preferred, whereby goals (or outcomes) are emergent and grow out of the environment in which evaluation is taking place (Patton, 1981; Patton, 1982; Richards, 1985). This coincides with the hypothesis that the project is probably not the only source of change within a community.

### Subjective and objective evaluation

It is tempting to talk about evaluating top–down and participatory projects as if they were distinct. This would be foolish, however, since both subjective and objective approaches can be used for evaluating either type of project. The appropriate approach will depend upon several factors. For instance, who will be using the evaluation results; what the purpose of the evaluation is; who is doing the evaluating; and when the evaluation is taking place.

An evaluation always has an audience in mind, someone who has requested that an evaluation be done. This 'someone' could be a funding agency, or it could be the management team of the organisation conducting the research, or the research team, or the community involved in the project. The purpose of the evaluation depends on who will be using the results, since each party has its own specific needs. A funding agency is generally more interested in how efficiently the research was conducted, whether it got value for money, and whether the project was finished on time. A research team is probably more inclined to want to know which methods worked most effectively in gathering information, where it can improve its practices, whether any important information was omitted, and whether the goals of the project have been reached. A community is more interested in knowing whether everyone was included in the research, whether the research was appropriate, and whether it took different groups and power structures into account (since this will give the research credibility in the eyes of the community members). Management is concerned about timeliness and efficient use of resources, about reaching the original goals, any other results that may have transpired, and whether personnel have performed as expected.

Subjective evaluations tend to be more suited to the needs of the research team and the community, since they will produce the information they seek most effectively. Objective evaluation tends to meet the needs of the funding agency or management, for the same reason.

Who is conducting it plays a key role in the type of evaluation to be used. If the same research team is also responsible for the evaluation, they are likely to use an approach which coincides with that of the project. Researchers implementing a participatory project are committed over the long term, and are interested in assessing progress along the way in order to be able to respond to new situations, and adjust methods where they are not achieving what they intended. Thus, such researchers will be inclined to use subjective evaluative methods. The team who built a dam may prefer an objective approach, since this will deliver the information they are after. Similarly, an outsider evaluating the participatory project may choose an objective evaluation method, if it is being done for management or the funding agency.

Not to be forgotten is the fact that the choice of evaluation type is itself subjective. Evaluators will be inclined to choose the method which fits with their own philosophy. Hence, one person may be inclined to use subjective evaluation when examining the effects of the newly built dam on people in nearby villages, and those who have been resettled in the process.

Finally, *when* the evaluation takes place will also determine the type that is used. If it is to inform learning throughout the implementation process, the subjective approach may be chosen. But it is often easier to use the objective approach if the evaluation is being conducted after the project has been completed. Again this will partly be determined by the type of information which is being sought.

Richards (1985) is critical of using an approach to evaluation which is dictated by its purpose. Rather, he would have evaluators choose a method commensurate with the type of project, and deduce the necessary information from there. We agree with him. Forcing (the) everyday life (of a project) to conform to the requirements of research does not make sense. Surely it is more expedient to look at everyday life, and draw conclusions from there.

Table 2 compares the subjective and objective approaches to evaluation.

## Applicability

Discussion has centred around the type of evaluation which is used for both participatory and non-participatory development projects. There is some argument, however, about whether evaluation is valid at all in a participatory context. It is sometimes argued that evaluation has its origins in top–down approaches, and therefore is intrinsically inapplicable to participatory projects. Our view is that subjective evaluation has evolved largely in response to the rise of participatory projects. But in any case, evaluation is an inherent part of people's everyday lives. We do not necessarily call it that, but we constantly process information as it becomes available and use it to make

| Table 2: Comparison of subjective and objective evaluations[4] | | |
|---|---|---|
| | **Subjective** | **Objective** |
| When evaluation takes place | Simultaneous with project: parallel process | After the fact: separate event |
| What is evaluated | Measures effectiveness or does not measure at all. Analyses social relations, power structures, and institutional factors | Measures efficiency, timeliness, value for money |
| Model | A complex system not explicable by a model | Reality is reduced to its smallest possible components |
| Type of activity | Learning process | Evaluation |
| Framework | Context-specific | Basic framework adjusted slightly for different situations |
| Nature of evaluation | Subjective, participatory, culturally based. Concerned with understanding human behaviour and development from the participants' own frame of reference. | Objective, scientific, and technocratic. Seeks facts or causes of social phenomena with little regard for the subjective states of individuals. |

(Table 2 summarises the experiences of FAO, 1988; Jiggins, 1995; Patton, 1981; Patton 1982; Richards, 1985; and Salmen, 1987.)

decisions about the future. Following the news is one example. Keeping a diary is another. This activity is not restricted to Western civilisation either: rural and indigenous communities have their own ways of doing the same thing. Early-warning systems and story-telling have the same functions. So, evaluation happens continuously. What is important is that the correct approach is used for the situation in question.

There are benefits and disadvantages in everything. Evaluating a project (using whatever approach) can never look at every aspect, and necessarily carries the danger of missing some major insight (Jiggins, 1995; Richards, 1985). Knowing that a project is going to be evaluated can lead to some bizarre situations, too. It may lead to inaction, because implementers are afraid of the consequences if something goes wrong, and it comes out in the evaluation. They may cover up things that took place and in so doing mask the real dynamics behind what happened. Or a show may be put on for the evaluators on the day they visit the project. All these will lead to incorrect conclusions. But not evaluating has pitfalls too. It exonerates project implementers from being accountable for the responsible use of resources. The opportunity for learning and improvement is also forfeited. In evaluating development projects, we need to be aware of these issues and interpret the results accordingly.

## Synthesis

In addition to the four main factors informing the type of evaluation to be chosen, underlying assumptions inherent in the project design will also be reflected. Thus it is often true that objective evaluation will be used to evaluate top–down projects, and subjective evaluation for participatory projects.

But both approaches have had a tendency to throw the baby out with the bath-water. Non-participatory development and objective evaluation follows the Western scientific paradigm, and in so doing ignores the important social interactions which affect the outcomes of a project – even those which set out to produce tangible outputs. Changing the environment will always have political ramifications (within the household, the community, the local authorities, or national government) which will influence the success of a project. Recognising that various aspects of life interact with each other would go a long way towards understanding why a given project turns out the way it does. Hence the need to look at how a project interacts with other factors, and vice versa. Further, objective evaluation often runs the risk of becoming so independent and objective that it loses sight of the needs of the participants, beneficiaries, and managers – and so is not relevant to them (IDRC, 1994).

Subjective evaluation tends to discount measurable goals such as efficiency, because 'participatory projects' are concerned with qualitative things such as gender or power relations. Further, interim goals are seldom set, because there is no telling how long it will take to reach them. This is a valid argument, but some broad objectives need to be set – otherwise practitioners are free to do as they please, with no accountability, and the capacity to waste a tremendous amount of resources. Wasting resources (whether time, money, or effort) does not enhance sustainability for instance, nor value for money, and does not make sense in the long run. Thus, measuring efficiency, timeliness, value for money, and so on is important. Paying attention to these aspects will hold practitioners more accountable for the resources they are using in the name of development. What may be necessary, though, is to find new ways of defining them, so that they can be used in a context where there are very vague goals, and no definite end to a project.

Unfortunately, even participatory evaluation is often concerned with looking at a 'project' in isolation. Often only the social interactions within the community itself are studied, ignoring the effect of the research team within the community. If these interactions were reviewed, it could lead to a better development process.

Another problem with objective evaluation is that it is often a one-off occurrence, to be performed at the end of a project. Subjective evaluation can be one-off, but often takes place on a continuous basis or at intervals throughout the project's lifetime. Objective evaluation could be valuable, if used at more than one point over a period of time. It would serve as a learning tool, and would encourage accountability.

## Conclusion

As development practices have evolved, so has evaluation. Generally, the underlying assumptions and approaches of both have been the same. This is true for both the participatory and non-participatory approaches. At first glance, it would appear that the subjective and objective approaches to evaluation are mutually exclusive. But each has some validity and, brought together, they form an improved approach to evaluation.

While a pendulum swings from one extreme to another, at some point it comes to rest in the centre. This discussion brings the pendulum to the centre by recognising that each approach has its place, but that each could learn from the other. An amalgamation of objective and subjective approaches can lead to a more informed evaluation outcome, and an enhanced development project or process. Finally, while any type of evaluation has its shortcomings, we should not be paralysed into inaction. Evaluation, while not always referred to as such, is a part of everyday life — and so demonstrates its usefulness in whatever we do.

## Notes

1   The terms 'goals' and 'outcomes' are used interchangeably in this article.
2   'Outputs' refers to tangible products resulting from a development project: for example, a dam or a number of houses. 'Outcomes' are what the project hopes to achieve as a result of the outputs: for example, capacity building or empowerment.
3   The question of who participates is, of course, an important question, but one which will not be dealt with here.
4   The information in Table 2 does not represent absolutes. Some which holds for the subjective column can just as easily hold for the objective column, and *vice versa*.

## References

Food and Agricultural Organization of the United Nations (FAO) (1988) *Participatory Monitoring and Evaluation*, Bangkok: FAO Regional Office for Asia and the Pacific.

Goulet, D. (1995) 'Authentic development: is it sustainable?' in *A Sustainable World: Defining and Measuring Sustainable Development* (Trzyna and Osborn, eds.), Sacramento: International Center for the Environment and Public Policy, California Institute of Public Affairs.

International Development Research Centre (IDRC) (1994) *Worksheets for Evaluation Planning*, Ottawa: International Development Research Centre.

Jiggins, J. (1995) 'Development impact assessment: Impact assessment of aid on nonwestern countries', *Impact Assessment* 13/1: 47-70.

Patton, M. Q. (1981) *Creative Evaluation*, Beverly Hills: Sage Publications, Inc.

Patton, M. Q. (1982) *Practical Evaluation*, Beverly Hills: Sage Publications, Inc.

Richards, H. (1985) *The Evaluation of Cultural Action*, London: Macmillan.

Salmen, L. F. (1987) *Listen to the People: Participant-Observer Evaluation of Development Projects*, Washington DC: The World Bank.

# Resources

Critical aid-watchers have long argued that development agencies, albeit unintentionally, depoliticise development. This may be to accommodate a particular worldview or policy agenda, or to allow them to tap into donor funding. All bureaucracies tend to perpetuate themselves, and aid agency staff are no different from other workers in being disinclined to court their own unemployment. Among development agencies themselves, we can identify three quite different positions concerning the methods that they use, and the wider approaches that these represent. The first is to treat these tools as though they were politically value-free, assuming that their use confers 'objectivity' on practitioners and their observations. The major official agencies are sometimes accused of promoting this technocratic view. The second is to see methods and tools as embodying the 'hidden agendas' of the organisations most closely associated with them, and hence not remotely neutral. In this reading, a tool that originated in, say, the corporate sector, necessarily bears the for-profit hallmark and cannot properly be applied to the non-profit sector. This line of thinking tends to be more associated with NGOs. The most common position is that of a pragmatic eclecticism: agencies take what they like from the smorgasbord of approaches and methodologies on offer, and simply ignore the bits that they dislike or find unpalatable. The problem is that if the links between methods and ideologies are ruptured, and the methods themselves are poorly understood or wrongly applied, the overall approach becomes incoherent and directionless.

This selected resources list includes some major theoretical works on development, a number of 'classic' texts on particular methods or approaches, and a range of critical readings on the issues. For ease of reference, the list has been organised under the following headings: background readings; information gathering and research; organisational change and organisational learning; monitoring, evaluation, and impact assessment; participation and capacity building; gender analysis and planning; environmental sustainability; multi-stakeholder partnerships; and humanitarian and emergency relief work. Where a book has been reviewed in Development in Practice, *this has been indicated; these reviews may be downloaded on a pay-per-view basis at www.tandf.co.uk/journals/carfax/ 09614524.html. Annotated lists of resources appended to previous titles in the* Development in Practice *Readers series are available free of charge at www.developmentinpractice.org*

*This selection was compiled and annotated by Alina Rocha Menocal with Deborah Eade, Deputy Editor and Editor respectively of* Development in Practice.

## Background reading

**Chang, Ha-Joon:** *Kicking Away the Ladder: Development Strategy in Historical Perspective*, London: Anthem Press, 2002, ISBN: 1 84 331027 9, 187 pp.

In this controversial book, Chang argues that developed countries did not become rich by adopting the 'good practices' and the 'good institutions' that they now present to poorer countries as the essential basis for development. He maintains that the industrialised nations are in this way 'kicking away the ladder' by which they climbed to the top, preventing the developing world from applying the very policies and institutions upon which they themselves had relied in order to develop.

**Dichter, Thomas:** *Despite Good Intentions: Why Development Assistance to the Third World has Failed*, Amherst: University of Massachusetts Press, ISBN: 1 55849 393 X

The author, himself a veteran aid-agency worker, surveys the history of development assistance from 1945, which has been premised on the belief that the industrialised countries could in some way engineer the acceleration of history in the less-developed world. He argues that the enterprise is internally flawed: the vast differences in power between the donors and recipients of aid, and the organisational imperatives to show 'results', conspire to keep the development industry in business and the unequal relationships intact. If the goal is for aid recipients to become autonomous, free of external control, then the first step has to be to reduce and not increase development assistance, since this serves principally to consolidate the power of the 'helpers'. For a full review, see *Development in Practice* 13(4).

**Escobar, Arturo:** *Encountering Development: The Making and Unmaking of the Third World*, Princeton, NJ: Princeton University Press, 1994, ISBN: 0 691 00102 2, 320 pp.

In this now classic presentation of post-development thought, Escobar offers a challenging critique of development discourse and practice, arguing that development policies deployed by the West to 'assist' impoverished countries are in effect self-reinforcing mechanisms of control that are just as pervasive and effective as colonialism was in earlier years. To capture the production of knowledge and power in development initiatives, Escobar uses case studies which illustrate how peasants, women, and nature, for instance, become objects of knowledge and targets of power under the 'gaze of experts'. He concludes with a discussion of alternative visions for a post-development era.

**Ferguson, James:** *The Anti-Politics Machine: 'Development', Depoliticization, and Bureaucratic Power in Lesotho*, Minneapolis, MN: University of Minnesota Press, 1994, ISBN: 0 8166 2437 2, 320 pp.

Based on a case study of a development project in Lesotho, this classic work is a searing critique of the development industry as a whole. The 'anti-politics machine' refers to the process through which outside 'development' agencies and experts wilfully turn the political realities of poverty and powerlessness into 'technical' problems which require an equally technical solution. Using an anthropological approach, the author analyses the institutional framework within which development projects are crafted, revealing how it is that, despite all the 'expertise' that goes into formulating them, these projects often betray a startling arrogance and deep ignorance of the historical and political realities of the communities whom they are intended to help.

**Fisher, William F. and Thomas Ponniah** (eds.): *Another World is Possible: Popular Alternatives to Globalization at the World Social Forum*, London: Zed, 2003, ISBN: 1 8427 7329 1, 320 pp.

The World Social Forum has swiftly become the focal meeting point for a diverse group of activists, practitioners, and analysts to identify alternatives to the current international economic system. This book is a compilation of some of the most cogent and constructive thinking by groups of indigenous people, trade unions, environmentalists, women's organisations, church groups, and students, among others, on issues concerning growth and equity, social justice, environmental sustainability, the importance of civil society and public space, new forms of democracy, and ethical political action.

**Harriss, John:** *Depoliticizing Development: The World Bank and Social Capital*, London: Anthem Press, 2002, ISBN: 1 84331 049 X, 149 pp.

Since the publication of Robert Putnam's work on the subject in 1994, social capital has been proclaimed by the World Bank and other multilateral institutions as the 'missing link' in international development. Harriss provides a meticulous critique of the concept of social capital, arguing that the Bank has embraced it precisely because it neatly sidelines issues of class relations and power. Social capital has thus been used in the dominant discourse as a tool to depoliticise development.

**Howell, Jude and Jenny Pearce:** *Civil Society and Development: A Critical Exploration*, Boulder, CO: Lynne Rienner, 2001, ISBN: 1 58826 095 X, 267 pp.

This book explores the complex relationship between civil society, the State, and the market in the context of democratic development. Drawing on case studies from Africa, Asia, and Latin America, the authors attempt to establish a common understanding of those key concepts and to clarify what the 'strengthening' of civil society, so often advocated by development agencies, may mean in practice.

**Ibister, John:** *Promises Not Kept: The Betrayal of Social Change in the Third World*, Bloomfield, CT: Kumarian Press, 2003, ISBN: 1 56549 173 4, 272 pp.

Now in its sixth edition, this classic text explores the links between the North and the South, and, more broadly, the issues of international poverty, in the context of a new US hegemony and the war on terrorism, post-11 September 2001. The author also surveys the prospects for justice in an increasingly globalised world.

**Ibister, John:** *Capitalism and Justice: Envisioning Social and Economic Fairness*, Bloomfield, CT: Kumarian Press, 2001, ISBN: 1 56549 122 X, 272 pp.

Can a capitalist economic system be a just one? How big a spread in incomes between the rich and the poor, for example, is consistent with social justice? And what commitment should a rich country like the USA make to foreign aid? In this book, Ibister addresses these and related questions, challenging readers to think creatively about the meaning of justice and how it can work towards social and economic fairness within the boundaries of capitalism.

**Kaplan, Allan:** *Development Practitioners and Social Process: Artists of the Invisible*, London and Sterling, VA: Pluto Press, 2002, ISBN: 0 7453 1019 2, 214 pp.

Kaplan views social development as a complex process of social transformation, not a technical operation. Drawing on his extensive experience as a development consultant in Africa and Europe, he argues that intentional social change is possible, and that learning is the path to self-discovery and self-awareness, 'enabl[ing] both the organism and the world with which it interacts to be lifted to a new level of existence'. See also *The Development Practitioners' Handbook*.

**Martinussen, John:** *Society, State, and Market: A Guide to Competing Theories of Development*, London: Zed Books, 1997, ISBN: 1 85649 442 X, 400 pp.

Intended as an introductory textbook to development theory, this provides a comprehensive and multi-disciplinary picture of development research since the 1950s, with a particular focus on the contributions of Southern intellectuals. The author presents a critical overview of some of the most important theoretical approaches and current debates in the field, including explanations of economic development and underdevelopment, the role of the State as an engine of growth, and the complex links that exist between civil society and development. For a full review, see *Development in Practice* 8(1).

**Momsen, Janet Henshall:** *Gender and Development*, London: Routledge, 2003, ISBN: 0 4152 6689 0, 216 pp.

Based on years of fieldwork, this accessible textbook underscores the importance of gender dynamics in development. The book contains many reader-friendly features, including case studies drawn from countries in Eastern and Central Europe, Asia, and Latin America, learning objectives for each chapter, discussion questions, annotated guides to further reading and websites, and numerous maps and photographs.

**Rahnema, Majid with Victoria Bawtree** (eds.): *The Post-Development Reader*, London: Zed Books, 1997, 1 8564 9474 8, 464 pp.

With contributions from leading scholars and activists from around the world, this volume presents some of the most critical thinking on development in recent years. Contributors both challenge the mainstream development paradigm and offer many innovative ideas for how to generate more humane and culturally and ecologically respectful development alternatives.

**Sen, Amartya:** *Development as Freedom,* Oxford: Oxford University Press, 1999, ISBN: 0 19 829758 0, 382 pp.

In many ways a summation of Sen's work over the past decade, this book argues that economic development needs to be understood as a means to extending freedoms rather than as an end in itself. In his view, the 'overarching objective' of development is to maximise people's 'capabilities' – their freedom to 'lead the kind of lives they value, and have reason to value'. The author also considerably expands the definition of development beyond a focus on material wealth to include issues related to inequality, tyranny, political structures, gender, and lack of opportunity and individual rights

**Thomas, Darryl C.:** *The Theory and Practice of Third World Solidarity,* Westport, CT: Praeger Publishers, 2001, ISBN: 0 275 92843 8, 344 pp.

This book examines the development of Third World solidarity as a reaction to the historic hegemony of the industrialised world. The author focuses on four generations of growing solidarity among developing countries: Afro-Asianism in the 1950s, non-alignment during the Cold War, the South vs the North in the 1970s, and South–South dialogue during the era of global restructuring in the 1980s and 1990s.

**Tornquist, Olle:** *Politics and Development: A Critical Introduction,* London: Sage, 1999, ISBN 0 761 95934 3, 208 pp.

In this comprehensive introduction to the principal analytical approaches used in political science, and their application to the study of Third World politics and development, the author presents a critical overview of the main schools of thought and illustrates how readers can develop their own analytical frameworks and perspectives.

**UNDP:** *Human Development Report*

The UNDP's annual Human Development Report was launched in 1990 as a counterweight to the *World Development Report* of the World Bank, which was viewed as focusing on economic issues to the exclusion of human and social development. The Bank's policies (particularly in the 'lost decade' of the 1980s) were having a detrimental effect on many developing countries, in part because of this neglect. Each HDR is thematic; topics have included gender, information technology, and human rights. The 2002 issue was entitled *Deepening Democracy in a Fragmented World*. UNDP has developed a range of economic and social measures in order to rank countries according to human development (the Human Development Index) and gender equity (the Gender Development Index) among other criteria. These indices persistently show that economic wealth, as measured by GNP and GDP, does not automatically correlate with the equitable distribution of resources or with the application of democratic principles.

**World Bank:** *World Development Report*

The World Bank's annual World Development Report is an influential publication, setting out the trends in development policy that will shape the Bank's own lending policies. Each issue focuses on a particular theme, such as poverty reduction, states and markets, transition economies, with milestone reports issued at the start of each decade. The 2003 WDR is entitled *Sustainable Development in a Dynamic World*; the subject of the 2004 volume is 'Making Services Work for the Poor'. Responding to criticisms about its lack of accountability, the Bank now incorporates extensive consultation in the preparatory process for each WDR, whereby trade unions, NGOs, and other public interest groups, as well as leading experts in the field, are involved in drafting and commenting on drafts. These submissions and commentaries are published on the Bank's website.

**UNRISD:** *Visible Hands: Taking Responsibility for Social Development*, Geneva: UNRISD, 2000, ISBN: 92 9085 032 9, 173 pp.

This sequel to *States of Disarray*, produced for the 1995 Social Summit, shows that few of the commitments made by UN member states have been backed with resources, and indeed that neo-liberal globalisation is in full spate, states are being further undermined by a rise in technocratic policy making, and the commitment to corporate social responsibility is little more than rhetorical. The report expresses the hope that rights-based development agendas will seize the public imagination and help to encourage reform of the international finance and trade organisation. For a full review, see *Development in Practice* 11(1):118-19.

## Information gathering and research

**Coghlan, David and Teresa Brannick**: *Doing Action Research in Your Own Organization*, London: Sage 2000, ISBN: 0 7619 6887 3, 152 pp.

This primer on action research and how to use it to understand organisations is structured in two parts. Part I covers the foundations of action research, including the research skills needed to undertake research, while Part II covers the implementation of an action-research project. The book addresses the advantages and potential pitfalls of undertaking action research in one's own organisation, as well as the politics and ethics involved. It also offers practical advice on such matters as selecting a suitable project and implementing it. Each chapter includes exercises, examples, and clear summaries.

**Gubrium, Jaber F. and James A. Holstein** (eds.): *The Handbook of Interview Research: Context and Method*, London: Sage, 2001, ISBN: 0 7619 1951 1, 982 pp.

Interviewing is the predominant mode of conducting research and gathering information in the social sciences. This ambitious volume offers a comprehensive examination of the interview as an integral part of society. With contributions from leading experts in a wide range of professional disciplines, the book addresses conceptual and technical challenges that confront both academic researchers and interviewers with more applied goals. The material covered is impressive in scope, ranging from interview theory to the nuts-and-bolts of the interview process.

**Thomas, Alan, Joanna Chataway, and Marc Wuyts** (eds.): *Finding Out Fast: Investigative Skills for Policy and Development*, London: Sage, in association with The Open University, 1998 0 7619 5837 1, 352 pp.

This book presents the key skills and approaches required to undertake policy-oriented research. Starting from the premise that policy decisions are typically made under severe time-constraints and on the basis of incomplete knowledge, the authors provide guidance on how to locate, evaluate, and use relevant information. The ultimate aim is to enable readers to become more competent investigators and to understand how to use research more effectively and critically evaluate research done by others. For a full review, see *Development in Practice* 9(1&2):202-4.

## Organisational change and organisational learning

**Chopra, A.J.:** *Managing the People Side of Innovation: 8 Rules for Changing Minds and Hearts,* West Harcourt, CT: Kumarian Press 1999, ISBN: 1-56549-098-3, 244 pp.

How do innovative ideas emerge in the face of deep-rooted organisational inertia and resistance to change? Chopra argues that such ideas will not be adopted without leadership, human energy, collaboration, and motivation. This 'how to' guide lists eight common-sense, though not always obvious, rules to change hearts and minds, and turns them into a series of tools aimed at facilitating change and innovation.

**Dixon, Nancy:** *The Organizational Learning Cycle: How We Can Learn Collectively,* Maidenhead: McGraw Hill, 1994, ISBN: 0 0770 7937 X, 176 pp.

Dixon analyses organisational learning as a powerful tool for self-transformation, arguing that, while organisations and individuals can learn independently of each other, growth is best achieved when organisational and personal development are combined and integrated. Thus, organisational learning requires the active involvement of the organisation's members in establishing the direction of change and in inventing the means to achieve it. To illustrate the different stages and types of learning involved, Dixon uses the Organisational Learning Cycle, whose four steps are the generation of information; the integration of new information into the organisational context; the collective interpretation of that information; and the authority to act based on the interpreted meaning.

**Eade, Deborah and Suzanne Williams:** *The Oxfam Handbook of Development and Relief,* Oxford: Oxfam GB, 1995, ISBN: 0 85598 274 8, 1200 pp.

Based on the work of Oxfam GB in more than 70 countries worldwide, this text synthesises the agency's thinking, policy, and practice in fields as diverse as social relations, human rights, advocacy, capacity building, popular organisation, education, health, sustainable agricultural production, and emergency relief. A gender perspective is incorporated throughout. Presented in three volumes, the Handbook reflects Oxfam's belief that all people have the right to an equitable share in the world's resources, and the right to make decisions about their own development. The denial of such rights is at the heart of poverty and suffering. For a full review, see *Development in Practice* 6(1):82-4.

**Foster, Marie-Claude:** *Management Skills for Project Leaders: What to do when you do not know what to do,* Basel: Birkhäuser Publishing, 2001, ISBN: 3 7643 6423 8, 202 pp.

Traditional models of management work best in situations characterised by simplicity, linearity, and continuity. However, given that chaos and uncertainty are the norm rather than the exception, such management models are of little assistance to aid agencies. Aimed at development managers and project leaders, this book outlines the critical skills that are required in this increasingly complex field, and focuses in particular on the importance of continuous learning among development workers and change agents.

**Hanna, Nagy and Robert Picciotto** (eds.): *Making Development Work: Development Learning in a World of Poverty and Wealth,* Somerset, NJ: Transaction Publishers, 2002.

The World Bank's Comprehensive Development Framework (CDF) initiative has been launched in 12 developing countries. Its four key principles are: a holistic long-term vision of development; domestic ownership of development programmes; a results-oriented approach; and stronger partnerships and collaboration between government, the private sector, and civil society. This book is divided into four sections, which examine each of these principles in turn. The concluding chapter identifies key lessons learned, and proposes that multi-faceted approaches which incorporate 'client empowerment' and social learning should replace top–down, 'one-size-fits-all' prescriptions.

**Khor, Martin and Lim Li Lin** (eds.): *Good Practices and Innovative Experiences in the South: Economic, Environmental and Sustainable Livelihoods Initiatives* (vol. 1), ISBN: 1 84277 129 9, 255 pp.
*Good Practices and Innovative Experiences in the South: Social Policies, Indigenous Knowledge and Appropriate Technology* (vol. 2), ISBN: 84277 131 0, 215 pp.
*Good Practices and Innovative Experiences in the South: Citizen Initiatives in Social Services, Popular Education and Human Rights* (vol. 3), ISBN: 1 84277 133 7, 260 pp.
London and New York, NY: Zed Books, 2001

These three volumes, jointly produced by Third World Network and UNDP's Special Unit for Technical Cooperation among Developing Countries, outline some of the best practices and innovative ideas that are being pioneered at the government, NGO, and community levels in developing countries. While the areas of experimentation are fairly diverse, all the experiences recounted here rely on the same basic principles: respect for local knowledge systems; harmony with the environment; equity; and democratic, participatory involvement. Providing examples of successful development efforts in Asia, Latin America, and Africa, the editors seek to contribute to the process of learning and replication elsewhere.

**Leeuwis, Cees and Rhiannon Pyburn** (eds.): *Wheelbarrows Full of Frogs: Social learning in rural resource management*, Assen: Koninklijke van Gorcum, 2002, ISBN: 90 232 3850 8, 480 pp.

The title of this book, taken from a Dutch metaphor, is used to illustrate the difficulties involved in social learning: how to keep all the frogs (i.e. the multiple stakeholders) inside a wheelbarrow (i.e. a platform for social learning), while manoeuvring across difficult terrain (i.e. resource-management dilemmas)? Contributors argue that success requires commitment, presence of mind, flexibility, and stability. Unlike interventions based solely on technological or economic grounds, social learning is 'an interactive process moving from multiple cognition to collective or distributed cognition': the shared learning of interdependent stakeholders is therefore critical to reaching better outcomes in rural resource management. Following a theoretical overview, the book addresses a variety of issues, including social learning in action in agriculture, and social learning and institutional change.

**Lewis, David and Tina Wallace** (eds.): *New Roles and Relevance: Development NGOs and the Challenge of Change*, Bloomfield, CT: Kumarian Press, 2000, ISBN: 1 56549 120 3, 272 pp.

As development NGOs become increasingly relevant in anti-poverty initiatives, they need to guard against allowing their independence and integrity to be compromised. The contributors, who include both researchers and practitioners, argue that it is only through engagement at all levels and through effective learning strategies that NGOs will make a real and sustainable contribution to poverty-reduction efforts worldwide. For a full review, see *Development in Practice* 11(4):538.

**Lindenberg, Marc and Coralie Bryant:** *Going Global: Transforming Relief and Development NGOs*, Bloomfield, CT: Kumarian Press, 2001, ISBN: 1 5654 9135 1, 271 pp.

Drawing on extensive international fieldwork and group discussions with NGO leaders, the authors argue that the major Northern-based NGOs in international relief and development are at the cusp of a process of re-definition and transformation. Changes in the international arena and the forces of globalisation are re-shaping the landscape that NGOs inhabit, presenting them with new challenges and opportunities. If they seize these challenges creatively, Lindenberg and Bryant suggest, they may become yet more influential and effective in their efforts to eradicate poverty and expand their work into new areas (peace building, advocacy, etc). However, if they fail to do this, they risk becoming outdated, or even obsolete. For a full review, see *Development in Practice* 13(1):123-7.

**Macdonald, Mandy, Ellen Sprenger, and Ireen Dubel:** *Gender and Organizational Change: Bridging the Gap between Theory and Practice*, The Hague: Royal Tropical Institute, 1997, ISBN: 90 6832 709 7, 156 pp.

How can organisations in both North and South become more gender-aware and more gender-sensitive? Illustrated with experiences of gender interventions in numerous organisations, this book presents a practical approach to changing gender dynamics that is built on consensus. It includes a 'road map' for organisational change; material on organisational culture, the change agent, and gender; strategies for developing more gender-sensitive practice; and guidelines for a gender assessment of an organisation. For a full review, see *Development in Practice* 8(2):247-8.

**Pettit, Jethro, Laura Roper, and Deborah Eade** (eds.): *Development and the Learning Organisation*, Oxford: Oxfam GB, 2003, ISBN 0 85598 470 8, 434 pp.

As development NGOs and official aid agencies embrace the idea of 'becoming a learning organisation', they are increasingly concerned with some form of knowledge generation and organisational learning. The literature on these issues has so far tended to come out of the private sector and reflect a Western worldview. Based on a special issue of *Development in Practice* (Vol. 12 Nos. 3&4), this book presents contributions from development scholars and practitioners from a range of institutional backgrounds worldwide, some introducing new approaches and models, others offering critical case studies of individual and group learning practice across cultures, and organisational efforts to put theory into practice. Among the lessons to emerge are that learning is hard to do, that we often learn the wrong things, and that huge gaps often remain between our learning and our behaviour or practice. There are clearly no simple recipes for success, but when learning breakthroughs do occur, the organisational whole can truly become more than the sum of its parts.

**Porter, Fenella, Ines Smyth, and Caroline Sweetman** (eds.): *Gender Works: Oxfam Experience in Policy and Practice*, Oxford: Oxfam GB, 1999, ISBN 0 85598 407 4, 342 pp.

This edited volume brings together contributions from 36 current and former staff of Oxfam GB and other national Oxfams, describing the organisation's efforts since 1985 to integrate gender-related issues into its work and culture. The process has not been an easy one, and these essays frankly record the many setbacks and struggles as well as marking progress and specific achievements. For a full review, see *Development in Practice* 10(1):122-5.

**Rao, Aruna, Rieky Stuart, and David Kelleher:** *Gender at Work: Organizational Change for Equality*, West Harcourt CT: Kumarian Press 1999, ISBN: 1 56549 102 5, 272 pp.

This volume analyses institutional barriers to gender equality and provides insights into the means and processes by which gender relations can be transformed. In-depth examples from diverse organisations and countries lay out strategies and approaches for transforming organisations into cultures expressing gender equity.

The authors pose new questions about how gender-responsive policies and practices can best be advocated.

**Smillie, Ian and John Hailey:** *Managing for Change: Leadership, Strategy and Management in Asian NGOs,* London and Sterling, VA: Earthscan, 2001-02, ISBN: 1 85383 721 0, 193 pp.

As the number of NGOs increases, so they need to work harder at preserving their distinctiveness and effectiveness. Drawing on their analysis of how nine successful NGOs in Asia are managed, the authors seek to identify the key characteristics of a sustained growth process, and the strategies, management styles, and organisational structures that are more likely to lead to success. For a full review, see *Development in Practice* 12(3&4):549-51.

## Monitoring, evaluation, and impact assessment

**Cracknell, Basil Edward:** *Evaluating Development Aid: Issues, Problems and Solutions,* Thousand Oaks, CA: Sage, 2000, ISBN: 0 7619 9403 3, 386 pp.

This book looks at the methodologies of evaluation in the area of development aid and some of the problems that are likely to arise. The author focuses on the vexed question of how to reconcile the requirements of objectivity, distance, and accountability with the realisation that some form of participation is essential in order to understand the impact of people-centred projects on the intended beneficiaries. Main topics include the history of development aid, evaluation of impact and sustainability, stakeholder analysis, and participation.

**Estrella, Marisol (ed.) with Jutta Blauert, Dindo Campilan, John Gaventa, Julian Gonsalves, Irene Guijt, Deb Johnson, and Roger Ricafort:** *Learning from Change: Issues and Experiences in Participatory Monitoring and Evaluation,* London: ITDG Publishing, 2000, ISBN: 1 85339 469 6, 288 pp.

A compilation of case studies and discussions drawn from an international workshop on Participatory Monitoring and Evaluation (PM&E) held in the Philippines in 2000, this volume provides an overview of relevant themes and experiences in this field. Part I offers a literature review of methodological innovations in PM&E practice worldwide. Part II presents case studies which illustrate the diversity of settings in which PM&E has been undertaken. Finally, Part III raises key questions and challenges arising from the case studies and the workshop proceedings, identifying areas for further research and action.

**Feinstein, Osvaldo N. and Robert Picciotto** (eds.): *Evaluation and Poverty Reduction,* Somerset, NJ: Transaction Publishers, 2001, ISBN: 0 7658 0876 5, 382 pp.

In his foreword to this volume, James Wolfensohn states that 'evaluation is a central aspect of any poverty reduction endeavor ... [It] is not just a scorecard ... [but] something that helps us change our behavior or influence the behavior of others'. The book itself is a collection of papers by leading development scholars and practitioners illustrating this point. Seeking to promote development effectiveness through social learning and problem solving, the contributors emphasise 'what works' in poverty-reduction programmes, including social funds and safety nets, anti-corruption programmes, and a vibrant civil society.

**Gosling, Louisa L:** *Toolkits: A practical guide to monitoring, evaluation and impact assessment,* London: Save the Children Fund, 2003, ISBN: 1 84187 064 1, 250 pp.

Designed to promote a systematic approach to planning, reviewing, and evaluating development work, SCF's Toolkits series includes a range of practical tools that can be adapted to suit different circumstances. Thoroughly revised and updated, this edition brings a commonsense approach to recent developments in monitoring and evaluation. It includes new chapters on impact assessment and monitoring and evaluating advocacy.

**Jackson, Edward and Yusuf Kassam:** *Knowledge Shared: Participatory Evaluation in Development Co-operation,* West Hartford, CT: Kumarian Press, 1998, ISBN: 1 56549 085 1, 272 pp.

This book analyses the theory and practice of participatory evaluation in a variety of contexts. The central argument is that such evaluation is a key ingredient in development, because it helps to mobilise local knowledge in conjunction with outside expertise to make development interventions more effective. With case studies from Bangladesh, El Salvador, Ghana, India, Indonesia, Kenya, Mexico, Nepal, and

St Vincent, the book is a guide to a community-based approach to evaluation that is a learning process, a means of taking action, and a catalyst for empowerment.

**Roche, Chris:** *Impact Assessment for Development Agencies: Learning to Value Change,* Oxford: Oxfam (in association with Novib) 1999, ISBN: 0 85598 418 X, 160 pp.

With a focus on the centrality of impact assessment to all stages of development programmes, the basic premise of this book is that impact assessment should not be limited to the immediate outputs of a project or programme, but should incorporate any lasting or significant changes that it brought about. After providing a theoretical overview, Roche discusses the design of impact-assessment processes and then illustrates their use in development, in emergencies, and in advocacy work. He ends by exploring ways in which different organisations have attempted to institutionalise impact-assessment processes and the challenges they have encountered in doing so. For a full review, see *Development in Practice* 10(2):261-2.

## Participation and capacity building

**Browne, Stephen:** *Developing Capacity through Technical Co-operation: Country Experiences,* London and New York, NY: Earthscan and UNDP, 2002, ISBN: 1 85383 969 8, 207 pp.

Based on various country studies, this book illustrates the importance of technical co-operation in fostering capacity development in a sustainable manner. The author also explores some of the opportunities lost when technical co-operation is used for purposes other than capacity building. Each case study provides a framework with which to evaluate what does and does not work in the use of technical co-operation for capacity development, and why.

**Blackburn, James with Jeremy Holland:** *Who Changes? Institutionalizing Participation in Development,* London: ITDG Publishing, 1998, ISBN: 1 85339 420 3, 192 pp.

This book explores the institutional changes that need to happen within the international development community to make participation and 'bottom–up' development a reality. Drawing together lessons and experiences from a number of agencies worldwide, the book considers the main issues confronting development professionals involved in

Participatory Rural Appraisal (PRA) practices. Is it possible to adapt PRA methods for large organisations? How can one identify and implement the kinds of organisational change needed in order to implement PRA effectively? The book also offers a checklist of practical considerations (including training, culture, monitoring, etc.) to be taken into account when promoting a participatory approach to development. For a full review, see *Development in Practice* 9(1):212-13.

**Chambers, Robert:** *Participatory Workshops: a Sourcebook of 21 Sets of Ideas and Activities,* London and Sterling, VA: Earthscan, 2002

Robert Chambers, based at the Institute of Development Studies (IDS) at the University of Sussex, is one of the most influential proponents of participatory development, in particular Participatory Rural Appraisal (PRA) and its myriad derivatives. This, his latest book, is a guide to interactive learning. Previous works, including *Rural Development: Putting the Last First* (1983) and *Whose Reality Counts? Putting the First Last* (1997), criticise top–down models of development in favour of participatory approaches and methods which view farmers in resource-poor areas as innovators and adapters, and recognise that their agendas and priorities should be central to development research and thinking. Chambers argues that the poor will be empowered only if the necessary personal, professional, and institutional changes take place within development and donor agencies.

**Cooke, Bill and Uma Kothari** (eds.): *Participation: The New Tyranny?,* London and New Jersey: Zed Books, 2001, ISBN: 1 85649 794 1, 207 pp.

The current focus on participatory development makes it important to question the concept of participation and ask whether it can live up to the expectations placed upon it. This provocative book asks what happens if participation degenerates into tyranny and the unjust and illegitimate exercise of power. The contributors, all social scientists and development specialists, warn of the potential pitfalls and limitations of participatory development. They challenge practitioners and theorists to reassess their own role in promoting practices which may not only be naïve in the way they presume to understand power relations, but may also serve to reinforce existing inequalities.

**Eade, Deborah:** *Capacity Building: An Approach to People-Centred Development,* Oxford: Oxfam, 1997, ISBN: 0 85598 366 3, 226 pp.

While many development agencies would see their role as being to enable people to sharpen the skills that they need in order to participate in the development of their own societies, these efforts will result in dependence rather than in empowerment if the agencies ignore or fail to support the existing strengths of the communities and organisations involved. 'Capacity building' is often used synonymously with 'training' but Eade argues that training alone is of little value unless the organisational, social, and political capacities exist to put it to effective use. The book outlines ways in which NGOs can work with people and their organisations in order to identify and build upon the capacities that they already possess. Particular attention is paid to the importance of a capacity-building approach in emergency situations.

**Smillie, Ian** (ed.): *Patronage or Partnership? Local Capacity Building in Humanitarian Crises,* Bloomfield, CT: Kumarian Press, 2001, ISBN: 1-56549-129-7, 224 pp.

While there is growing recognition that capacity building at the local level is an essential ingredient for long-term development, strengthening local capabilities is easier said than done, and an appropriate balance must be struck between the interventions of outsiders doing something in the midst of an emergency, on the one hand, and building longer-term local skills, on the other. Focusing on case studies from Mozambique, Bosnia, Sierra Leone, Sri Lanka, Haiti, and Guatemala, this book examines this dilemma from a local perspective, and examines a number of constructive possibilities as well as examples of bad practice. For a full review, see *Development in Practice* 12(1):105-7.

**VeneKlasen, Lisa** with **Valerie Miller:** *A New Weave of People, Power & Politics: An Action Guide for Advocacy and Citizen Participation,* Oklahoma City: World Neighbors, 2002, 346 pp.

This thought-provoking training guide for the promotion of citizen participation implicitly challenges advocacy as it is conventionally undertaken, and offers a persuasive vision of how much more effectively it could be done. It is divided into three parts: Understanding Politics, Planning Advocacy, and Doing Advocacy. Part I examines the basic definitions of politics and advocacy, democracy and citizenship, power and empowerment. Part II focuses on how to envisage citizen-centred advocacy, and contains several exercises aimed at helping readers to think strategically about their place in 'the big picture', defining and analysing problems, and comparing alternative strategies. Part III addresses practical issues such as media work, mobilisation, leadership, 'insider' tactics, and coalitions and alliances. The annexes include notes for trainers, and each chapter contains exercises and discussion points aimed at helping readers to think more creatively about the potential of advocacy.

## Gender analysis and gender planning

**Datta, Rekha and Judith Kornberg** (eds.): *Women in Developing Countries: Assessing Strategies for Empowerment,* Boulder: Lynne Rienner Publishers, 2002, ISBN: 1 58826 039 9, 190 pp.

This volume considers the various strategies of empowerment used at the international, national, and sub-national levels. Rather than offering a universal definition of the term, the multiple case studies reveal the differences in empowerment experiences in different parts of the world and the level(s) at which they occur.

**Goetz, Anne Marie** (ed.): *Getting Institutions Right for Women in Development,* London and New Jersey: Zed Books, 1997, ISBN: 1 85649 526 4, 248 pp.

Gender and Development (GAD) or Women in Development (WID) initiatives have been promoted since the mid-1970s, but have not succeeded in dismantling the power structures that still subordinate women in the family and in the economy. Offering a gendered analysis of development agencies, this book presents a conceptual framework for exploring the internal politics and procedures of institutions that design and implement policy, which is then used to analyse empirical case study material. Topics addressed include how to help organisations to internalise or institutionalise gender equity, and how to make accountability to women a routine part of development practice. For a full review, see *Development in Practice* 9(1):204-6.

**Guijt, Irene and Meera Kaul Shah:** *The Myth of Community: Gender Issues in Participatory Development,* London: ITDG Publications, 1998, ISBN: 1853394211, 282 pp.

This book explores the ways in which women can become more appropriately and equally involved in participatory development projects, and ways in which gender issues can be more meaningfully addressed. With contributions from four continents, the volume provides a variety of viewpoints and perspectives from those most closely involved in participatory approaches to development, with a particular emphasis on the need to avoid assuming that community members share homogeneous interests. For a full review, see *Development in Practice* 9(3): 347-9.

**March, Candida, Ines Smyth, and Maiyetree Mukhopadhyay:** *A Guide to Gender-Analysis Frameworks,* Oxford: Oxfam GB, 1999, ISBN: 0 85598 403 1, 96 pp.

The authors outline the main analytical frameworks for gender-sensitive research and planning. Such a framework can be useful for setting out the various elements and factors to be considered in any analysis, and for highlighting the key issues to be explored. It may outline a broad set of beliefs and goals, or be more prescriptive and give a set of tools and procedures. This guide draws on the experience of trainers and practitioners and includes step-by-step instructions for using a range of frameworks, as well as summaries of the advantages and disadvantages of using them in particular situations.

**Molyneux, Maxine and Shahra Razavi** (eds.): *Gender, Justice, Development, and Rights,* Oxford: OUP, in association with UNRISD, 2002, ISBN: 0 1992 5644 6, 504 pp.

Contributors analyse the mixed impact of the prevailing emphasis in the international development agenda on rights and democracy, at a time when neo-liberal policies have resulted in reduced social services, and have been accompanied by rising income inequalities and record levels of crime and violence. Theoretical essays and case studies examine these issues through a gender lens.

**Moser, Caroline:** *Gender Planning and Development: Theory, Practice and Training,* London: Routledge, 1998

This book explores the relationship between gender and development, and presents the conceptual rationale for a tool now referred to as the 'Moser framework' of strategic and practical gender needs. Drawing on Maxine Molyneux's earlier work on gender roles and interests, Moser identifies methodological procedures, tools, and techniques to integrate gender into planning processes and emphasises the role of gender training. More recently, Moser has focused on gender and conflict, and, with Fiona Clark, is author of *Victims, Perpetrators or Actors? Gender, Armed Conflict, and Political Violence* (Zed Books, 2001). For a full review, see *Development in Practice* 12(2):230-2.

**Murthy, Ranjani K.** (ed.): *Building Women's Capacities: Interventions in Gender Transformation,* New Delhi: Sage Publications, 2001, ISBN: 81 7829 064 2, 383 pp.

The editor brings together papers on development initiatives conducted throughout India with the aim of strengthening the capacities of rural women. A critical theme is how to empower women not only economically, but also socially and politically. Equally important is the recognition that men need to be sensitised to gender issues if initiatives aimed at empowering women are to succeed. The volume draws conceptual, methodological, and practical lessons from the experiences described, in an attempt to further promote effective capacity building among women.

**Parpart, Jane L., Shirin M. Rai , and Kathleen Staudt** (eds.): *Rethinking Empowerment: Gender and Development in a Global/Local World,* New York, NY: Routledge, 2002, ISBN: 0 4152 77 698, 272 pp.

This volume offers a holistic definition of empowerment, based on four dimensions. First, empowerment needs to be analysed in global and national as well as local terms. Second, our understanding of power itself needs to be more nuanced. Third, individual empowerment is not merely driven by agency but rather takes place within a context of structural constraints. Finally, empowerment should be seen as both a process and an outcome.

**Townsend, Janet et al.**: *Women and Power: Fighting Patriarchies and Poverty*, London: Zed Books, 1999, ISBN: 1 85649 803 4, 200 pp.

This book explores the creative empowerment strategies that rural women in Mexico have developed in order to confront the challenges they face and to change their lives for the better. The authors argue that it is often poor women in poor countries, rather than those in wealthier ones, who fight the hardest for their empowerment.

**United Nations :** *Women Go Global*, CD-ROM, New York, NY: United Nations, ISBN: 9 2113 0211 0

An interactive, multimedia CD-ROM, surveying some of the most important milestones that have shaped the international agenda for promoting gender equality. It offers extensive coverage of the four UN conferences on women held in Mexico City, Copenhagen, Nairobi, and Beijing, the parallel non-government forums, and the 23rd Special Session of the General Assembly. The CD-ROM also includes relevant documents from the UN and the NGO community, as well as a bibliography, links to key websites and archives on women's history, and the profiles of more than 200 leading figures fighting for women's rights.

**Valk, Minke, Henk van Dam, and Angela Khadar** (eds.): *Institutionalising Gender Equality: Commitment, Policy and Practice – A Global Sourcebook*, Amsterdam: KIT Publishers in association with Oxfam GB, 2001, ISBN: 0 8559 8459 7, 172 pp.

This volume analyses the experiences of organisations that are incorporating women and gender considerations in their policies, not only in projects and programmes but also in their own internal workings. It includes an annotated bibliography and a list of relevant websites.

**Williams, Suzanne with Janet Seed and Adelina Mwau:** *The Oxfam Gender Training Manual*, Oxford, Oxfam GB, 1995, ISBN: 0 85598 267 5, 630pp.

Drawing on the experience of gender specialists all over the world, this best-selling manual contains authoritative guidance on how to run a successful gender-training programme. It offers field-tested training activities and handouts taken from a wide range of sources and shaped into an accessible and flexible set of training modules. The manual is also available in Spanish and Portuguese. For a full review, see *Development in Practice* 6(2):180-81.

## Environmental sustainability

**Blowers, Andrew and Steve Hinchliffe:** *Environmental Responses,* West Sussex: John Wiley & Sons Ltd., 2003, ISBN: 0 470 85005 1, 320 pp.

This book is the last in a series sponsored by The Open University entitled 'Environment: Change, Contest and Response'. It addresses both the impact of human actions on the environment and the technical, economic, and political responses that societies make when confronted with environmental change. The book is richly illustrated and draws on examples from all over the world.

**Dale, Ann:** *At the Edge: Sustainable Development in the 21ˢᵗ Century,* Vancouver: University of British Columbia Press, 2001, ISBN: 0 7748 0836 5, 224 pp.

Winner of the 2001 Outstanding Research Contribution Award for Public Policy in Sustainable Development of the Canadian government, this book is a call to action at a time when new ideas are urgently needed to address global environmental problems. The author argues that sustainable development, which she defines as the process of reconciling conflicting ecological, social, and economic needs, is the fundamental human imperative of the twenty-first century. Warning that this will not be realised without strong leadership by governments at all levels, she stresses that what is needed is a new framework for governance, based on human responsibility and a recognition of the interconnectedness of human and natural systems.

**Helmore, Kristin and Naresh Singh:** *Sustainable Livelihoods: Building on the Wealth of the Poor,* Bloomfield, CT: Kumarian Press, Inc., 2001, ISBN: 1 56549 132 7, 129 pp.

This is an informal handbook on the sustainable-livelihoods approach to poverty alleviation, an approach that places the assets and priorities of the poor at the centre of development planning and action. Drawing on experiences in three African countries, the book outlines the Participatory Assessment and Planning for Sustainable Livelihoods methodology, while it also argues that science, technology, investment, and sound governance are necessary ingredients for development projects to succeed.

**Puttaswamaiah, K.** (ed.): *Cost–Benefit Analysis With Reference to Environment and Ecology,* Somerset, NJ: Transaction Publishers, 2001, ISBN: 0 7658 0706 8, 430 pp.

Social Cost–Benefit Analysis (SCBA) is now regarded as an essential tool in the formulation, appraisal, and evaluation of development projects. This volume presents a comprehensive overview of cost–benefit analysis in its theoretical and applied dimensions. Intended primarily for analysts and planners, the book explores how SCBA is being used to identify and assess public projects in both developing and industrialised countries.

**Woolard, Robert and Aleck Ostry:** *Fatal Consumption: Rethinking Sustainable Development,* Vancouver: University of British Columbia Press, 2001, ISBN: 0774807873, 280 pp.

With contributions from both academics and practitioners, this book explores the problematic relationship between two opposing logics: a culture based on consumption, and the need to promote sustainable development. The book analyses the present situation and counter-balances a discussion of the opportunities for change with a frank examination of the barriers to such change.

## Multi-stakeholder partnerships

**Alsop, Ruth, Elon Gilbert, John Farrington, and Rajiv Khandelwal:** *Coalitions of Interest: Partnerships for Processes of Agricultural Change,* New Delhi: Sage Publications, 2000, ISBN: 81 7036 890 1, 308 pp.

While significant rural policy reforms have been carried out in India, large sections of the agricultural population have failed to benefit from them. Examining the agricultural sector in the semi-arid region of Rajasthan, this book establishes the need for what the authors call process monitoring (PM), or the interaction and collaboration between different stakeholders: various levels of government, NGOs, and farmers' groups. They conclude that practical mechanisms are needed to bring about the consensus necessary to effect change through interaction among multiple stakeholders, and that PM is the key tool for such coalitions to work.

**Brinkerhoff, Jennifer M.**: *Partnership for International Development: Rhetoric or Results,* Boulder, CO: Lynne Rienner Publishers, Inc., 2003, ISBN: 1 58826 069 0, 205 pp.

While partnerships have been hailed as a strategy that can deliver better development outcomes, evidence of their contributions to actual performance has remained largely anecdotal. Brinkerhoff sets out to give a clear definition of the concept and a roadmap for how to achieve meaningful partnership results. Case studies of partnerships for public service, corporate social responsibility, and conflict resolution are also discussed.

**Reich, Michael, ed.**: *Public–Private Partnerships for Public Health,* Cambridge, MA: Harvard University Press, 2002, ISBN: 0 6740 0865 0, 208 pp.

Can public–private partnerships (PPPs) between corporations and governments, international agencies, and/or NGOs provide global solutions to global health problems? Exploring the organisational and ethical challenges that PPPs face, the author focuses on ventures that seek to expand the use of specific products to improve health conditions in poor countries, and argues that such ventures can be productive but also problematic. In each chapter, the book draws lessons from successful as well as more troubled partnerships in order to help guide efforts to reduce global health disparities. For a full review, see *Development in Practice* 13(2&3).

**Robinson, Dorcas, John Harriss, and Tom Hewitt** (eds.): *Managing Development: Understanding Inter-Organizational Relationships,* London: Sage, in association with The Open University, 1999, ISBN: 0 7619 6479 7, 352 pp.

This book sets out to explain the dynamics of inter-organisational relationships in the development context. Moving beyond concepts of co-operation and partnership, contributors explore a wide variety of issues, including how diverse relationships can be; how competition, co-ordination, and co-operation are all constantly at play; how changes in institutional imperatives, terminology, and political agendas have yielded new types of organisational relationship; and how such relationships can be worked out in practice. The volume also provides examples and case studies to illustrate ways of managing the real-life complexities of the development process.

**Tennyson, Ros:** *Managing Partnerships: Tools for Mobilising the Public Sector, Business and Civil Society as Partners in Development,* London: The Prince of Wales International Business Leaders Forum, 1998, ISBN: 1899159843, 124 pp.

The author seeks to provide development practitioners with the skills and confidence they need to develop cross-sectoral initiatives with the public sector, business, and civil society. Topics include how to plan and resource partnerships; how to develop cross-sectoral working relationships; and how to develop action learning and sharing programmes. The appendices offer checklists, tips on how to manage cross-sectoral encounters, and notes on action research and impact assessment.

## Humanitarian and emergency relief work

**Rieff, David:** *A Bed for the Night: Humanitarianism in Crisis,* New York, NY: Simon & Schuster, 2002, ISBN: 0 684 80977 X, 384 pp.

Rieff argues that humanitarian organisations now work in an ever more violent and dangerous world in which they are often betrayed and manipulated, and have themselves increasingly lost sight of their purpose. The civil wars and 'ethnic cleansing' that marked the 1990s have shown that humanitarian aid can only do so much to alleviate suffering, and sometimes can cause harm in its efforts to do good. Drawing on first-hand reports from a number of conflict areas, the author describes how humanitarian organisations have moved away from their founding principle of political neutrality and have slowly lost their independence.

**The Sphere Project:** *The Sphere Handbook: Humanitarian Charter and Minimum Standards in Disaster Response,* Geneva: The Sphere Project, 2000, ISBN: 9 2913 9059 3, 322 pp.

An international initiative aimed at improving the effectiveness and accountability of disaster response, the Sphere Humanitarian Charter and Minimum Standards in Disaster Response spells out the rights and minimum standards that organisations providing humanitarian assistance should guarantee to those affected by natural disasters. The Charter is based on the principles and provisions of international humanitarian, human rights, and refugee law, and on the principles of the Red Cross and the NGO Code of Conduct. The Handbook sets out Minimum Standards in five core sectors: water supply and sanitation, nutrition, food aid, shelter and site planning, and health services. Also published in French, Russian, and Spanish

**Terry, Fiona:** *Condemned to Repeat? The Paradox of Humanitarian Action,* Ithaca: Cornell University Press, 2002, ISBN: 0 8014 8796 X, 304 pp.

The author, who is the former head of the French section of Médicins sans Frontières, argues that humanitarian organisations often fail in their mission to alleviate suffering, and may even exacerbate it, because of their shortsightedness. Terry maintains that agencies deploy aid in unthinking ways, without taking the wider political context into account and without investigating or considering the ramifications of their aid. Drawing from case studies of refugee camps in Pakistan, Honduras, Thailand, and the Democratic Republic of Congo, she shows how aid that was intended to help refugees often ends up in the hands of the combatants.

**Wood, Adrian, Raymond Apthorpe, and John Borton** (eds.): *Evaluating International Humanitarian Action: Reflections from Practitioners,* London and New Jersey: Zed Books 2001, ISBN: 1 85649 976 6, 224 pp.

Based on the experiences of those engaged in humanitarian programme evaluations and on the lessons that they learned in the process, this book analyses humanitarian assistance in terms of both how it is (and should be) delivered and how it is (and should be) evaluated. With case studies from four continents, including Central Asia and the Balkans, the volume addresses the context in which evaluations of humanitarian assistance take place; the process of doing evaluations; and lessons to improve evaluations in the future. For a full review, see *Development in Practice* 12(3&4):551-3.

# Addresses of publishers

**Anthem Press**
PO Box 9779, London SW19 7 QA,
UK.
www.anthempress.com

**Birkhäuser Publishing**
Viaduktstrasse 42, CH-4051
Basel, Switzerland.
www.birkhauser.ch

**Cornell University Press**
Sage House, 512 East State
Street, Ithaca, NY 14850, USA.
www.cornellpress.cornell.edu

**Earthscan Publications**
120 Pentonville Road, London
N1 9JN, UK.
www.earthscan.co.uk

**Harvard University Press**
Holyoke Centre, Cambridge,
MA 02138, USA.
www.hup.harvard.edu

**Heinemann,**
PO Box 6926, Portsmouth,
NH 03802-6926, USA.
www.heinemann.com

**ITDG Publishing**
103-105 Southampton Road,
London WC1B 4HL, UK.
www.itdgpublishing.org.uk

**James Currey**
73 Botley Road, Oxford OX2 0BS,
UK.
www.jamescurrey.co.uk

**John Wiley & Sons**
The Atrium, Southern Gate,
Chichester, West Sussex
PO 19 8SQ, UK.
www.wileyeurope.com

**Lynne Rienner Publishers**
1800 30th Street, Boulder,
CO 80301, USA.
www.rienner.com

**KIT Publishers**
Mauritskade 63, PO Box 95001,
1090 HA Amsterdam,
The Netherlands.
www.kit.nl/publishers

**Koninklijke van Gorcum**
Industrieweg 38, 9403 AB
Assen, The Netherlands.
www.vangorcum.nl

**Kumarian Press**
14 Oakwood Avenue, West
Hartford, CT 06119 2127, USA.
www.kpbooks.com

**McGraw Hill**
2 Penn Plaza, 12th Floor,
New York, NY 10121-2298, USA.
http://books.mcgraw-hill.com

**Oxfam GB**
274 Banbury Road, Oxford
OX2 7DZ, UK.
www.oxfam.org.uk/publications

**Oxford University Press**
Walton Street, Oxford OX2 6DT,
UK.
www.oup.co.uk

**Pluto Press**
345 Archway Road, London
N6 5AA, UK.
www.plutobks.demon.co.uk

**Praeger Publishers**
88 Post Road West, Westport
CT 06881, USA.
www.greenwood.com

**The Prince of Wales
International Business Leaders
Forum (IBLF)**
15-16 Cornwall Terrace,
Regent's Park, London,
NW1 4QP, UK.

**Princeton University Press**
41 William Street, Princeton, NJ
08540, USA.
http://pup.princeton.edu

**Routledge**
11 New Fetter Lane, London
EC4P 4EE, UK.
www.routledge.com

**Royal Tropical Institute**
Mauritskade 63, P.O.Box 95001,
1090 HA Amsterdam,
The Netherlands.
www.kit.nl

**Sage Publications**
M-32 Market, Greater Kailash-I,
New Delhi 110 048, India.
www.sagepublications.com

**Save the Children Fund**
17 Grove Lane, London
SE5 8RD, UK.
www.savethechildren.org.uk

**Simon & Schuster**
Mail Order, 100 Front Street,
Riverside, NJ 08075, USA.
www.simonsays.com

**The Sphere Project**
PO Box 372, 1211 Geneva 19,
Switzerland.
www.sphereproject.org

**Transaction Publishers**
390 Campus Drive, Somerset,
NJ 07830, USA.
www.transactionpub.com

**United Nations Publications**
Room DC2-0853, Dept. I004,
New York, NY 10017, USA.
www.un.org/Pubs/index.html

**UNRISD**
Palais des Nations, CH-1211
Geneva 10, Switzerland.
www.unrisd.org

**University of British Columbia Press**
2029 West Mall, Vancouver, B.C., Canada V6T 1Z2.
www.ubcpress.ubc.ca

**University of Massachusetts Press**
PO Box 429, Amherst, MA 01004, USA.
www.umass.edu/umpress

**University of Minnesota Press**
111 Third Avenue South, Suite 290, Minneapolis, MN 55401, USA.
www.upress.umn.edu

**The World Bank**
1818 H Street, NW, Washington, DC 20433, U.S.A.
publications.worldbank.org

**World Neighbors**
4127 NW 122 Street, Oklahoma City, OK 73120 USA.
www.wn.org

**Zed Books**
7 Cynthia Street, London N1 9JF, UK.
www.zedbooks.demon.co.uk

# Index

# Development in Practice Readers

*Development in Practice Readers* draw on the contents of the acclaimed international journal *Development in Practice*.

> 'The great strength of the Development in Practice Readers *is their concentrated focus. For the reader interested in a specific topic ... each title provides a systematic collation of a range of the most interesting things practitioners have had to say on that topic. It ... lets busy readers get on with their lives, better informed and better able to deal with relevant tasks.'*

(Paddy Reilly, Director, Development Studies Centre, Dublin)

The series presents cutting-edge contributions from practitioners, policy makers, scholars, and activists on important topics in development. Recent titles have covered themes as diverse as advocacy, NGOs and civil society, management, cities, gender, and armed conflict.

There are two types of book in the series: thematic collections of papers from past issues of the journal on a topic of current interest, and reprints of single issues of the journal, guest-edited by specialists in their field, on a chosen theme or topic.

Each book is introduced by an overview of the subject, written by an internationally recognised practitioner, researcher, or thinker, and each contains a specially commissioned annotated list of current and classic books and journals, plus information about organisations, websites, and other electronic information sources – in all, an essential reading list on the chosen topic. New titles also contain a detailed index. *Development in Practice Readers* are ideal as introductions to current thinking on key topics in development for students, researchers, and practitioners.

For an up-to-date list of titles available in the series, contact any of the following:

- the Oxfam Publishing website at www.oxfam.org.uk/publications
- the *Development in Practice* website at www.developmentinpractice.org
- Oxfam Publishing by email at publish@oxfam.org.uk
- Oxfam Publishing at 274 Banbury Road, Oxford OX2 7DZ, UK.

> 'This book [Development, NGOs, and Civil Society] *will be useful for practitioners seeking to make sense of a complex subject, as well as for teachers and students looking for a good, topical introduction to the subject. There is a comprehensive annotated bibliography included for further exploration of many of the issues.'*

(David Lewis, Centre for Civil Society at The London School of Economics, writing in *Community Development Journal* 36/2)

# Development in Practice

*Development in Practice* is an international peer-reviewed journal. It offers practice-based analysis and research on the social dimensions of development and humanitarianism, and provides a forum for debate and the exchange of ideas among practitioners, policy makers, academics, and activists worldwide.

*Development in Practice* challenges current assumptions, stimulates new thinking, and seeks to shape future ways of working.

It offers a wide range of content: full-length and short articles, practical notes, conference reports, a round-up of current research, and an extensive reviews section.

*Development in Practice* publishes a minimum of five issues in each annual volume: at least one of the issues is a 'double', focused on a key topic and guest-edited by an acknowledged expert in the field. There is a special reduced subscription for readers in middle- and low-income countries, and all subscriptions include on-line access.

For more information, to request a free sample copy, or to subscribe, write to Oxfam Publishing, 274 Banbury Road, Oxford OX2 7DZ, UK, or visit: www.developmentinpractice.org, where you will find abstracts (written in English, French, Portuguese, and Spanish) of everything published in the journal, and selected materials from recent issues.

*Development in Practice* is published for Oxfam GB by Carfax, Taylor and Francis.